THE CHARACTER

Dr Wesley Carr

The Character of Wisdom

Essays in Honour of Wesley Carr

Edited by

MARTYN PERCY
Lincoln Theological Institute, University of Manchester, UK

and

STEPHEN LOWE
Bishop of Hulme, Diocese of Manchester, UK

ASHGATE

Published by
Ashgate Publishing Limited
Gower House
Croft Road
Aldershot
Hampshire GU11 3HR
England

Ashgate Publishing Company
Suite 420
101 Cherry Street
Burlington
VT 05401-4405
USA

Ashgate website: http://www.ashgate.com

British Library Cataloguing in Publication Data
The character of wisdom: essays in honour of Wesley Carr
   1. Carr, Wesley, 1941– 2. Church of England 3. Church of England – Liturgy –
Theology 4. Theology, Practical 5. Pastoral Theology – Church of England
I. Percy, Martyn II. Lowe, Stephen III. Carr, Wesley, 1941–
230.3

Library of Congress Cataloging-in-Publication Data
The character of wisdom : essays in honour of Wesley Carr / edited by Martyn Percy,
Stephen Lowe. – 1st ed.
     p. cm.
Includes bibliographical references and index.
   ISBN 0-7546-3417-5 (hardcover : alk. paper) – ISBN 0-7546-3418-3 (pbk. : alk.
paper)
   1. Pastoral theology–Church of England.   I. Carr, Wesley.   II. Percy, Martyn. III.
Lowe, Stephen, 1946–

  BX5175.C44   2004
  283'.42–dc22

                          2003024696

ISBN 0 7546 3417 5 Hardback
    0 7546 3418 3 Paperback

Typeset by MHL Production Services Ltd, Coventry.
Printed and bound in Great Britain by MPG Books Ltd, Bodmin, Cornwall.

Contents

Part Three: Theology, Church and World

Part Four: Response

Contributors

Revd Prebendary Dr Paul Avis is Secretary of the Council for Christian Unity, London

Revd Duncan B. Forrester is Emeritus Professor of Theology, University of Edinburgh

Revd Canon Robin Gill is Michael Ramsay Professor of Theology, University of Kent

Rt Revd Stephen Lowe is Bishop of Hulme, Diocese of Manchester

Revd Dr Christopher Moody is Vicar of Market Harborough

Dr Anton Obholzer is a former Director of the Tavistock Centre, London

Revd Emma Percy is Vicar of Holy Trinity, Millhouses, Sheffield

Revd Canon Dr Martyn Percy is Director of the Lincoln Theological Institute, University of Manchester

Rt Revd Dr Alastair Redfern is Bishop of Grantham, Diocese of Lincoln

Dr Edward R. Shapiro is Medical Director of The Austen Riggs Center, Stockbridge, Massachusetts, and Associate Professor of Psychiatry, Harvard Medical School

Revd Angela Tilby is Vice-Principal of Westcott House, Cambridge

Revd Dr Francis Ward is a parish priest in Manchester

Rt Revd Dr Tom Wright was formerly Canon Theologian of Westminster Abbey, and is now Bishop of Durham

Introduction

This volume is dedicated to the Very Revd Dr Wesley Carr. It has been put together as an appreciation of his ministry and work in the Church of England, and to mark his substantial contribution to theology and public life that spans five decades. Wesley Carr was ordained in the 1960s, and is currently Dean of Westminster Abbey. During this period, as a minister and academic, Wesley Carr has been one of the most prolific and prescient authors in the field of pastoral theology for many years. One of the hallmarks of a diligent scholar is the persistence, thoroughness and depth with which they engage their subjects. In the case of Wesley Carr, we can also add range and breadth to the list of virtues. In a ministry lasting more than 35 years, his seminal writings and influential views have ranged far beyond pastoral theology, to take in church–state relations, theology and the media, and task and process in organizations, to name but a few.

Arthur Wesley Carr was born in 1941. He studied at Jesus College Cambridge, graduating in 1964. Three years later, at the age of 26, he was ordained in the diocese of St Albans, where he served his curacy at Luton with East Hyde. He moved from there four years later, becoming successively Tutor and Chaplain at Ridley Hall in 1971. His next move took him north, where he held the prestigious Stephenson Fellowship in the department of Biblical Studies at Sheffield University, and completed the publication of his doctoral thesis on angels and demons. During this time he was also honorary curate of Ranmoor parish church, where he is still remembered with affection. In 2003, Sheffield University honoured Wesley with an honorary Doctor of Divinity.

The mid-1970s brought fresh challenges for Wesley Carr. He was appointed Chaplain of Chelmsford Cathedral in 1974, becoming a Residentiary Canon in 1978 until 1987. During this time he held other posts, including being the Deputy Director of the Centre for Research and Training from 1974 to 1982, and then Diocesan Director of Training from 1976 to 1984. In 1987 he was appointed Dean of Bristol Cathedral, a post he held until his appointment as Dean of Westminster Abbey in 1997. His time at the Abbey has been full and colourful, and has seen him preside over several landmark events such as the funeral of Diana, Princess of Wales, and the funeral of Her

Royal Highness, the Queen Mother. During his tenure as Dean, he has also instituted a number of key and necessary reforms. As readers will doubtless be aware, some of these have attracted national interest.

For example, on the one hand, Dr Carr has been responsible for modernizing the structures and procedures of the Abbey, thereby ensuring that the nation's foremost and best-loved church is managed with greater transparency and efficiency. At the same time, and on the other hand, his reforms have also restored something of the sacred and sentient atmosphere of the Abbey, turning it back into a place of quiet and prayer, even in the midst of the hustle and bustle of countless tourists and the demands of grand state occasions. This is no small achievement: recovering a place of prayer and demarcating a substantial sacred space in the middle of a major capital city, adjacent to the Houses of Parliament. Westminster Abbey will always be a place for the idle tourist; but it has also been preserved afresh as a space for worship and solitude.

The essays in this volume are divided into three sections, each dealing with an area of ministry or scholarship with which Wesley Carr has been associated. Many of the essays address some of Dr Carr's seminal publications, such as *The Priest-like Task* and innovative writing projects such as *Say One For Me*. But some essays are more generally concerned with programmes and issues that have arisen in the wake of his influence on ecclesial thinking and practice. The sections are:

- Shaping the Church
- Pastoral Theology and Christian Ministry
- Theology, Church and World.

Perhaps inevitably, such distinct sections are somewhat artificial, but they have been preserved in the book to remind readers of the varied territory and concerns that have typically preoccupied Wesley's thinking, writing and consultancy work in nearly 40 years of ministry. The essays in each of the three sections consist in turn of two types. Half the essays are 'academic' in their ethos and remit, are shaped by research, and are intended to be intellectually demanding in a particular way, whilst remaining accessible for the general reader. The other essays are shorter, more meditative and popular in character, but are intended to be no less rigorous in their thinking. It was always our expectation, as editors, that the different styles of essay offered by each writer would reflect Wesley Carr's own adept commitment to considerable variety in forms of communication.

As for the title of the volume – *The Character of Wisdom* – it seemed to present itself quite naturally. In times of significant change, most gurus of management and business studies agree that what you do not want is a manager; what you do need is a leader. A leader is someone who can *inspire* – not only by example, but also by their own creative thinking, imagination, tenacity and acuity. A leader is also someone who can elicit the gift that is already present in others; leadership is not implanted – it is drawn out of the best by the best. Furthermore, the wisdom that leaders embody is usually made up of three distinct elements: intelligence, experience and goodness.

Many in the church will be very aware that there is a world of difference between management and leadership. Leaders can take you through a crisis, and lift a body, organization or people beyond the problems that beset them. Managers, in contrast, tend towards compromise and accommodation. Problems are deliberated and perhaps dealt with, but the people under their control are seldom delivered from the looming crisis. All too often, the besetting problems are deflected, hidden, and ultimately passed on to the next generation. And assuming one accepts this characterization, one can immediately see that that what separates inspiring ecclesiastical figures from more ordinary ones is the true gift of leadership (which must always include grasping the proverbial nettles), as opposed to those who simply (and sometimes valiantly) attempt to manage.

For example, one can think of many senior ecclesiastical figures who are experienced and full of goodness, but who lack genuine intelligence. One can think of a number who are intelligent and good, but who lack experience. And one can think of a few who are intelligent and experienced, but who are deficient in goodness. When the milk of human kindness was being served out, they seem to have opted for the skimmed variety. These figures, by and large, tend to manage well. But alas, all too few embody intelligence, experience and goodness in ample and suitable proportionality. The church today is in need of figures who can genuinely embody 'practical wisdom' – leaders who will inspire, by their example, thought and reasoning. The writer of *Proverbs*, of course, adds a fourth quality to wisdom – spirituality. That is to say, waiting on God, listening, and seeking the will of God – knowing that all human wisdom, where it is truthful in the heart, comes from God and returns to God: 'the Lord *gives* wisdom'.

That said, the wisdom of God is not 'something' that is in the possession of only a few. Strictly speaking, it is a gift that is part of the whole church and can be exercised and discerned by any number of individuals or groups at various times. Moreover, the wisdom of God is not something that is necessarily 'learned' in any conventional sense, as though at school or college. It is sometimes formed out of spiritual experience, as much as it may also come from the ordinary life of the church, or from worship. It is no accident that spiritual directors and mystics talk about 'the school of prayer' or 'spiritual lessons'. As such, they are pointing to a different kind of knowledge, and to a different aspect of the theological formation of the church that is not enslaved to pre-formed curricula. It is, rather, concerned with developing spiritual, theological, pastoral and ministerial habits that are critically self-aware, and are unafraid of asking demanding questions.

This leads us to say, finally, that a festschrift should never be an occasion in which to indulge in hagiography. True, each of the writers in this volume has written because they appreciate certain aspects of Wesley Carr's writing or thinking, and the contribution that he has made to pastoral theology and to the wider church. But each writer has also engaged critically with their subject, and therefore with Wesley's work. Of course, the pursuit of wisdom would demand nothing less than a critical-friendly interaction. But it is also a tribute to Wesley that he welcomes this approach, and has been generous enough to write a response to the contributions contained within this volume. It is our hope, as editors, that the essays here will reflect something of the character of wisdom that can be widely encountered in theology and the church today, as well as testifying to the inherent wisdom in the ministry of an exceptional and gifted individual, to whom this collection is dedicated.

Martyn Percy and Stephen Lowe

PART ONE
SHAPING THE CHURCH

Chapter 1

The Priest-like Task: Funding the Ministry of the Church of England

Martyn Percy

One of the most vexing questions faced in the Church of England today is this: how can it be afforded? The question permeates almost every level of debate on structure, viability and mission. From theological colleges to continuing ministerial education, and from diocese to national headquarters, there is no escaping the financial vagaries and uncertainties that question every appointment, initiative and commitment. An editorial in *The Economist* (US edition) explains the problem plainly:

> The Church of England is suffering from poverty. It has been in a financial fix before, most famously in the 1980s when the Church Commissioners lost money in high-risk commercial property deals. The commissioners, who manage the church's large portfolio of stock exchange and property assets, do better now ... [but] the current problem is that the church has underestimated how much it will have to pay in pensions ... the income from the Church Commissioners that would normally go to the parishes to support the everyday work of the church now largely has to make good the shortfall ... [income handed] over to the parishes has dropped ... retired clergy live longer ... As a result, the dioceses, which rely for their income largely on gifts from churchgoers, are being asked to provide an extra eleven million pounds a year to keep the church running. Already it is estimated that three-quarters of the dioceses are in the red. The dioceses are urgently exploring ways of preventing the church from going broke ....[1]

Yet this analysis only scratches the surface of the problem. As I have recently argued (Percy, 2002: 336–341), the Church of England has yet to adapt to the emergent paradigm in which it finds itself; one in which a comprehensive national ministry is now funded by *congregations* rather than its parishes. True, as a 'spiritual public service' to the nation, the Church of England continues to enjoy a high

---

[1] 'Counting the Doomsday Option: Church of England – Another Public Service is In Crisis', *The Economist*, (US edition), 1 September 2001.

degree of public support at many levels. Occasional offices (e.g., baptisms, weddings, funerals), national religious rites and service (e.g., at times of national grief or celebration, or involvement in politics, education and social situations) and in regional representation (e.g., regeneration initiatives, etc.) all underline the fact that the Church of England continues to serve its people. But its people do not fund the church, and have only done so haphazardly throughout its history.

In bygone eras, the tithing of the whole community supported the local parish church – both the building and the clerical stipend. Up until the sixteenth century, non-payment of tithes could mean excommunication; non-attendance could merit a fine. But fines were always difficult to collect and seldom imposed; excommunications were almost unheard of. The practice of tithing was always haphazard, and it waned quickly in direct proportion to the growth of industrialization throughout the eighteenth and nineteenth centuries (see Pounds, 2000: 213ff; Russell, 1980: 128; and Percy, 2003). Parliamentary reforms in 1836 tried to regularize tithing by replacing the notoriously chaotic 10% levy imposed on all produce (e.g., hay, milk, fish, cheese, and any other harvest), with a rental charge imposed on land. But even this could not last, and in 1864 the law abolished the 'Church Rate' (which had been re-imposed in 1661). The practice of paying a tithe on land was finally abolished by the Tithe Act of 1936.

What the Church Rate had tried to do was to put established religion on a more comfortable footing, as it obliged parishioners to support their parish church financially (irrespective of their beliefs). But the cultural and industrial revolutions of the seventeenth and eighteenth centuries questioned this arrangement intensely. Parliament passed the Toleration Act in 1689, enshrining religious freedom in law: and the freedom to worship where you wished inevitably inferred permission to support your own religion in your own way – and not to subsidize the established church. By the last quarter of the nineteenth century, the foundations for the present anomaly were already laid, namely the bifurcation of the economy of the parish with that of the welfare of the parish church. However, parish churches were to be open and available to their respective resident populations, and were to minister to them accordingly. But the cost of that ministry was borne, not by the parish, but by the congregations themselves, and in collaboration with the Ecclesiastical Commissioners.[2] In the twentieth century, further reforms to the financing of the Church of England placed more power in central and diocesan hands. In 1976 the Endowments and

---

[2] The Church Commissioners were created in 1948, an amalgamation of the Ecclesiastical Commissioners and Queen Anne's Bounty (Russell, 1980: 268).

Glebe Measure vested all land and its management in the hands of the diocese.

For Church of England congregations and their ministers, there are three interrelated problems that need addressing which will have a bearing upon the future provision of parochial ministry. The methodology used for reflection is primarily drawn from the field of practical theology. Here, it is my contention that in order to reform or afford the ministry of the Church of England in the future, local congregations and their narrativity will need to be listened to and understood as the place where emergent structures and theologies of ministry are rediscovered. The corresponding recommendations arise out of a 'problem-posing' theological strategy that locates the debate in the grounded reality of parish and diocesan life, rather than in 'ideal' theologizing on the nature of gift, reciprocity or mutuality.

As readers will recognize, the basis for this agenda lies in two works by Wesley Carr. *The Priest-like Task* (1985), has become a 'modern classic' of pastoral theology reflecting on the nature of priesthood; *Say One For Me* (1992) is a remarkable and prescient study of the Church of England that tries to foresee its future, exploring its changing shape and role in the modern world. Another feature of Wesley Carr's work that has shaped this essay also needs mentioning: his deep and abiding interest in religious organizations. For many years Wesley has acted as a consultant or mentor to parishes, dioceses and various bodies within the Church of England, helping them with structure, strategy and mission. This work has, for the most part, been undertaken quietly and discreetly, but its impact has been considerable. This festschrift partly bears testimony to this. Having said that, this essay does not discuss either of the books I have just mentioned, nor does it describe Wesley's less well-known consultancy work – that task is undertaken by other contributors. Rather, this essay begins where both the books mentioned end, and attempts to examine how the Church of England might address itself to the urgency of its financial situation and the funding of its mission and ministry. There are three concerns to mention briefly.

The first concern to outline is the rising cost of ministry and the manner in which the money is raised by the church. Most dioceses have a 'quota' or 'parish share' system for each parish, and calculate the worth of the parish using a variety of complex formulae. The income raised from the parishes supports the work of the diocese (i.e., its central infrastructure, which may be concerned with parsonages, legal matters, development, mission, education, etc.) and makes contributions to clergy pensions and stipends. In addition to this, money raised by the congregation must pay for the expenses of ministry and the upkeep of the church and its buildings. Clearly, some congregations, for a variety of reasons (e.g., size, wealth, geography, etc.) raise more money than others. Yet the problem that is now emerging is that many congregations see the significant amounts of money they contribute to parochial ministry, and to their own churches, is being swallowed up in central diocesan infrastructures.

For example, my own parish church (in the diocese of Sheffield), a financially comfortable (but by no means wealthy) congregation, finds that for every pound given in the collection plate, the diocese takes 82%, which it then uses to support itself and redistribute to poorer parishes. The effect of this 'tax' is deleterious upon the morale of the congregation, which finds that in spite of the significant monies it raises, it struggles to fund adequately its own local ministry and pay for the upkeep of its buildings (Percy, 2002: 340). Furthermore, it is important to stress that this 'tax' is voluntary – 'it is not a legally enforceable obligation'. Indeed, as Hill (2001) points out the levying of the quota 'in the form of a quasi tax may be unlawful', since the authority of Parliament is not behind it. Some parishes that can afford to pay their clergy directly, and do not wish to contribute to the diocese, may be allowed to do so in law, although it would not make them popular with the bishop or other parishes in the diocese (Hill, 2001: 76).

Second, this leads to questions about the necessity of so much diocesan infrastructure, and the viability of other churches. A century ago, there were no 'diocesan centres' employing large numbers of staff. A parish church, it must be said, normally understands its need of a bishop, but it is normally less clear about the need for a large number of diocesan employees. The multiplication of centres and staff over the last 50 years has led to the enhancement and intensification of 'diocesan identity', and the deepening and extension of what a regional resource can offer to the local. To be sure, this has been a valuable (but expensive) development. But fundamentally, parishes remain the basic unit of ecclesial order and identity in the Church of England. Parishes need a bishop (occasionally), but a diocese seldom. The concerns of parochial congregations remain endearingly local and contextualized, focused around the state of the church (building) itself and the availability and effectiveness of ministerial provision (Percy, 2002: 87). Anything provided after that is a welcome extravagance; but increasingly, the financial accountability of dioceses is becoming an issue for parishes (see Laughlin in Percy and Evans, 2000: 49–73).

And in terms of the viability of churches, there is an increasing historical consciousness amongst the laity that questions the apparently inalienable 'myth' that most communities have always been served by a local parish church. In Sheffield, for example, the nineteenth century opened with there being only three churches

(Odom, 1917: 8). To cope with the increasing population, the Ecclesiastical Commissioners divided the town in 1846 into 25 parishes. By 1914 (the year the diocese was created), that number had increased to 47, serving a population of some 450,000. But many of these churches were built by specious 'popular' or 'local' subscription rather than levy, or by private endowment. In other words, the character of many mid to late Victorian foundations for parish churches was primarily *congregational*, even if parochial concerns also motivated the agenda.

Third, the evolution of clerical stipends is probably incomplete, and at its present stage, problematic. There is, for example, an obvious incoherence in paying a parish priest of 25 years' service and considerable experience and expertise little more than someone who has just emerged from theological college. The former may have significant numbers of dependants (children of college age that need funding, frail parents that need financial support, etc.); the latter may have no dependants at all, but their 'living allowance' is virtually the same. The stipend takes no account of the income of a spouse either. It is, paradoxically, a kind of proto-socialist form of payment. All receive more or less the same income, irrespective of the range of responsibilities, output, capacity and ability of the person. Housing is standardized. Of course, the origins of the 'standardized' stipend are well understood, even if it is a relatively recent development; a valiant attempt to address the substantial inequalities that existed under the previous systems of glebe land (Russell, 1980: 238), absent incumbents and private patronage. But the present difficulty is that where there was once some social equivalence in clergy pay, clerical incomes have now fallen dramatically in comparison to other professions.

For example, in 1957, the average clerical income was one fifth of the pay of barristers, doctors, solicitors and dentists – a radical shift from the comparative parity of the mid-nineteenth century. Today, as Russell notes, 'a clerical family with no other income other than a stipend and with two children qualifies for ... income supplement ... in some parishes both the vicar and assistant priest are dependent on social security for some part of their total income ... ' (Russell, 1980: 269). Furthermore, it should be noted that those clergy who are 'preferred' (i.e., promoted) in the church, perhaps becoming a canon residentiary, archdeacon, dean or bishop, do receive higher stipends. However, this leaves many priests with considerable experience and expertise, exercising valuable ministries, on a 'basic' stipend, and potentially resentful.

These three financial problems are, I hold, all interrelated, and rooted to the future of ministerial provision in the Church of England. But how are they to be addressed? What strategies might there be to enable the priest-like task to continue and flourish? In what follows, I want to first of all outline how practical theology, in conjunction with James Hopewell's stress on local narrativity, can help the church address the multiplicity of issues. Then secondly, I want to reflect upon the Church of England's self-understanding of ministry and identify specific strategies that might enable the future organization of the church.

Practical Theology and the financing of ministry

A theologian, on being approached by an earnest young student, was asked: 'What is your methodological starting point?'. The theologian replied simply: 'A theologian is always beginning in the middle of things'.[3] The wit, clarity and acuity of the reply says something important about the nature of theology, and with what it is engaging. If Practical Theology begins anywhere at all, it is in the recognition that the nature of theology is both practical and public as it seeks to make some sense of the relationships between belief and practice, faith and the world, and church and society. But this involves some openness at the very heart of the theological endeavour, since Practical Theology is a listening and reflective discipline; it does not seek to be dogmatic in its engagements:

> Practical Theology is a critical and constructive reflection within a living community about human experience and interaction, involving a correlation of the Christian story and other perspectives, leading to an interpretation of meaning and value, and resulting in everyday guidelines and skills for the formation of persons and communities (Poling and Miller, 1985: 62).

There are, of course, several other ways of describing the discipline and its focus. For Pattison and Woodward, Practical Theology is 'a place where religious belief, tradition and practice meet contemporary experiences, questions and actions and conduct dialogue that is mutually enriching, intellectually critical and practically transforming' (2000: 7). For Elaine Graham (1996) it is transforming practice – the articulation and excavation of sources and norms of Christian practice; a form of *phronesis* (practical wisdom) that helps churches to practise what they preach and preach what they practise (Pattison and Woodward, 2000: 104). For Duncan Forrester, it is 'the theological discipline which is primarily concerned with the interaction of belief

---

[3] Rowan Williams, *On Christian Theology*, Oxford, Blackwell, 2000: xiii.

and behaviour' (Bowden and Richardson, 1983: 455). And for Don Browning, Practical Theology is utterly fundamental:

> ... all theological thinking ... is essentially practical. The social and intellectual context in which theology is brought into conversation with the vision implicit in pastoral practice itself, and with the normative interpretations of the faith handed down in the traditions of the church. Theology thus arises from practice, moves into theory, and is then put into practice again (Browning, 1991; Pattison and Woodward, 2000: 6).

For our purposes here, one of the best examples of a Practical Theology occurs in James Hopewell's work in the field of Congregational Studies. Hopewell sees practical theology as something that begins in the middle, with hermeneutics that *then* follow:

> an analysis of both local congregational idiom and the way the gospel message confronts and yet is conveyed by that language would be a better starting point for efforts to assist the local church. Rather than assume that the primary task of ministry is to alter the congregation, church leaders should make a prior commitment to understand the nature of the object they propose to improve ... many strategies for operating upon local churches are uninformed about the cultural constitution of the parish ... (1987: 11)

Studying congregations, of course, is something that is not taught at theological college. The roots of this absence lie in a profound deficiency in the notion of theological education, and in an impoverished understanding of theology – of how God acts in the world. Where Practical Theology can help the churches is in retrieving the questions, definitions and shape of theology from the idealized to the concrete. Thus, the theological enterprise is something richer and more empathetic:

> To ponder seriously the finite culture of one's own church, given the promise of God's redemptive presence within it, opens up a vast hermeneutical undertaking. The congregation recedes as primarily a structure to be altered and emerges as a structure of social communication within which God's work in some ways already occurs. The hermeneutical task is not merely the mining of biblical revelation in ways meaningful to individuals. It is more basically the tuning of the complex discourse of a congregation so that the gospel sounds within the message of its many voices (Hopewell, 1987: 11).

The turn towards narrativity is one of the more striking features of Hopewell's work. How and what congregations *recollect* identifies their *plot* and its course or cycle. Without recollection, congregations drift; with it, they narrate their lives together in communion with God, and in the midst of triumph and tragedy, opportunity and adversity, and more besides. So, in telling the story of the congregation, we unravel its plot:

> ... church culture is not reduced to a series of propositions that a credal checklist adequately probes. The congregation takes part in the nuance and narrative of full human discourse. It persists as a recognizable storied dwelling within the whole horizon of human interpretation (Hopewell, 1987: 201).

But in what way is money or finance a serious theological issue for a congregation? Clearly, congregations tell stories about money and funding all the time. They also listen to the stories of others: poor clergy on low incomes, the Church Commissioners losing substantial sums, 'the clergyman down the road who does nothing, but is paid the same as our tireless priest', the church up the road 'with plenty of financial reserves', 'the amazing fundraising scheme or stewardship development of a neighbouring parish', 'the sacrifice of a single benefactor', the 'looming crisis in pensions', and more besides. Whatever balance sheets and financial reports might be issued by the diocese or the Church Commissioners – in other words, whatever the facts or spin – it is *stories* about money that also constitute the lives of congregations and condition their expectations.

Hopewell sees money as a powerful symbol in the life of the congregation: 'money is frequently an *emotion*-laden metaphor that both expresses and provokes the identity of a particular congregation' (1987: 8). The symbolization is diverse. Some hide its symbolization altogether: the subject is seldom mentioned, money or cheques are presented in sealed envelopes, discreetly, and all campaigning is done quietly (but efficiently). At another congregation, money may function as 'a potent expression of superabundance and fertility': it is a sign of spiritual fecundity. At another church, money is seen as an agent of the material and an adversary to the spiritual, and its power to dominate agendas is fiercely resisted. Still at another parish, financial difficulties become the foundation for expressing disappointment with the world (which ignores the congregation), the lack of resources from the wider church, and the apparent 'success' of neighbouring churches, which is resented. In this last form of symbolization, the lack of money is normally correlated with the loss of – power and membership.

These insights are important for three reasons.. First, the presence or absence of income and capital, however that is construed in a congregation, is part of the overall *symbolization* within their theological framework. A congregation sees that its wealth or poverty says something about their relationship with God and the world (e.g., blessing, suffering solidarity, social marginalization, empowering-pivotal centrality within a locality, etc.). Second, money is an issue for the *orthopraxis* of the congregation or denomination; its use is *value-laden*. It may be obvious that it is not easy to pay the heating bills year on year, but that will not stop the same congregation raising money for a new window, or the restoration of a beloved pulpit. Third, income and capital remain stubbornly part of the *local* narrativity of a congregation first and foremost (inevitably), and is therefore not easily assigned a role in a larger regional or national 'plot'.[4] In other words, before congregations worry about the fiscal viability of a diocese, they are first and foremost concerned with their leaking roof, the expenses of their minister, and adequately endowing local outreach, of which a care of buildings is inevitably a part. Correspondingly, there is understandable resentment or reticence about large amounts of income 'disappearing' into central or regional sources, since the local, historically, invariably precedes the meta-structures of the hierarchy, which often lack definition or comparable narrativity.

Ministry and money

Paying proper attention to congregations and their fiscal narratives is an important theological and ecclesial task. It serves to remind church leaders and dioceses that the primary resourcing of the Church of England is from the local *to* the local. Moreover, the local and the congregational are theologically significant locations where the story of witness and its recollection continues to shape and characterize the ministry of the church. Too often dioceses or central church structures assume that the meta-organization is essential and that the local is small and therefore expendable. In truth, the reverse is true. The Church of England survived more than adequately for many centuries without the substantial national, regional and diocesan resources it presently enjoys. For many parishioners, their primary experience of the Church of England is a local one, occasionally tempered with a visit from the bishop, or an incident in the media in which the Church of England, as 'established' religion, provides occasion for what Wesley Carr calls 'national gossip'.

---

[4] On this, see N. Ammerman, *Organizing Religious Work*, Hartford Institute for Religious Research, July 2002, in which the authors compare ten mainstream denominations in the USA, and note that local congregations invariably resist and resent the larger regional or national organizing structures.

Behind these assertions lurks a deeper question: what kind of creature is the clergyperson? It is normal for most trained clergy today to assume that they are 'professional', and that in being ordained, they join, in effect, a profession. But this understanding of the clergy is comparatively recent, and a brief understanding of the history is essential if we are to move forward with the parallel financial questions. In Anthony Russell's ground-breaking *The Clerical Profession* (1980), we are introduced to the idea that the clergy only became 'professionalized' in the late nineteenth century, as they gradually lost their stakeholdings as landowners, gentlemen, magistrates, almoners, arbitrators, essayists, political figures and generators of improvement in health, education and overall social well-being. The rapid industrialization of society squeezed clergy out of many 'soft' mainstream public roles or diffuse role obligations, and created the pressure for a new intensification of identity, or what we call 'professionalization':

> As a result of these processes, the clergy of the mid-nineteenth century were disposed to accord greater significance to that central and irreducible religious function of the priestly role, the leadership of public worship. In this element of his role at least the clergyman had a monopoly of legitimate function. In an age which came to accord high status to those who possessed socially useful technical knowledge, the clergy, by their emphasis on liturgical studies, attempted to become technologists of the sanctuary (Russell, 1980: 40).

The Oxford Movement helped this process along, with its emphasis on frequent celebration of Holy Communion. Less than 50 years earlier, most English people had been used to receiving the sacrament only once a year. The Evangelical revival also encouraged the intensification of professional identity, with an emphasis on discipline, systematic visiting, and schools for preaching and catechizing. Within a very short time, English clergy began to dress differently from other 'gentlemanly professions' in everyday wear by sporting dog-collars, something they had not done previously. Furthermore, clergy were now being 'trained' at special theological colleges rather than taught divinity at university (another new development), which also enhanced the emerging professional identity.[5]

This rapid development in professionalization would normally be something that is welcomed in the vocational or occupational spheres of work. But in ministry, its status as a 'profession' has never been

---

[5] For an American perspective on the nineteenth century, see D. Scott (1978).

something that could be easily agreed upon. Neither, for that matter, has it ever been something the Church of England could easily afford. As Russell notes, the number of paid clergy dropped steadily throughout the twentieth century: there were 25,000 in 1901, and less than half that number 100 years later (Russell, 1980: 263). The number of residential theological colleges in the same period has dropped from 40 to 10. Yet in the midst of this, clergy have shown a marked reluctance to be reformed in line with other professions, even as their social and cultural 'capital' has steadily declined. The Paul Report of 1964 (*The Deployment and Payment of Clergy*) recommended the abolition of freehold, but aligned it with better proposals for pay and working conditions. The Report and its recommendations were defeated by the Church Assembly, the precursor to the General Synod. The Morley Report of 1967 (*Partners in Ministry*) made similar suggestions on the security and status of clergy, but it too was defeated by the clergy, who feared for the loss of their freehold. The attitude of the clergy towards too much professionalization is summed up neatly in a letter to *The Times*, written by a clergyman in 1957:

> the parochial clergy of the Church of England are becoming transformed into the salaried members of a diocesan staff, living in houses provided and maintained for them on incomes fixed and guaranteed by diocesan stipend funds (Russell, 1980: 271).

The disdain towards equality and uniformity expressed in this letter may seem paradoxical to some. After all, do the clergy not want to be treated like professionals, in which their rights, privileges and salaries are guaranteed? The answer is both 'yes' and 'no'. 'Yes', in the sense that they want to be regarded as specialist purveyors of knowledge, rites and techniques – 'technologists of the sanctuary'. But 'no' in the sense that they do not want to be rationalized or organized into a properly hierarchical or accountable body, in which their right to freedom and dissent is jeopardized.

Perhaps inevitably, various categories of minister have sprung up in the gap created by the smaller numbers of paid priests in the Church of England, and also to reflect the ambivalent attitude that prevails in relation to ministerial provision. As Russell candidly notes, 'proposals have been placed before the Church in almost every decade in the last 120 years'. Schemes have ranged from a voluntary diaconate (first proposed in the mid-nineteenth century, but regularly resurrected as an idea) to Auxiliary Pastoral Ministry (APMs), which was later to become known as Non-Stipendiary Ministry (NSMs). Many dioceses now have Ordained Local Ministers (OLMs). In addition to these categories, the number of 'sector ministers' – chaplains in hospitals, the armed services, prisons and education – has risen significantly. The blurring of the boundaries between full-time and part-time ministry, and the emergence of 'house-for-duty' clergy, has also meant that there are difficulties in specifying what constitutes 'professional' ministry in the Church of England; it no longer means 'paid', if it ever once did.

Having a very basic understanding of the convoluted evolution of 'professional' ministry is important if we are to return to the question of financing the ministry of the Church of England in the near future. We have already noted that nationally, resources are stretched. We have also noted that at the level of the local congregation, much of the narrativity about funding is conditioned by anxiety and pressure. Clearly, the impasse has to be broken. One answer may be to have more and more OLMs and NSMs, but this might undermine the value of those who are in paid full-time ministry. There is also some ambivalence about providing more and more 'cheaper' clergy, which hitherto, few in the Church of England have been willing to face. At what point does the 'supplement' become a major part of the staple diet? Other solutions will undoubtedly include reducing the number of churches in cities, towns and villages, in effect reversing the avaricious tendencies of the Victorians, who built too many churches.[6] But the closure and merger of parishes creates resentment, and of course whilst saving some money, may also lead to the further loss of income: a parish church that no longer exists ceases to contribute funds to its diocese. Another solution may be to slim down diocesan staffing to skeletal levels, sharing out the work across regions (trans-diocesan) or amongst ministers. But each of these options is fraught with difficulties, and will not make a decisive difference to the endemic financial crisis the ministry of the Church of England faces.

Power in partnership

So how might the problem be addressed? The advantage of the approach taken by Practical Theology is that it takes seriously the grounded experience of the life of congregations. Furthermore, it also adopts a 'problem-posing' stance in addressing issues, which it borrows from Liberation Theology. The other dimension the methodology permits is a thematic approach rather than a dogmatic

---

[6] In consulting Odom's history of Anglican churches in Sheffield, it is interesting to note that some of those churches built in the mid and late nineteenth century did not even survive to be counted amongst the congregations of the city when the diocese was inaugurated in 1914 (Odom, 1917: 31).

or systematic one, and in what follows, I want to suggest that the key to resolving the problem lies in the rehabilitation and redevelopment of the notion of *partnership*, a major foundation of the Morley Report (1967). However, when the Morley Report deployed the term, it meant a reconfiguration of relations between clergy and the hierarchy. I am using the term rather differently, to infer the establishment of mutual *trust* between congregations and the hierarchy in the mutual support of clergy and parochial ministry. The appeal to trust implies a sense of reliability, commitment, strength, confidence, expectation and responsibility. It is my view that the modern structuring of dioceses (and their method for collecting quota payments) no longer demonstrates adequate trust in congregations and their ability to minister locally in ways that they deem to be suitable.[7] I am conscious that the proposals set down here are only lightly sketched at present, but I also hold that the ideas laid out could lead to a productive and fruitful strategy for developing the future parochial ministry in the Church of England.

First, there should be a new sense of the partnership that forms the paradigm for ministry: between parish, congregation, diocese and priest. This partnership, recognizing that the main funding comes from the congregation, could be more substantially enhanced if there was a redistribution of capital resources, increasing the stakeholding of congregations in the development of local ministry. At present, local Church of England congregations do not own their churches or vicarages. Clergy must usually live in tied-housing, all of which is policed by a diocesan hierarchy, which the congregation funds. However, I believe that the lack of ownership (but increasingly coupled to their financial *obligations*) is an extremely difficult dilemma for the Church of England to address. Increasing payments to central and diocesan centres, but no incremental increase in, say, running of the affairs of the church, is a dis-empowering experience, and ultimately a rudimentary recipe for revolution: 'no taxation without representation'. To address this, I want to suggest that the Church of England needs to find more flexible ways of building financial partnerships with local congregations and parishes, in order to enable the mission of the church locally and nationally.

One way forward would be for the Church of England to sell much of its tied-housing stock to local congregations. Parishes or con-gregations, in a few instances, would be able to buy such properties outright, and would thereafter hold the property for future incumbents in trust, the management of the housing becoming the responsibility of

---

[7] For a useful meditation on trust, see O. O'Neill (2002).

the congregation, but in line with agreed minimum standards laid
down by the diocese. For congregations that could not afford to own
tied-housing, the option of a mortgage would be available, or a split
option whereby the diocese and congregation jointly owned the house,
or shares therein. Bills for maintaining the tied-housing would be the
responsibility of the owner or owners. For congregations in UPA or
inner city parishes, where ownership was either undesirable or un-
economic, the diocese concerned could continue to own and invest in
tied-accommodation for clergy.[8] A simple scheme such as this would
create and release substantial new funds to invest in mission. It would
also begin to allow clergy the freedom to choose between tied-housing
and a stipend, or a salary and a housing allowance. Where a clergyperson wished to invest in housing themselves, the housing allowance
could be paid by the parish from the proceeds of renting the tied-
housing.[9] In some cases, congregations could insist that the tied-
housing and the church were an integral unity, and that the local
expectation for ministry would continue to be that any clergyperson
becoming the incumbent of the benefice would need to live in the tied-
house provided, and that this would be a condition of accepting the
post.

Second, this flexibility could also begin to pave the way for
parishes, congregations and dioceses to enter into a new partnership on
patterns of pay for clergy. If parishes were given more autonomy over
the resources that they are already stewards of, new patterns of
ministry might emerge from the material *and* the spiritual. In reality,
this has already begun: we have already mentioned the rise in the
phenomenon of the 'house-for-duty' priest. In many rural areas, there
is no reason to doubt that the provision of pastoral care is more than
adequate under such arrangements. Furthermore, we have already
alluded to the fact that clergy should be properly regarded as 'semi-
professional'. With greater flexibility, churches can determine whether
or not they need someone full-time or part-time as their parish priest,
and the level of expertise that is required. Furthermore, suppose that,
within certain limits, parishes were also able to set levels of

---

[8] Of course, clergy would not be permitted to purchase tied-housing, as this would
complicate local church polity when it came to new appointments.

[9] This is increasingly becoming an issue for the clergy. The rising number of parish
offices attached to churches, coupled with working spouses, means that many clergy
choose to keep their tied-housing primarily as a family home, and not as a place of
work. Furthermore, rising house prices may mean that some clergy are now forced to
take out substantial first-time mortgages upon retirement, or, enter into joint equity
deals with the Church of England Pension Board. Greater flexibility on housing and
incumbency in the future might help clergy to avoid some of the economic problems
that many presently face.

remuneration? This would encourage a more realistic appraisal of many ministries, and allow congregations to value experience, responsibility, energy, challenge and more besides. Of course, there are some who would complain that this is precisely what the stipend system sought to get away from: the creation of inequality. But in reality, the enforcement of equality can be potentially morale-sapping and incoherent. Again, a partnership on pay and conditions between congregations, parishes, clergy and the diocese might open up rich possibilities for the re-evaluation of ministry. In UPA, inner city and certain rural areas where increased pay differentials might be problematic, the diocese should be able to guarantee minimum standards, and perhaps add the novel twist of providing incentives to contemplate such ministries. The 'liquid' capital that would be created from the sale of tied-housing could easily be used to augment mission and ministry in areas that were identified as being especially needy or vital to the overall work of the church.[10]

Third, an appropriate adoption of pay differentials for clergy would allow a partnership between parishes, clergy, congregations and the diocese to emerge, and then to continually value the experience and expertise of their clergy, independent of any type of preferment.[11] The recognition that there are *four* partners in parochial ministry might begin to tap new sources of revenue for certain types of work: urban regeneration, community development or certain types of youth work. (In many dioceses, this has already happened, with certain types of funding from government in effect 'buying' the time of a clergy-person.) For the clergy, although minimum standards would need to be maintained, the effect of adopting pay differentials would be to create a richer diversity of possibility within the Church of England. Can one, for example, envisage a future in which a clergyperson turns down the offer of a Suffragan Bishopric, because the pay would be no more (or perhaps less?) than they presently receive as a Team Rector of seven years standing, and following 25 years of ministry? The decision may come down to weighing up other pros and cons. Would the responsibility of serving one town or large urban council estate be more appealing than the endless rounds of confirmations, church fetes and clergy interviews that might be the lot of the average Suffragan Bishop? At present, with stipends linked *only* to preferment, the Church of England simply does not create the right *material*

---

[10] In the USA, for example, many dioceses can augment the salaries of UPA and inner city priests, precisely because the suburban parishes own their own tied-housing.

[11] A recent review of stipends suggests linking the pay of clergy to teachers and head teachers, but bearing in mind that the tied-housing is worth several thousand pounds per year. See Turnbull (2001).

conditions in which imaginative (or even vocational?) decisions can be made about an individual's future.[12]

Finally, it may be that dioceses need to *listen* to their local congregations more deeply than ever, and begin to build a missiological strategy that is more collaborative and less hierarchical. With congregations now mainly responsible for funding the priest-like task, and this being done on an entirely voluntary basis, dioceses will have to show that they are increasingly accountable to their main benefactors. I suspect that this will lead to leaner diocesan structures in the future, and, perhaps, slimmer national-central structures. Indeed, I would go further and suggest that a reasonable goal to strive towards would be the radical *shrinkage* of the parish quota system and diocesan infrastructure. Heavy pruning of diocesan and central staffing levels would allow congregations to take more responsibility for the money they generate, and invest this locally in mission and ministry.[13] But such a move would not represent the 'collapse of the system'; far from it. If this evolution can be conceived of in terms of *trust* and *partnership*, it may well be that even more resourcing emerges from local situations to enable the work of the church. Instead of the typical congregational experience of financial disempowerment – being bled dry year on year by an increasingly demanding hierarchy – the Church of England might discover that it has hidden riches at local levels that have hitherto remained untapped. But to tap such resources will require partnership and the establishment of trust; the central giving way to the diocesan; the diocesan giving way to the congregational; the congregational re-engaging with the local; and to close the circle, the local redistributing to the national and regional. It will require a far more flexible approach to mission and ministry to enable the priest-like task of tomorrow: nothing less than a radical practical theology of the church and its financing to imagine what the future might be. It will require a recognition that ministry is now a partnership between laity and hierarchy, and is not simply a matter of what the diocese provides.[14]

---

[12] The issue of payment and gender discrimination belongs to another essay, but we do note that women cannot be consecrated (or paid) as bishops: their salaries or stipends are 'capped'.

[13] For example, in many episcopal dioceses in the USA, congregations contribute between 5% and 12.5% to their dioceses. The congregation remains responsible for fixing and paying the salary of the clergy, which it does through the diocese. The congregation also maintains and normally owns any tied property. The bishops' diocesan staff will probably number no more than 15 persons. By the same token, many parishes can afford several staff working in ministry locally, because they are not paying sizeable sums to the diocesan quota.

[14] Indeed, my research reveals that some large evangelical congregations – which provide sizeable contributions to diocesan funding – are now arguing that their

We began this essay by briefly noting three interrelated financial problems that have implications for the future provision of pastoral and priestly ministry: the lack of money at national, diocesan and parochial levels. Under the present arrangements, the laity of Church of England (congregations) are still being treated as though they were providing marginal supplements to enable ministry. But in reality, they are now substantially underwriting the cost of ministry. Yet in return for this, they have received no incremental increase in their capacity to shape and form local ministry. Congregations have been slowly educated by the Church Commissioners into becoming 'fundamental units of funding' for the ministry of the church (Percy, 2002: 337). And as we have seen from our discussion, some congregations accept their lot stoically, and others cheerfully, depending on their world view. But this, I venture, cannot continue indefinitely: there are finite limits on the burden of central or diocesan 'taxation' that can be tolerated by most congregations.[15]

Our solution to this problem is a sharing out of the economic power that has hitherto supported the ministry of the Church of England, and the creation of trust between partners. It is to allow congregations to come into their own as important constituents within the overall equation for funding ministry, and to give them a stake and responsibility within that framework. Partnerships are, when all is said and done, a vital sign of commonality, and involve a mutual commitment that fosters vision, shares authority, and is clear about interests. The idea of conceiving a new partnership between clergy, diocese, congregations and parishes is to re-determine the value and need of ministry in any given context, and to create the conditions whereby the church could respond more adequately to changing social situations. To achieve this, the sale (or mortgaging) of tied-housing would generate significant funding that could be used in existing or new areas of ministry.[16]

---

financial support should allow them a much greater say in the shaping of ministry in those parishes that their giving supports. In other words, the evangelical parishes are seeking the status of partner or stakeholder; they want a say in how the diocese spends the money it receives from them. In many cases, such initiatives do not represent any kind of colonialization, but rather demonstrate a desire to move from maintenance to mission in some of the neediest areas of any given diocese.

[15] Furthermore, there are already signs that a few congregations in the Church of England that object to certain of its theological stances (e.g., on sexuality or gender) already either withhold part of their quota payment, or may even go so far as to pay their clergy directly, no longer contributing to the diocesan purse or to the Church Commissioners.

[16] For example, I estimate that the sale of three quarters of the tied-housing stock in the Diocese of Sheffield would create an endowment fund of around £30,000,000. The interest from this fund could then support new mission initiatives, supplement stipends

Furthermore, such a programme would also usher in a new era of flexibility for clergy (and congregations), on agreed working hours, pay and conditions; creating, in effect, a significant new pastoral subsidiarity based on *trust*. Trust is that underrated theological virtue which is seldom appealed to in the ongoing debate on the financing of ministry. Trust and partnership might create a situation where appropriate decisions on pastoral provision would be made at the most appropriate level, which would often, but not always, be the local. Such a move would take some of the very best customs and arrangements of the past (prior to the standardization of housing and stipends), and blend it with the demands of the present and future, with the need for reflexivity and imagination in a new economic and ecclesial climate. It is precisely this kind of *phronesis* (practical wisdom) that the Church of England may need to contemplate urgently, if the priest-like task is to be adequately funded and supported in the future. The alternative is less palatable:

> ... when great institutions decline they do not suddenly fall over a precipice; they simply slide down the slope, a little further each year, in a genteel way, making do in their reduced circumstances, like a spinster in an Edwardian novel ... .[17]

The power and potential of the Church of England will undoubtedly lie in ever deeper local partnerships. There will need to be a marked shift away from the quasi-socialist paternalism of diocesan and central structures, which presently deprive local churches of the pleasure, desire and incentive in giving, precisely because congregations are conferred with almost no authority in how their gifts are to be reified and deployed. In short, more say for local congregations in how their money is spent might lead to more gifts being offered. But until a relationship of trust – rather than a system of taxation – is established as the true basis for funding the ministry of the church, we won't really find out what the future could be like. We will be condemned to struggle forever in the creeping penury of the present – fewer and fewer, paying more and more, for less and less.

---

and generally enable ministry in the locality. Discreet research in northern dioceses suggests that something approaching two-thirds of parishes could afford to 'buy-back' their benefice housing, creating an enormous pool of funds for generative mission in deprived areas, as well as providing sufficient resources to increase clergy pay where appropriate.

[17] Lord [Kenneth] Baker, from a speech in the House of Lords, and quoted in *The Economist*, 16 November 2002: 11.

References

Ammerman, N. (ed.), *Organizing Religious Work*, Hartford Seminary, Hartford, 2002.

Bowden, J. and Richardson, A., *A New Dictionary of Theology*, London, SCM, 1983.

Browning, D., *A Fundamental Practical Theology, Descriptive and Strategic Proposals*, Philadelphia, Westminster, 1991.

Carr, W., *The Priest-like Task*, London, SPCK, 1985.

Carr, W., *Say One For Me*, London, SPCK, 1992.

Graham, E., *Transforming Practice*, London, Mowbray, 1996.

Hill, M., *Ecclesiastical Law* (2nd edn), Oxford, Oxford University Press, 2001.

Hopewell, J., *Congregation: Stories and Structures*, London, SCM, 1987.

Morley, W. (ed.), *Partners in Ministry*, London, CIO Publishing, 1967.

Odom, W. *Fifty Years of Sheffield Church Life – 1866–1916*, Sheffield, J. Northend, 1917.

O'Neill, O., *A Question of Trust*, Cambridge, Cambridge University Press, 2002.

Pattison, S. and Woodward, J., *The Blackwell Reader in Pastoral and Practical Theology*, Oxford, Blackwell, 2000.

Paul, L. *The Deployment and Payment of Clergy*, London, CIO Publishing, 1964.

Percy, M. *Salt of the Earth: Religious Resilience in a Secular Age*, Sheffield, Sheffield Academic Press, 2002.

Percy, M. and Evans, G. (eds), *Managing the Church? Order and Organisation in a Secular Age*, Sheffield, Sheffield Academic Press, 2000.

Percy, M. 'Finding Our Place, Losing Our Space: Reflections on Parish Identity' in Coleman, S. (ed.), *Religious Identity*, London, Ashgate, 2003.

Poling, J. and Miller, D., *Foundations for a Practical Theology of Ministry*, Nashville, Abingdon, 1985.

Pounds, N. *A History of the English Parish Church*, Oxford, OUP, 2000.

Russell, A., *The Clerical Profession*, London, SPCK, 1980.

Scott, D. *From Office to Profession*, Pennsylvania, University of Pennsylvania Press, 1978.

Turnbull, R., *Generosity and Sacrifice: The Report of the Clergy Stipends Review Group*, London, Church House Publishing, 2001.

Williams, R., *On Christian Theology*, Oxford, Blackwell, 2000.

Chapter 2

The Shaping of Institutions

Anton Obholzer

It has long been a mystery – at least to me – what the factors are that cause the shape and shaping of an institution. It is, of course, a given fact that social, political and historical factors both conscious and unconscious make up the ingredients that determine an institution's shape, but I have never felt that these factors alone are sufficient to explain the differences between institutions. Even if we incorporate concepts arising from psychoanalysis, systems theory and from the group relations field, the resulting explanation still seems thin.

So, for example, a psychoanalytic systems approach that would see an institution 'representing' or 'unconsciously carrying' some aspects of the whole on behalf of the whole system makes sense but does not, in my view, necessarily take us that much further. An embodiment of this would, say, explain the Tavistock as representing the psychosocial approach to mental health in United Kingdom society at large while the Maudsley dealt with the biological mental illness element on behalf of the whole system. This explanation makes sense but still avoids the question of why one or the other, and what makes for the 'choice' of one or other institution to carry something on behalf of the whole.

It could, of course, be a case of the right institution starting up at the right place at the right time, thus a version of the view that successful revolutionaries are those that get the timing right – those that 'arise' at the wrong time are dead, buried and long forgotten. There is, in my view, a lot to be said for this perspective on institutions, particularly if they give 'voice' to a new 'need' they are to an extent revolutionary. If that is so, it of course raises the question of what process determines who initiates the founding of an institution at that time. It is, I think, by now clear that the capacity to think new ideas or, put another way, the courage to abandon old ideas and to view problems in a different way often happens in several unconnected places in the world at more or less the same time. It is as if the world 'state of mind' has reached a certain readiness to think a new idea and that this sometimes happens at different and often unconnected places. At times like this, what is then required are 'thinkers' who are prepared to 'think new thoughts' and to give expression to the 'new thoughts' in the systems that are

looking for an outlet. It is presumably by this means that thinkers
emerge who gather around them people who are engaged with the new
idea(s) and so institutions are born.

It is a question of importance whether the above thinkers are
actually the originators of the idea or whether they are merely the
psychological/ organizational 'midwives' to the process. The answer is
probably a combination of the two in which certain individuals have
more receptive psychological 'antennae' to pick up the signals about
societal change that are available to be picked up in the global 'ether'.

It seems to me to be important to give some thought to how these
processes come about, because it is these individuals who become the
'founder members' of institutions and who thus have a major influence
on the shaping of institutions. If the above hypothesis is correct,
namely, that founder members have particularly sensitive antennae to
what developments would be appropriate and bearable at the time, and
if they get their timing right, then one might assume that this quality of
'supersensitive in-touchness' would be a quality that would remain as
an attribute of the leader and of the organization. In effect, the opposite happens. No sooner is the organization founded than a relentless
process of ossification and bureaucratization sets in. The organization
moves on and increasingly becomes 'encrusted' with all sorts of rules
and regulations, which create an atmosphere the very opposite of
creativity. Before long, the situation arises in which the organization
itself becomes 'the establishment' that finds it difficult to tolerate
difference and creativity within its own boundaries. We thus have a
situation in which the 'shape' of the organization is pre-determined
and where any 'shaping' processes, particularly ones that are
generated within, are strongly resisted. Change processes from within
therefore have either to be powerful enough to foment and sustain a
rebellion or else they are wiped out.

It does, of course, raise the question of by what psychological and
institutional processes an organization that at its foundation is at the
zenith of societal 'in-touchness', within a relatively short period gets
to be out of touch and after that increasingly out of touch, and
therefore increasingly resistant to reshaping.

The traditional psychoanalytic perspective, with which I agree,
would be that unconscious defensive processes against the pain
inherent in the primary task of the organization, would begin to take
over and therefore creeping institutional rigidity would result and
pervert the primary task of the organization. The primary task would
thus become subverted and the new 'task' would be to put in place and
maintain defensive structures to protect and shield the staff from the
pain. This would therefore cause the institution to turn increasingly
'inward' and to be less and less in touch with external reality.

I have no problem with the above formulation, but feel that whilst it applies perhaps particularly in the people-changing sector, I am less convinced about it in the manufacturing and 'city' industries. It is as if the founders and 'founder state of mind' needs to be one of complete openness in order to get the institution off the ground, and then almost immediately the opposite becomes true – that the shutters need to come down in order to ensure that no 'alien thoughts' enter the system, putting the tender new institutional organism at risk. This, perhaps, also explains why institutional founders who continue to have new ideas leave or, more often, get thrown out in order to have 'new ideas' 'elsewhere' – sometimes founding a string of institutions – whilst their original organization then carries on in 'as if' mode in a model that bases itself on a rigid stylization of the original idea.

It is as if it is too painful, and also too risky for survival, to keep an open mind once the institution has 'found its feet', and instead the tendency is to consolidate the early gains surrounding the founding date, the founding fathers, and the founding idea(s). For a time, such institutions thrive, drawing in more staff and other resources, often following the model of a charismatic leader surrounded by acolytes. The power and emotional radiance emanating from such a leader often suppresses normal institutional conflicts and rivalries, and instead staff find their place at 'the feet' of the leader, each one 'basking' in their own quiet personal place of institutional transferential glory. And so, the institution gets off the ground, has a 'direction of travel' and a sense of purpose and enthusiasm. At the same time, the first signs of institutionalization appear: letterheads, mission statements, 'nobles' on the letterhead, and so on. The organization moves from being mean and lean to becoming increasingly bourgeois and institutionalized. In turn, those members that find themselves stifled rebel and either leave or are ejected. Thus, the first steps of the shaping of an institution are taken.

But I am sure that I am not the first person to have observed that institutions often take on some of the emotional qualities of the founding father(s)/mother(s). This is understandable, given the fact that the new institution arises from nothing in the sense of there not being a forerunner, and so it is not surprising that just as in vernacular architecture which uses as the building materials that which comes to hand on or near the building site, the same happens symbolically with institutions. One might argue that in creating an institution they thus use 'what comes to hand' in terms of approaches to problem-solving, states of mind and emotional qualities that are being recycled. The 'tabula rasa' of the institution, inasmuch as it ever existed, becomes colonized by qualities held in the behaviour and minds of the early founder members. This 'vernacular' approach to institution building is not necessarily a bad thing, for surely it makes sense for methods and

approaches to problem-solving and management that have been found
to be effective in the past or in other settings to be usefully applied in
the new setting. The problem lies not in the application but in the fact
that it often happens unconsciously and therefore without thought and
institutional debate relating to problem and task.

Just as in the case of institutional defences, the problem is the
'thoughtless' falling into a style and pattern of behaviour. In institutional defences against anxiety and pain, the problem is not so much
that there are defences but the fact that the anxieties and pain are not
aired and thought about, but that there is an emotional 'short-circuit'
where the causes are not got in touch with and thought about, and the
'remedy' is applied unconsciously. This therefore means that the
opportunity of thinking about and implementing the most psychologically and cost-effective way of dealing with the problem does not
happen, and the staff and institution are saddled with an unconsciously
generated, ineffective, and emotion- and resource-expensive system of
functioning.

I am postulating that the same mechanism is at play at the foundation stage of institutions. Thus, anxiety-inducing issues arise at the
foundation stage of a new institution. The institution then falls into a
problem-solving flight from anxiety that has a twin effect. On the one
hand, 'vernacular' solutions are rustled up as mentioned above – the
solutions often being based on the experience and experiences of the
founder(s). On the other hand, the problems and the solutions or
pseudo-solutions do not surface. In fact, they are swept under the
carpet so that there is no debate about the problem nor an open
approach to the solution. I believe that it is these mechanisms that
make for the shaping of the institution at its founding phase. There is
therefore often no documentation of how foundation practices were
decided upon, nor a formal record of what they are. Instead, a culture
arises of 'protecting our tradition' (in effect, based on the inner-world
defensive mechanisms of the founders), and of making sure that that
tradition is not veered from – it being about 'the way things have
always been done here'.

At the early stage of an institution, these mechanisms can at times
function quite well. There is certainty about how the work might be
done, the 'state of mind' that one might affect as a member of staff,
and a sense of certain clarity about the future.

As the institution in this model has, however, not set itself up for
ongoing change and as the outside world that commissions the
institution's services is in a constant stage of transition, trouble is often
not that far away. The trouble that then arises means that the clarifying
and problem recording and solving work that needed to have been
done at the beginning now has to be done at a later and much more

complicated stage. Symbolically speaking, it is as if the original foundations and foundation stone has got 'silted over' by a series of layers of institutional silt, and if the organization has to change, the original foundation and with it the primary task has to be exposed. To continue with the vernacular architecture simile, it is like a scenario in which the location of the service stop-cocks (e.g., water, gas, etc.), have been forgotten and overgrown and at the time of crisis or change or renovation, they have to be located and turned off before the new phase of work can be embarked on.

My hypothesis is thus that at a time of change, the basic structure of the organization, its task, its changes and risk to the workers, the hopes and expectations of the founders, and so on, have to be recovered or rediscovered and residual and unconscious matters dealt with before the organization is in a fit state to move to the next phase of its existence. This, of course, then leads on to the question of what it is that drives the need for organizational change or the reshaping of institutions. My experience is that the pressure for change is almost invariably a pressure from 'outside' – thus, a pressure from the other side of the institutional boundary is perceived. That is not to say that internal pressures do not arise or cannot be effective in the sense of change.

In cases like that, there is often an attempt to draw in an outside consultant and to then subvert the consultancy role into a leadership role so that the incumbent head can 'slip away'. Other factors that make institutions more amenable to change and therefore to reshaping have to do with a change in size, and therefore a change in the innate dynamic of the institution.

At other times, a change in legislation affecting the institution or the industry within which the institution functions makes for a need for change. Technological advances in the industry also make for pressures of change, as do retirement pressures in family businesses where there are perhaps not enough family members able or willing to be drawn into the business, and thus requiring the move from a family business state of mind to an organization that is more open and accountable.

There is, of course, also the question of time. The common fault is to believe that change can be delivered shortly after a decision to change has been made. In fact, it takes a long time for the juggernaut of change to get moving and 12–18 months for a process of change to show some effect is about par for the course.

It is not unusual for an external pressure to find an in-house counterpart that is prepared to work with or cooperate with a process of change. And, of course, it is not unusual in history for so-called 'traitors' to open the city gate or some other entrance point to allow

the 'outside enemies' to overrun the defenders of the status quo. There
are many factors that can lead to an in-house greater openness to
change. Illness of an incumbent senior office-bearer (often kept secret
within) is not an uncommon factor.

In my experience, these internal factors mostly make for a
willingness or more often a tendency or a vulnerability for external
change agents and pressures to find a leverage point – it is much rarer
for this to be a purely 'internal' process. As mentioned before, in cases
where there is by and large an internal pressure for change, the
likelihood is much more that those wanting change either form a semi-
autonomous 'enclave' within the whole or, more usually, are ejected to
go off and form a discrete and separate entity.

On the reshaping of institutions

If the above is true about the origin of shaping institutions, how about
the reshaping of institutions? From the perspective of the leader or the
leadership of an instiution, it is obviously essential to have an understanding of institutional processes if the process of change/reshaping is
to be initiated from within. That means it is necessary to have a
balanced perspective of the history of the institution – 'balanced' here
means neither an idealized venerating perspective nor one that
denigrates the past.

At the same time, it is not enough for there to be an 'in-house'
feeling of the need for change – that by itself only makes for the
previously-described process of either encapsulation or else of
ejection. Change from within must therefore link with external change
elements that might be constructively and effectively harnessed in the
service of change. This, in my view, is also in line with the leadership
role, which I see as being astride a porous boundary between the inside
and outside of the organization whilst being responsible for and in
charge of the ebb and flow of information, and particularly of 'reality'
across the boundary.

It would also seem to me that just as in the foundation phase of an
institution the 'timing' must be right and the leader must have the
capacity to 'time' and 'surf' the societal wave, so in the restructuring
of an organization. Thus, trying to reshape an organization from within
– if there is no internal pressure for change and particularly if there is
no external pressure – makes the chances of failure extremely high. It
needs to be assumed as a given fact that within any institution to be
reshaped, the majority opinion will be against change. That does not
necessarily mean that this resistance to change will manifest itself in
an open way. Far from it. Often, particularly in institutions in which

staff are anxious about job losses, resistance manifests itself as what might be termed 'fulsome support'. The effect of this support, or better named pseudo-support, is, however, a dragging of feet and a slowing down of change that effectively functions at least as resistance to change and at worst results in actual sabotage of the change process. This is to be taken for granted and regarded as a normal parameter of the institutional 'reshaping' debate. It is obviously important for there to be adequate time for debate; it equally needs to be noted that the hallmark of the resistance grouping is that there is never enough time or debate and that more is always required. Management of this effective use of time/time wasting difference of opinion is one of the key tasks of the reshaping of institutions.

I mentioned previously the importance of reviewing the primary task of the institution – both from the perspective of the trajectory the institution had travelled since it had been founded, but also from the perspective of the primary task for the future – taking into account external and internal pressures bearing on the task of the institution. The primary task, of course, also has to be seen in the context of the viability of the institution in its setting. There is no point in either continuing with or setting out on a particular course if the viability of the institution cannot be, at least to a substantial degree, assured by taking that pathway.

The concept of the primary task is itself an interesting and contentious one. Many nowadays see it as a restrictive concept that attempts to squeeze the organization into a straitjacket of sorts, thus cutting down on the flexibility of tasks so fashionable nowadays. But Miller and Rice, who coined the original concept, never saw or intended the primary task as restrictive in the above sense. They described the primary task as a 'heuristic' concept against which the work of the institution needed to be 'held' from time to time. It was thus more of a 'roughish' compass direction than a specific and restrictive compass bearing, the idea being that if there is no clarity or perhaps better relative clarity about the strategic direction of the institution, then it is very difficult to assess whether inside or outside pressures are likely to have a beneficial or a detrimental effect on the organization.

Of at least equal interest is the question of who determines the primary task of the organization, or who has the right to determine it. There is often a whole collection of stakeholders who would claim to have that right, starting with the founders, the funders, the staff, the clients, the community, among others. In practice, it is unusual for any one of these parties to have the definitive say over what the primary task is to be: in practice, what happens is that through a series of negotiations and compromises, a composite primary task is agreed and from then on it takes a fair degree of monitoring and ongoing negotiations to see that the agreement is maintained. Should the question then arise, either from internal or external sources, about the need for the primary task to be re-defined, then the whole process of negotiation between the stakeholders is stirred up again and eventually a decision reached that represents the power status of the stakeholders at the point of negotiation.

The whole process of negotiation as described above of course looks as if all of this happens on a purely conscious 'above board' process. In reality, a great deal of what goes on is 'below board', unspoken and often unconscious. The latter factors often refer to defensive processes arising from a process of defending against the psychic pain arising from the job. Just as in industrial processes in mines where the miners get coal-dust in the lungs with resultant lung disease, so in 'industrial' processes at the emotional coalface, the workers get symbolic 'dust' in the mind, and this latter takes the form of work processes that are unconsciously determined and act to shield the workers from the pain of the work. In effect, because the processes are not thought through, not in touch with what the problem is, and not geared to finding a solution, the end result is often both destructive of the workers and likely to blight the institution. But these defensive processes 'sloshing about' in the symbolic basement of the institution often make for the raw material that then finds itself transformed into anti-task processes. The anti-task ideas in reality, of course, are presented by the relevant stakeholders as valuable contributions to the institutional debate on the primary task, and it is sometimes a difficult process to disentangle anti- from on-task contributions to the debate.

Engaging with the process of change

In working at shaping and reshaping the organization, the technical question, of course, arises: how to involve the membership of the organization, and perhaps more importantly, where to start. Any organization consists fundamentally of its members, and if they are not engaged then, in practice, all one has is at best a business plan and at worst a piece of paper. Ideally, one would want the process of change to start simultaneously and equally at a variety of places throughout the organization – something that is perhaps best represented by 'open space' technology. In reality, however, it is much more likely for the change process to start in one or other sector or level of the organiza-tion and from there to spread through the rest of the organization. There are, however, risks to this way of proceeding, for those that are 'in the lead' of change are then lumbered with having to do the running on behalf of all, while the rest are at risk of falling into a passive/dependent state of mind, on the one hand 'waiting to be told' what to do next, on the other hand basking in the certainty of 'knowing best' what needs to be done but not having to put it to the test at all.

We are thus talking about getting the balance between leadership and followership right. Too 'solid' a leadership performance and one risks a passive, dependent followership, too fragile a leadership and the institution is engulfed by anxiety that paralyses it. Getting it wrong and needing to make adjustments to the trajectory of change is commonplace and inevitable. Without taking the risk of making mistakes, no progress can be achieved. Equally, not taking any decisions and 'leaving things as they are' is unfortunately not an option as the environment is constantly changing, requiring a constant adaptation process on the part of the institution. Maintaining the status quo is thus the equivalent of managing oneself into ossification. In a few rare instances where the task is to run a mausoleum, there is perhaps a certain charm inherent in this approach, but it certainly does not work in the majority of institutions.

A further dilemma is the question of to what extent worst-case/best-case scenarios should be spelt out. There is little doubt that in order for the change/transitional process to be effective, both elements are necessary. The risk, however, is of falling into an obsessive indecisiveness that halts progress or of working up possible negative scenarios to such an extent that all hope is lost. At this point – or preferably before this point – it is always advisable to have some good consultancy on-tap from someone who has either been there before and thus has the experience, or from somebody who is experienced at not falling into a panic at times of stress – someone who can retain a capacity to think when many around are losing their heads.

In conclusion

This paper explores some elements of institutional functioning that affect the shaping of institutions. The care strand that is explored is the concept that many of the assumptions on which both past and present behaviour is based are unconsciously held and therefore only accessed with difficulty as part of the process of change. Drawing in outside perspectives from a variety of sources, including consultancy, can help to remedy the situation and facilitate change.

Chapter 3

The Church of England Between Memory and Hope

Paul Avis

Over the centuries, the diocese of Exeter and the county of Devon have given the Church of England three of its greatest theologians. In chronological order they are John Jewel, Richard Hooker and Samuel Taylor Coleridge. The first two made their major contribution in the second half of the sixteenth century, the last in the first half of the nineteenth. The first was a bishop, the second a priest and the third a layman. This trinity of divines gives me my starting point for a reflection on the Church of England in memory and hope, in tradition and in mission, on the need to conserve the past and to build for the future.

By his writing and preaching Jewel consolidated the Anglican settlement at its fragile birth under the young Elizabeth I. A generation later Hooker feared for the Church of England at the hands of radical reformers within and helped to secure its future. Coleridge made trial of his age (as Newman put it) and set the Church on a fresh course of intellectual and imaginative renewal at a time when searching minds (such as Thomas Arnold) believed that it was finished. The emergence of Jewel, Hooker and Coleridge (among many others, of course), at the time when they were sorely needed, suggests that theological leadership is raised up in due season. I mention Coleridge first before reverting to the sixteenth century and then doing a hop, a skip and a jump to the present.

Coleridge was born at Ottery St Mary in 1772 and died at Highgate in 1834. Coleridge's father had been schoolmaster of the market town of South Molton (where I served as assistant curate in the extensive team ministry in the late 1970s), tucked under the edge of Exmoor. Coleridge senior went on to become vicar and headmaster at Ottery St Mary, east of Exeter, and this is where Samuel Taylor spent his early boyhood, in the valley of the River Otter. Though best known as a poet, critic and philosopher, Coleridge wrote on a range of theological issues, from Church and State to the inspiration of Scripture. He was immersed in the Anglican divines of the sixteenth and seventeenth centuries and championed Martin Luther and the Reformation. The rediscovery of

the Reformation by Julius Hare, F.D. Maurice and others in the mid-
nineteenth century, as a riposte to the later Oxford Movement's
dismissal of the Reformers, stems from Coleridge's inspiration. His
theological insights are to be found also in *Aids to Reflection* and in his
marginalia to earlier writers. Much of Coleridge's output has not yet
been 'received' by Anglicans, absorbed into the theological
bloodstream by a process of critical engagement. Nevertheless, just as
Hooker is our greatest theologian among the clergy, Coleridge must
surely rank as the Church of England's greatest lay theologian, a much
more creative and supple thinker than Gladstone, another contender as
the leading lay theologian of the Church of England.[1]

John Jewel was born at Great Torrington in North Devon in 1522
and died in 1571. He achieved recognition by a series of polemical
sermons of which the first and the last were preached at St Paul's
Cross in the City of London at the beginning of Elizabeth I's reign in
1559–60. Jewel's intervention at this point was critical. Elizabeth's
hold on the realm was rather tenuous and her personal position was
vulnerable. The constitutional religious settlement was balanced on a
knife-edge. All but two of the serving bishops declined to support the
shift to moderate Protestantism.

Jewel transformed the situation by turning a defensive theological
posture, directed against continuing Roman Catholic claims, into a
theological offensive. In the St Paul's Cross sermons he enumerated
27 medieval beliefs and practices, mostly concerned with the
Eucharist, and offered to convert to Rome forthwith if it could be
proved that any one of these could claim support from Scripture, from
the Fathers or from the ancient General Councils. Jewel's backers
(Archbishop Parker and the court) held their breath, fearing that he had
over-reached himself. But Jewel's challenge was not met. He was
rewarded with the bishopric of Salisbury and proved to be an excellent
bishop.[2]

Jewel followed up his preaching triumph with the first major defence
of the English Reformation and of the reformed English Church. The
Apologia Ecclesiae Anglicanae (1562) was little longer than a tract, but

---

[1] Coleridge, S.T., *Collected Works*, Princeton, Princeton University Press; London,
Routledge and Kegan Paul, 1972. On Coleridge and the Reformation see Avis, P.,
*Anglicanism and the Christian Church: Theological Resources in Historical
Perspective*, revised and expanded edition, Edinburgh, T. & T. Clark/Continuum,
2002, pp. 265–71. For Coleridge's views on Church and State see Avis, P., *Church,
State and Establishment*, London, SPCK, 2001, pp. 50-51. Both Avis (2002) and Avis
(2001) contain sections on Gladstone's ecclesiology.

[2] See Booty, J.E., *John Jewel as Apologist of the Church of England*, London,
SPCK, 1963; Southgate, W.M., *John Jewel and the Problem of Doctrinal Authority*,
Cambridge MA, Harvard University Press, 1962.

it made up in strategic importance what it lacked in length. Then, as though to show that he was not to be dismissed as an author merely of homiletic fireworks and slim volumes, Jewel responded at multi-volume length to criticisms of the *Apologia* from Stephen Harding, a Roman Catholic. Jewel's *Defensio Apologia Ecclesiae Anglicanae* was a theological blockbuster if ever there was one. With massive learning and enormous polemical skill Jewel succeeded time and again in manoeuvering his opponents into appearing to directly contradict the theological authority of the Fathers. No wonder that the *Apology*, translated by Lady Bacon, was chained up in every church to settle parish pump theological arguments and that Archbishop Parker wanted it appended to the Articles of Religion. Jewel provided the first sustained vindication of Anglican ecclesiology.

Richard Hooker was born at Heavitree, now a suburb of Exeter, but then a separate village, in 1554 and died in 1600 at Bishopsbourne, near Canterbury. In his *Of the Laws of Ecclesiastical Polity* Hooker provided the most accomplished and profound interpretation of Anglicanism ever given. He is the primary architect of an enduring Anglican ecclesiology – an idea of the Church of England that is neither torn from its pre-Reformation roots nor a muted echo of the continental Reformers.[3] Well might Izaak Walton claim that 'he that praises Richard Hooker, praises God, who hath given such gifts to men.'[4]

On the Cathedral Green at Exeter stands a statue of Hooker, seated and holding a volume of what is presumably his great work (with other volumes at his feet). He looks much older than the 46 years that were his allotted span, ground down with arduous study, no doubt! He is bearded, grave and venerable. Until a few years ago, the statue was unprotected and attracted graffiti from the passing trade of the city centre. Hooker was accessible – and vandalized. The Dean and Chapter took steps to remedy this: they fenced him in and planted a hedge of prickly thorn bushes around him. Now he is inviolable – but perhaps a little more remote.

I take that as a parable of how we are prone to treat our Anglican heritage. Either we ignore and neglect our tradition, as though it had nothing relevant to offer us today, or we idealize and romanticize it, put it on a pedestal, fence it round as holy ground, and make it remote and unusable. What we find difficult to do, it seems, is to indwell that tradition, wrestle with it and let it pervade and enrich our thinking and our prayer. We are not good today at 'receiving' (to use the term that is

---

[3] On Hooker's ecclesiology see Avis, P., 2002, pp. 31–51. On his view of Church and State see Avis, P., 2001, pp. 45–7.

[4] Walton, I., *The Lives of John Donne, Sir Henry Wootton, Richard Hooker and Robert Sanderson*, London, OUP, 1927, p. 220.

now indispensable in ecumenical theology) the resources of the tradition – diverse, contradictory and sometimes wrong-headed though they may be. If intellectual progress is made within what Alastair MacIntyre calls 'tradition-constituted enquiry', we Anglicans are not in a position to make much headway.[5] The theological imagination must inhabit the past life of the Church, as well as the Scriptures and the creative, nodal points of contemporary culture. Scripture, tradition and reason must be brought into conversation. Ultimately, they must come together and co-inhere in an integrated working of authority in theology and Church.

The Communion of the Saints, an article of the Creed, has a backward, tradition-constituted reference as well as a forward, eschatological one. Echoing Edmund Burke's words about society when revolutionaries set out to draw a line after the past, we may say that the communion *(koinonia)* of the Church 'is a partnership not only between those who are living, but between those who are living, those who are dead, and those who are to be born'.[6] The past is largely a lost world to most Anglicans, in spite of the liturgical calendar and all its commemorations. Our backs are turned to it. But as Simone Weil says in *The Need for Roots*:

> It would be useless to turn one's back on the past in order simply to concentrate on the future. It is a dangerous illusion to believe that such a thing is even possible. The opposition of future to past or past to future is absurd. The future brings us nothing, gives us nothing; it is we who in order to build it have to give it everything, our very life. But to be able to give, one has to possess; and we possess no other life, no other living sap, than the treasures stored up from the past and digested, assimilated and created afresh by us. Of all the human soul's needs, none is more vital than this one of the past.[7]

I am convinced that no one – but no one – can enrich Anglican theology more than Hooker himself, as he has done continuously for four centuries. Of course, Hooker is no more a timeless theologian than any other mortal can be. In spite of his assumed air of moral and

---

[5] MacIntyre, A., *After Virtue*, London, Duckworth, 1981. An admirable attempt to retrieve considerable swathes of the English Anglican tradition of spirituality is Rowell, G., Stevenson, K. and Williams, R., *Love's Redeeming Work*, Oxford: Oxford University Press, 2001. On the idea of reception see Avis, P., ed., *Discerning the Truth of Change in the Church: Reception, Communion and the Ordination of Women*, Edinburgh and London, T. & T. Clark/Continuum, 2003.

[6] Burke, E., *Reflections on the Revolution in France*, London, Dent (Everyman), 1910, p. 93.

[7] Weil, S., *The Need for Roots*, trans. A. Wills, London, Routledge, 1952, p. 51.

theological superiority, he was actually deeply implicated in the cut and thrust of polemic himself. He was so accomplished at it that it barely shows. But surely we have to confess that Hooker wears amazingly well. Hooker still has so much to offer us. His writings can still inspire and inform our reflection and prayer. We need more of his unwavering, calm, cultured, profoundly rooted spirituality. He can help us to know who we are as a church and as a communion. Hooker is our theological contemporary in the quest for true Anglican identity in the ecumenical context. It would be salutary if more of us immersed ourselves in Hooker, unworthy even to blow the dust off his wonderful writings though we are!

This enduring quality of Hooker's thought almost certainly has something to do with his own theological method – specifically the way that his argumentation soars above the theological squabbles of the day and takes every issue back to first principles. W. Speed Hill, the General Editor of the Folger Library edition of Hooker's works, suggests that 'this sense of his church's continuity with its own past is reinforced by Hooker's reluctance to cite from contemporary English advocates of conformity, such as Thomas Bilson, John Bridges, Matthew Sutcliffe, John Whitgift and Richard Bancroft, whose treatises he must have been familiar with.'[8]

When Hooker was appointed Master of the Temple at the age of 34, he found a rather formidable junior colleague already in residence. Walter Travers, a militant Calvinist and Presbyterian, was Lecturer (an independently financed assistant curate) for the evening sermon. Disappointed at not himself being appointed Master, Travers engaged in a running challenge to Hooker's position and his theology. The battle of the sermons began.[9]

Travers had already received Presbyterian ordination at Antwerp and subsequently refused episcopal ordination in the Church of England. Sacked by Archbishop Whitgift from his Readership at the Temple, Travers was allowed to retain his stipend and lodgings there. With their master still much in evidence, Travers' disciples made Hooker's life a misery. Though the dispute between Hooker and Travers at the Temple was initially about such doctrines as justification and predestination, it turned inevitably in the direction of Church

---

[8] Speed Hill, W., in McGrade, A.S., ed., *Richard Hooker and the Construction of Christian Community*, Tempe AZ, Medieval and Renaissance Texts and Studies 165, 1997, p. 16. However, it is apparent that contemporary sources underlie, strongly in places, Hooker's argument.

[9] See Haugaard, W.P., 'The Hooker-Travers Controversy', The Folger Library Edition of the Works of Richard Hooker, ed. W. Speed Hill, 5 vols, Cambridge: MA, Folger Library, 1977–93, V, Supplement I, pp. 264–9.

order – the shape of the Church and its ministry – and so prompted
Hooker's life's work.

Writing to Archbishop Whitgift to request a quiet country living,
one that would take him away from strife with his presbyterian
adversaries at the Temple Church, Hooker confessed that the
controversy there had prompted him to begin 'a treatise, in which I
intend a justification of the Laws of our Ecclesiastical Polity'. The
biographer of Walter Travers, Hooker's opponent, comments: 'Thus,
what began as an answer to a silenced Presbyterian preacher,
eventually became an answer to all who have ever questioned the
orthodoxy and catholicity of the Church of England.'[10]

Hooker gave shape to the reformed English Church. While
wholeheartedly sharing in the Reformation's rediscovery of the free,
unmerited grace of God in Jesus Christ, he vindicated the Church of
England's continuity with the Church of the Middle Ages and the
Early Fathers. It must be significant for Anglicanism that the writings
of its greatest divine are concerned, almost without exception, with the
nature of the Christian Church. It is a well-worn fallacy that
Anglicanism has no special doctrines of its own, a fallacy that has
been robustly refuted by Stephen Sykes in various writings.[11] Its
special doctrines are in the understanding of the Church itself, the
theological self-definition of Anglicanism and consequently its
ecclesiology as a whole.[12] Hooker points us to the Church, and
through the Church, to Christ. For him, the life of the Church – its
teaching of the faith and study of the Scriptures; its offering of prayer
and worship; its sacraments of baptism and the Eucharist; its pastoral
care and concern for its people – is the life of grace, a source of
strength, guidance and holiness for the Christian.

Hooker's polemic was not aimed, as Jewel's was, at the Roman
Catholic challenge to Anglicanism. It was directed at a different target:
the Puritan threat to the liturgy and polity of the Church of England
which, Hooker believed, was in danger of passing away like a dream.
He begins his Preface to the *Ecclesiastical Polity* with these words of
foreboding and resistance:

> Though for no other cause, yet for this; that posterity may know we
> have not loosely through silence permitted things to pass away as in a
> dream, there shall be for men's information extant thus much

---

[10] Knox, S.J., *Walter Travers: Paragon of Elizabethan Puritanism*, London,
Methuen, 1962, p. 88.

[11] Sykes, S.W., *Unashamed Anglicanism*, London, Darton, Longman & Todd,
1995, gathers the relevant papers together.

[12] Cf. Avis, P., *The Anglican Understanding of the Church*, London, SPCK, 2000.

concerning the present state of the Church of God established amongst us, and their careful endeavour which would have upheld the same. (*EP* Preface 1, i)[13]

To counter this threat, Hooker fights by fair means and foul, and the Puritans were unable to answer his arguments. Even more than Jewel, Hooker was virtually unanswerable. 'The Christian Letter' put out in 1599 by anonymous reformists in response to Hooker's first five books was little more than carping and spluttering. But it struck home when it parodied Hooker's fears, stated in his Preface, that the Church of England would pass away as in a dream. 'When men dream they are asleep, and while men sleep, the enemie [i.e. Hooker] soweth tares ... Therefore wise men [i.e. the reformists] through silence permit nothing to pass away as in a dream.'[14] Hooker's marginal comments on the 'Christian Letter' show that he was deeply riled, his patience tried beyond endurance.

Hooker knew that the reformed English Church was fragile; it was at serious risk from enemies within and without. He was afraid that the Church of England, a church both catholic and reformed, had no future. It was a real possibility. The Elizabethan Church survived, however, thanks not only to the theological justification provided by Hooker but also to the ruthlessness of Archbishops Whitgift and Bancroft in crushing opposition through state power and thus ensuring a period of relative calm. The quarter century that followed Hooker's death in 1600 has sometimes been regarded as a golden age of the Church of England. Its scholarly achievements have never been in doubt: *clerus britannicus stupor mundi* refers to this period. But recently the Jacobean Church has been singled out by historians for its pastoral strength. Kenneth Fincham[15] scotches the common caricature of the Jacobean bishops as a pack of timeserving careerists who cared little for their spiritual responsibilities. In the period of political stability under James I and VI, pastoring and preaching were renewed.

Of course, Hooker's premonitions of disaster were only deferred, and came home to roost during the Civil War. Many despaired of the Church of England and indeed of Christian civilization. Lucius Cary, Lord Falkland, one of the most brilliant lay theologians that the Church of England has ever had, courted death with a broken heart at the second battle of Newbury and perished at the age of 34.[16] After the

---

[13] Hooker, R., *Works*, ed. J. Keble, Oxford, OUP, 1835, I, p. 125 (Preface to *Of the Laws of Ecclesiastical Polity*).

[14] Folger edn, I, p. 6.

[15] Fincham, K., *Prelate as Pastor: The Episcopate of James I*, Oxford, Clarendon Press, 1990.

[16] On Falkland see Avis, 2002, pp. 85–88.

Parliamentary victory in the Civil War, the Church of England as we know it was demolished. Anglicanism as an ecclesial ideal was destroyed: the Prayer Book was proscribed; the Christian Year was abolished; the episcopate was banned; the supreme sacred symbol of the Church, the King, was executed and Archbishop Laud before him. An Anglican writer, looking back on the seventeenth century, said that the Church of England had been 'crucified between two thieves': the Puritans and the papists. But during those hidden years of Anglicanism – that are only now being adequately researched – theologians such as Hammond and liturgists such as Cosin were preparing for the day when Church and monarchy would be restored, as they were in 1660, and the Book of Common Prayer could be reimposed, as it was of course, in 1662.

Hooker was not the only Anglican luminary to fear for the future of his Church. In every generation, it seems, his forebodings have been echoed by some of the most gifted and perceptive of Anglican divines. Joseph Butler, author of the most subtle of all Anglican works of Christian apologetic *The Analogy of Religion, Natural and Revealed* (1736), as Bishop of Bristol, is said to have declined the see of Canterbury in 1747. He believed it was 'too late to try to support a falling Church'. Even if this refusal is apocryphal, it is of a piece with the well known words of the 'Advertisement' prefixed to the first edition of the *Analogy*:

> It is come, I know not how, to be taken for granted, by many persons, that Christianity is not so much a subject of inquiry; but that it is, now at length, discovered to be fictitious. And accordingly they treat it, as if, in the present age, this were an agreed point among all people of discernment; and nothing remained, but to set it up as a principal subject of mirth and ridicule, as it were by way of reprisals, for its having so long interrupted the pleasures of the world.[17]

Fears for the Church of England were never far from the surface towards the end of the seventeenth century and in the first decades of the eighteenth. 'The Church in danger' was an overused but not unwarranted slogan. The Church of England was widely thought to be buckling under the onslaught of Dissenters, deists, unitarians and other enemies of the Established Church, not least the heterodox within her own clerical ranks. In his *Letter to a Convocation Man* (1697) the High Church agitator Francis Atterbury, later Bishop of Rochester, painted a desperate picture of an age when 'such a settled contempt of

---

[17] Butler, J., *The Analogy of Religion, Natural and Revealed, to the Constitution and Course of Nature*, London, George Bell and Sons, 1889, p. 37.

Religion and the Priesthood have prevailed everywhere; when heresies of all kinds; when Scepticism, Deism and Atheism it self [sic] over-run us like a Deluge ... when the Trinity has been as openly denied by some ... when all Mysteries of Religion have been decried as Impositions of Men's Understandings ...'.[18]

How little Butler foresaw the resurgence of various streams of vital Anglican religion that was already springing up within the Church of England: the interacting Evangelical revival and Methodist movement, and the High Church revival, pastoral, theological and sacramental, that a time of comparative political stability fostered.[19]

Moving into the next century, we find Thomas Arnold, the Broad Church Headmaster of Rugby, despairing of the Church of England at the time of the First Reform Bill in 1832. Troubled by agricultural disturbances, and possessed of a sense of the impending dissolution of the old order, Arnold accepted that constitutional change was inevitable. He supported the moral and educational aspects of reform rather than the political agenda. But where, he wondered, would reform on secular, Enlightenment, utilitarian principles end? There was a danger of arriving at a secular constitution, like that of the United States of America, where no religion was recognized and there was no state-sponsored Christian education. In these circumstances one could not commend the Church by invoking 'our glorious constitution' or our 'pure and apostolical Church', as was the manner of some. Arnold knew that working people (on the land and in the burgeoning industrial towns) had no respect for either. Therefore, 'one must take the higher ground', not trying to preserve institutions for their own sake, but upholding the eternal principles that they both embody and distort. 'The Church, as it now stands, no human power can save.'[20]

Even Arnold could not foresee the strength and energy of Victorian religion, invigorated by the Evangelical revival and the Oxford Movement. At home it generated societies, missions, schools, church building, theological colleges, theological controversy, a hunger for

---

[18] Atterbury, F., *A Letter to a Convocation Man. Concerning the Rights, Powers and Privileges of that Body*, London, 1697, p. 2. On Atterbury and the High Church platform generally see Avis, 2002, pp. 77–81, 131–56.

[19] On the mainstream High Church revival, far less well known than the Evangelical and Methodist movements, see Mather, F.C., *High Church Prophet: Bishop Samuel Horsley (1733–1806) and the Caroline Tradition in the Later Georgian Church*, Oxford, Clarendon Press, 1992; Nockles, P.B., *The Oxford Movement in Context: Anglican High Churchmanship 1760–1857*, Cambridge, Cambridge University Press, 1994.

[20] Stanley, A.P., *Life of Arnold*, London, Ward Lock & Co., 1891, p. 184. See further for Arnold on the Church: Avis, 2002, pp. 271–8 and on his views of the national church, Avis, 2001, pp. 54–6.

published sermons, huge increases in the numbers of parochial clergy – even devout Anglican Prime Ministers (e.g. Gladstone and Salisbury).[21] Overseas it produced a consecrated missionary movement and the incipient Anglican Communion.[22]

Reflections

In these rather selective examples, drawn at a venture from four centuries, we see a pattern of threat giving rise to despair, followed by unforeseen spiritual renewal generating fresh energies and new theological and institutional paths for English Anglicanism. Does this pattern suggest anything to us today? It is not difficult to see parallels. Alarming indications of decline, numerical and financial, have been with us for some time. The established Church is comparatively marginalized in civil society. Its bishops and clergy are often derided, though not as virulently as in the past. The Church of England is affected by the paradox of decline in institutional religion, on the one hand, and the burgeoning of various forms of spiritual searching outside of official channels, as it were.

Our own ecclesiastical history teaches us not to be despondent. The prophets of doom, however reluctantly so – Hooker, Falkland, Butler, Atterbury and Arnold – misread the signs of the times. Let us not make the same mistake. The undeniable inroads of secularization (the diminishing impact of the Church on public life) should not blind us to the fact of real spiritual hunger and receptivity around us. That is particularly evident in the way that cathedrals and the greater churches, not least Westminster Abbey, draw thousands every week to their sources of spiritual refreshment. Pluralism (the recognition by law of a plurality of faith communities) should not deceive us into assuming that the role of a national church is *passé*. The great national shrines, Westminster Abbey and St Paul's, acquire an almost sacramental significance, as vessels of God's grace in Christ at times of national mourning and national celebration. The Church of England still feeds the multitude with the bread of life episodically. The

---

[21] On the institutional aspects of the nineteenth century religious revival see Burns, A., *The Diocesan Revival in the Church of England c.1800–1870*, Oxford, Clarendon Press, 1999.

[22] On the global impact of Anglicanism see Sach, W., *The Transformation of Anglicanism: From State Church to Global Communion*, Cambridge, Cambridge University Press, 1993; Jacob, W.M., *The Making of the Anglican Church Worldwide*, London, SPCK, 1997.

strategy must be to sustain this pastoral provision week by week in every community of the land.[23]

No one is taking this national mission away from us. Very few are telling us we are not wanted. But the traditional Anglican mode of mission – a profoundly pastoral one – can go by default. It can be lost through lack of vision, courage and energy. There is little enforced marginalization; mainly voluntary exile from the heart of the nation's life. Edward Norman's recent book *Secularisation*, though cast as a diatribe against the modern Church of England, contains a central, sound message that should not be overlooked: the marginalization of the Church is largely self-inflicted. The Christian faith has not been rejected. But the message of redemption has been muted and the cutting edge of mission has been blunted. Most people probably believe that the Church stands for a form of sentimentalized welfare humanism. The faith is not inculcated in season and out of season. Christianity is defended intellectually by only a few.[24]

We should not be reconciling ourselves to decline, to a 'bit part' in national life, but praying and working for the renewal of the Church that will generate fresh energies for mission. Revival, an awakening among the people, not internal exile, may lie ahead if we are ready for it.

Hooker shows us a Church among the people and for the people. Now we need, I believe, to transpose Hooker's vision of a Church wedded to the nation to our own situation, one that is marked by secularization and pluralism. The Church of England's missiological commitment to the community cannot any longer be on the basis of state-enforced religious uniformity or an Anglican religious monopoly (those were destroyed centuries ago). It must find its ground in an understanding of mission and ministry – ministry in the cause of mission – that will give it a rapport with individuals, households and communities, especially at the symbolic milestones of life, the rites of passage that the Church sanctifies through her occasional offices. That engagement at the level of personal, familial and communal faith provides the platform and spiritual power base – the ecclesial credibility, in fact – for the Church's simultaneous mission in terms of civil society, as an institution among institutions, and for its engagement with the State (an equally missiological issue). So let us turn to the question: how can the Church, acting in the spirit of Richard Hooker, strengthen its links with the population and respond to the spiritual longing and questioning that we find all around us?

---

[23] The ideas on pastoral method and strategy that follow are developed in Avis, P., *A Church Drawing Near: An Applied Theology of Mission and Ministry*, Edinburgh and London, T. & T. Clark/Continuum, 2003.

[24] Norman, E., *Secularisation*, London, Continuum, 2002.

In a society undergoing secularization, we need to take the persistence – indeed the resurgence – of the sense of the sacred in our culture seriously. As a Church we need to address both the public forum of social policy and the private forum of individual conviction and personal religious experience. We should demonstrate that we value, nay prize, the ordinary parochial way of being a Christian, where the life of the Church and the life of the local community interpenetrate. We need to make it clear that we do not restrict our appreciation of religious experience to our own particular fold, but recognize the grace of God and the presence of the Holy Spirit working beyond the political structures of the Church. Thus we can help individuals to make the essential connection between their most deeply cherished moments and the unique gospel entrusted to the Christian Church.

In a society that is being secularized, the Church should speak boldly to the conscience of the nation by enunciating moral and religious principles that are in danger of being overlooked or eclipsed. But it should speak at the same time to the heart of the individual who has an awareness of a sacred realm and experiences intimations of the reality of God, but who has not yet identified these glimmerings with the gospel of Christ.

If mission is understood like this, in the pastoral mode – as the leading edge of the ministry of word, sacrament and pastoral care – it must be offered on as broad a front as possible, through a multiplicity of points of access: sacred persons (clergy and other representative ministers); sacred places (parish churches and chapels; churchyards and crematoria chapels; quiet rooms in secular institutions, etc.); and sacred occasions (not only Sunday worship, but on every occasion that is significant for the values of the community, in season and out). The Church must take the risk of exposing its gifts of grace all along the boundary with an increasingly secular society. Deeply implicated in the structures of community and civil society, in a way that I am sure Hooker would approve, it needs to be perceived as welcoming the spiritual aspirations of individuals, couples and families, of communities, organizations, institutions and societies. Not condemning them for their shortcomings, but if anything erring on the side of charitable presumption, giving the benefit of the doubt, not breaking the bruised reed or quenching the smouldering flax. The Church vindicates its place in society when it is seen to be committed to nurturing the wholeness of human beings, strengthening the bonds of family and community and deploying its pastoral resources where the volume of human need is greatest.

Chapter 4

Task: A Transcendent Notion

Edward R. Shapiro

As a theologian, Wesley Carr's interest in institutions brings an abiding interest in the transcendent. His mind moves quickly from the individual through institutions to society. Re-examining our jointly authored work, *Lost in Familiar Places*, I will describe from the perspective of a working colleague Wesley's focus on the way individuals are inevitably working 'on behalf of,' and the implications of that notion for grasping the dynamic shaping of institutions and their links to society.

Wesley Carr and I wrote a book together, trying to bring our two vastly different worlds into some congruence to consider the experience of being 'lost in familiar places' (Shapiro and Carr, 1991). From his perspective as an Anglican priest and mine as a Jewish psychoanalyst, we had jointly discerned an experience of disorganization in our constituents and ourselves. The book, which took us several years and some shared vacations on both sides of the Atlantic to write, allowed us to negotiate our different professional languages and perspectives to outline an approach that might allow individuals to locate themselves in the confusing swirl of rapid social change. It is from that experience of writing together that I can speak about how Wesley Carr uses his theological perspective to shape his thought. In what follows, I shall briefly review the basic concepts we developed together and then focus on the second half of our book, in which his thinking takes the lead.

The editors of this volume invited an examination of Wesley Carr's pastoral theology and its contribution to the 'shaping of structures.' The theoretical filter through which I know Wesley's ideas about these issues is the study of organizations and groups, derived from the tradition of the Tavistock Institute for Human Relations. Wesley has consulted to my organization (Shapiro and Carr, 1987), thought with me about this kind of work (Carr and Shapiro, 1989), and joined me in consulting to other organizations (Shapiro and Carr, 1991). While I brought to our collaboration the views of an individual psychoanalyst and family theorist, Wesley brought the perspective of the religious institutional leader focused on organizational and social dynamics.

Task

The basic conceptualization behind the Tavistock tradition derives
from the thought of Wilfred Bion (1961). Bion's seminal notion was
that people in groups and organizations are consciously and
unconsciously linked by their commitment to the group's task. An
organization's primary 'task' – that which is necessary for the
organization's survival – is carried out on behalf of its larger context,
which may be as vast as society. For example, hospitals take care of
the ill so that society can have healthy members. 'Task,' therefore,
connects individuals to that which transcends them as individuals and
the organization as a group; it links individuals to particular sets of
shared values and beliefs (Shapiro and Carr, 1991; Shapiro, 2001).
This transcendent notion, which has been further elaborated by many
authors including the two of us, has about it something faintly
idealistic, perhaps even 'religious.' At the very least, the notion of task
is heuristic, for it serves as a lens through which to study aspects of
group members' rational and irrational behaviors.

Attention to how individuals work at or avoid the group's task
illuminates group dynamics and the nature of irrational group interaction. So, for example, a family, conceived as a social organization,
has the task of facilitating the mastery of developmental tasks for each
of its members. Family members' rational and irrational behavior in
relation to this task can illuminate some of the dynamics of the larger
society of which the family is so central a part. For example, a family
torn by divorce may be unable to provide a working example of
heterosexual collaboration for the child at particularly vulnerable
developmental periods, leading to an internalized picture of gender
confusion representing aspects of society's changing picture of
appropriate gender roles.

Social structures are shaped by and shape human connections.
Wesley Carr focuses his thinking on the notion of joining – whether as
conscious decision or through unconscious relatedness. As an
organizational leader, he sees how membership evokes complex
dynamic connections to larger forces that are out of our awareness. For
example, he describes the often denied and unconscious influence that
larger group entities have on us as individuals: a professional organization, a religious tradition, a nation. He sees how such connections
are mobilized at times of national emergency or during profound
personal anxiety, such as birth or death, exercising a powerful
influence. With Erik Erikson (1968), he notices that our identities are
inevitably 'identities in context,' underlining how we are shaped
within social institutions and among the chronic uncertainties and
ambiguities of social interaction.

A story

In his writings and in his speaking to congregations, Wesley Carr often uses stories to put into ordinary language the ideas that he wishes to convey. Following his lead, I will offer one such story, presented to me at a recent English conference in a discussion about ethnicity. Tom, a black social worker and church member reported the following: 'I was on a bus, during the firemen's strike, and a group of black teenagers began harassing the bus driver. None of the white passengers moved or intervened in any way. As the teenagers' harassment grew in intensity, I thought with some irritation and anxiety, 'Why do *I* have to do this?' Finally, I got up and spoke to the group of kids about the current tensions in the environment and the dangers of their behavior and asked them if they could contain themselves, which they did. I did not like the role I was in.'

This story concisely conveys many of the issues that Wesley Carr grasps so clearly in his thinking. An individual finds himself, almost against his will, in a role – and feels pulled in ways he can't fully articulate or discern into a risky engagement with a task that transcends his personal needs. Tom says, 'Why do *I* have to do this?' This man is 'lost in familiar places.'

The story raises a number of questions. Who says he 'has to?' Are the pressures he experiences coming from his personal psychology or from the social surround? And, for whom is he responding? Dr Carr and I write, 'The more we become aware that our experience of ourselves is affected by others, not just in our families but in the larger contexts in which we live, the less sure we seem to become about where our individual experience begins and ends' (Shapiro and Carr, 1991: 63).

Tom's second comment is similarly puzzling. He says, 'I did not like the role I was in.' Does this mean the role is 'not I'? Each individual, in some situations, may choose a role (making it feel like part of the self). Alternatively, he may find himself in a role as a consequence of factors beyond his grasp (unconscious family dynamics, hidden ethnic identifications), making it feel somewhat alien to the self. Under whose authority does Tom take up this role and task – and on behalf of whom? Is he acting in his role as an adult, a social worker, a church member, a black man? Does it matter? And, if he has the time to reflect, what sense does he make of what he has just done?

An interpretive stance

From the acknowledgement that in our social interdependency, 'I' cannot with any certainty be differentiated from 'not I,' Wesley and I developed the notion of the 'interpretive stance.' This stance takes individual experience, places it in the context of a role, links it with external evidence, and attempts to discern the relevant context that is affecting that experience. We suggested that individuals, paying attention to their experience, could make sense of their place in the social surround. They can begin to locate themselves, and this mapping of their experience also maps the social surround.

We wrote about organizations as 'intermediate' containers of experience, suggesting that organizations are more graspable by individuals through the experience-containing boundaries of their roles and the organization's task. Organizational experience in role, therefore – though often confusing – is more coherent than attempting to locate oneself within the vast ambiguity of 'society.' The organization's task provides a central connection to the larger world. Individuals join (both consciously and unconsciously) the organization's primary task, linking their values, ideals and beliefs to their role performance (Shapiro, 2001). We defined organizational role as a function of the particular task, and as the place where the individual and the context meet.

On behalf of

The relevant context consists of others in related roles, each acting 'on behalf of' something larger. We take in others' communications, not only through their language but also through their behaviors and the unconscious pressures they put on us to conform to their needs. And, we often act on behalf of others in ways we do not fully see. Sometimes this happens through an unconscious family agenda that we live out for the generations before us, sometimes through a role we take up in an organization or through some other symbolic function for society, as in our story about Tom.

Let us pursue our story by examining Tom's role in his church organization. Wesley Carr focuses on the social pressures that help shape organizations and are symbolically transmitted within them, affecting individuals in particular roles. In his study of a church in our book, for example, he connects an internal organizational controversy about the placement of a statue of Mary to the tensions in the surrounding neighborhood about ethnicity, religion, the toleration of differences, social devaluation, competition and belonging. Through this examination, he raises for scrutiny the symbolic function and social task of religious institutions, which individuals carry in their role as members.

Religion

Wesley Carr argues that the primary task of religious institutions is to help contain irrationality (as it relates to ideas about that which transcends human knowing) and dependency on behalf of the larger community. He notes that a major function of religious organizations is 'to bring people together,' linking them through their inter-dependency and organizing them around their feelings about the transcendent. He suggests that leaders in these institutions, who are at the boundary between the organization and the outside world, can generate hypotheses about these dynamics, as they are being experienced and managed within the organization, so that members of the religious community can begin to negotiate their social relatedness to the larger social community.

Wesley notes that religious organizations deliberately acknowledge dependency through belief in God, pastoral activities and acts of worship. Like art, religious bodies acknowledge the irrational aspects of daily life without presuming that such aspects are pathological. Religion both affirms dependency (which society can devalue as 'immature') and deals with emotions, like fear, love, grief, guilt and anxiety.

Because of this focus, Wesley suggests that the social task of religious institutions is to enable individuals to face the connections between their interdependency and their feelings about the transcendent by providing a managed and contained context for both. He argues that the unconscious interaction between members of the society and its religious institutions constitutes a key symbolic containment (a 'holding environment'), which provides for safe regression and the possibility of empathic connections between members of the larger society. The ritual and symbols of religion facilitate a shared regression in which problematic feelings and experiences (around dependency and the search for transcendent meaning) can be dealt with in a constructive rather than chaotic manner. Regression, in this sense, refers to a type of psychological fusion with the larger whole, which links us to something beyond the self and beyond our grasp: the transcendent. Dr Carr further suggests that both the activity of church members and the unconscious relatedness of those in the outside world to religious institutions may facilitate a general social regression away from isolation and toward interdependency in the service of a society's survival and development. Such unconscious connections to these social issues through his church membership might have served, in part, to mobilize Tom (through regression) in his reactions to the actions of the disruptive teenagers.

How is such organizational influence transmitted in religious institutions? There are two central areas of religious ritual that address these social issues, and Dr Carr elaborates these ideas in his other writings as well. The first is the ritualized affirmation of the transitions – or, what he refers to as the 'ultimate boundaries' – of life, including the entry into the world and the exit from it. Rituals are linking phenomena, allowing for recognition of connections to the past, to cultural heritage, and to the significant developmental transitions (birth, adolescence, marriage and death). For believers and unbelievers alike, such rituals allow for constructive regression and joining, which furthers the development of both participants and others. In *The Birth of Tragedy*, Nietzsche sees the action on stage as the constitution of tragedy, insofar as the individual actors separate themselves out from the chorus/music and therefore suffer. We suffer as individuals by experiencing the individual/group tension in the temporary fusion we share, and then give up.[1] Recapturing that interconnectedness, however temporary, allows for further development.

The second major area for religious ritual is in the service of certain public events, particularly around death. For example, Dr Carr speaks of the national service in London managed by religious leaders after the Falklands victory in 1982, noting that the service needed to attend in a more complex way than the simplistic victory that was politically expressed, incorporating the conflicting feelings of rage, grief, jubilation, horror and vindictiveness. Within the publicly held ritualized celebration, religious spokespeople could offer a more complex, linking interpretation that allowed integration of disparate groups into a diverse community. In their identification with this linking interpretation, individuals could regress and develop out of their highly differentiated, often narcissistically invested, and conflicting positions into a more unified identification with a complex society. Another, more recent, example, with the same task but in a very different setting, was the funeral of Diana, Princess of Wales. This kind of managed regression and search for a greater sense of connectedness can allow individuals to transcend their narrow ethnic or other subgroup identities into a larger sense of relatedness to shared ideals. These ideas have application through American religious practices as well as in Britain. Possibly, Tom was influenced through this kind of relatedness to the national tensions around the firemen's strike.

---

[1] I am grateful to Dr John Muller for this point.

Illusion and delusion

Dr Carr focuses on the space between 'illusion' and 'delusion'. The first constitutes the normal range of fantasies with which most of us live our lives (e.g. that we will not die, that we are good people). These are explorable illusions and testable with others. In contrast, 'delusion' is a pathological state in which a person constructs an idiosyncratic, untestable world in which to live. Religious bodies, he asserts, have an interpretive function, which can provide individuals and various groups with a focus for projecting the irrational parts of themselves, which emerge from deep within the self, where the difference between illusion and delusion is often difficult to discern.

Dr Carr states that religious institutions keep alive the ultimate illusion – the notion of God – used to contain destructive aggression. Churches themselves do not contain illusions; instead, the act of professing God has that function. He outlines the conflict around the individual's need for an object on which to depend and the contemporary positivistic assumption that belief in God is a delusion. In their focus on the other world – God, life after death, a spiritual dimension to existence – religious institutions represent for the larger society a major area of human life that many feel is irrational. Commitment to such notions can support personal risk taking and surrender, as in Tom's engagement with the troublesome adolescents.

The role of citizen

Society uses the issue of difference (skin color, ethnicity, religious or sexual preference) as initial containers for projections used to stabilize the chaos individuals feel about living in the 'unstructured large group' of society. If, as an isolate, I cannot find or negotiate recognizable connections with others, I can at least begin to recognize that I am 'not them'. If 'they' are white, I can at least be 'black' and locate myself in a discernable subgroup with which I can feel a kind of membership. It allows me to make some sense of an otherwise dauntingly complex world that can feel incomprehensible. Wesley Carr notices this effort at simplification, suggesting that the dynamic of polarization can allow individuals to 'focus anxiety, aggression, alienation and other unmanageable feelings derived from the chaos of living in an international society' (p. 170).

In our story, feelings of membership in a 'black' subculture could have allowed Tom to recognize some of the social forces mobilizing the anger and rebellious acting out of the black adolescents and moved him toward an empathic identification with them against the (white?)

authority of the bus driver. This, in conjunction with his larger social identification (through his church membership?) with the British culture and the momentary threat to it during the fireman's strike may have precipitated a conflict within him. This could have led to his recognition that only he, in the bus, could face the adolescents' aggression (since he also felt it) that he could intervene to help them recognize the social consequences of acting it out.

In Tom's intervention, he offered the adolescents an identification with his multiple roles – black adult man, church member, citizen – so they could place their reactions in a more contained structure. Such a formulation is an example of Wesley Carr's idea that we mutually negotiate such 'institutions-in-the-mind' in order to 'manage in a controlled way our inevitable unstructured regressions in the face of the imminent and threatening power that society represents' (Shapiro and Carr, 1991: 171). Such roles within institutions – related to institutional tasks – 'begin to enable the individual to establish sufficient self-definition to be able to examine and then competently assume the necessary range of social roles within society' (p. 172). In our story, Tom has to filter his experience through the range of roles he has in his 'institutions in the mind,' so that he can take up, however reluctantly, the effective role of a participating citizen.

We can now begin to answer some of the questions Tom raises. First, he asks, 'Why do *I* have to do this?' Based on the ideas Wesley Carr has developed, we would approach this question by the examination of Tom's several roles. The first would be Tom's role as a black male adult. Through this role, Tom can feel the anger of black youths without being too afraid of it; he is one of them. Secondly, through his role as church member, he has identified with the transcendent interdependency that belief in God entails.

Tom says, 'I did not like the role I was in.' In response to Wesley's ideas, we would consider the importance of ritual in Tom's life – possibly the rituals in his church and those carried out in the larger society. As Wesley describes, such rituals provide space and symbols for containing diverse feelings, allowing for a regression away from isolated differentiation toward the uncovering of transcendent connections. Wesley points to the shift from isolation toward a negotiated interdependence and work on the nature of that dependency. That Tom does not 'like' the role he is in, points to the conflict in roles he is experiencing and, with reflection, might lead to an internal inquiry about a significant social tension he is containing between ethnic identity and citizenship.

This complex inquiry 'on behalf of' the larger society is, I would suggest, contained in Tom's question, 'Why do *I* have to do this?' Wesley Carr's contribution would suggest that this tension represents a question for all of us – that it lies behind the experience of being 'lost in familiar places' – and that the exploration of the answer underlies the experience of living 'on behalf of.' I suspect that Wesley would refer to this experience as 'The Way of the Cross.'

Final comments

The methodology we developed in our book has extensive practical application. Using the interpretive stance we developed, Wesley and I have consulted to organizations as diverse as psychiatric hospitals, group study organizations and law firms. The interpretive stance, which allows a negotiated perspective on group and organizational irrationality, can be used to help individuals take up task-related authority to realign groups and organizations with shared values, tasks and social aims.

Wesley Carr's insight into the inextricable link between individuals and their social institutions provides a structure for examining our participation as individuals in society's developing systems of beliefs and values. Work on this transcendent social relatedness and interdependency through the medium of responsible role and task commitment lies at the heart of taking up responsible authority as a citizen.

As a theologian, Wesley Carr has found a way to integrate his beliefs with a deep psychological approach to the way human beings work and live together. In our book, the presence of a perspective on, and deep commitment to, the transcendent permeates his thought.

References

Bion, W.R., *Experiences in Groups*, London: Tavistock, 1961.

Carr, A.W. and Shapiro, E.R., What is a 'Tavistock interpretation?', in Carr, A.W. and Gabelnick, F. (eds), *Proceedings of the International Symposium*, Washington: A.K. Rice Institute, 1989.

Erikson, E.H., *Identity, Youth and Crisis*, New York: W.W. Norton, 1968.

Shapiro, E.R. and Carr, A.W., Disguised countertransference in institutions, *Psychiatry*, (1987) 50: 72–82.

Shapiro, E.R. and Carr, A.W., *Lost in Familiar Places: Creating New Connections between the Individual and Society*, New Haven: Yale University Press, 1991.

Shapiro, E.R., The changing role of the CEO, *Organizational and Social Dynamics*, (2001) 1: 130–42.

PART TWO
PASTORAL THEOLOGY
AND CHRISTIAN MINISTRY

Chapter 5

Revisiting Teams

Stephen Lowe

Introduction

Whether many clergy and laity like it or not team ministries are all around us in the Church of England. On their effective functioning diocesan bishops depend through their staff meetings. Teams in chapters, hitherto clerical and now with laity, administer the cathedrals of the land. At parish level many dioceses have a clear policy to encourage the development of more team ministries and many clergy coming from theological colleges and training courses positively seek the opportunity to work in a team context. It is now nowhere near so difficult to recruit into them and those in the larger teams particularly show much greater enthusiasm for this model of ministry. The isolation that has bedevilled so many working in difficult urban contexts is certainly challenged by team ministry as well as the more effective deployment of a shrinking body of stipendiary clergy. Wesley Carr has played a key role in institutional consultancy particularly within the Church of England and this paper reviews his writing, some of his own practical consultancy and offers a critique of the current practice of team ministry within the Church.

A critical view of team ministries

Team ministries have got themselves a bad name. When Wesley Carr wrote *The Priest-like Task* in 1985, many of the team ministries in the Church of England were struggling, riven by built-in inequalities amongst themselves and a laity who felt that a team ministry had been imposed on them with little obvious benefit. Twenty years on there have been some substantial changes and some of Wesley's critique of team ministry can now no longer be justified.

In 1995 the Team and Group Ministries Measure came into force, which gave an opportunity for greater equality between team rector and team vicars. Good practice now gives all members of the team the same leasehold term of office. In many dioceses the model of team ministry has changed with a team benefice and a number of parishes both retaining their own Parochial Church Councils (PCCs) and church wardens. The team council can then be seen more clearly to add value to the pattern of ministry in the parish.

Carr identifies three problems inherent in team ministries. (Carr, 1985: 66) The first concerns the nature of authority within a team. He points out that all team members derive their authority from the bishop and by implication the rector has no greater authority than any other team member.

Second, 'dependence cannot be worked with unless the ministry provides dependability.' Parishioners, he suggests, are faced with a choice of ministers of apparently equal authority with the consequence that the task of the team may become that of dealing with the implications of these situations rather than with the actual expectations of the people.

Third, Carr believes that teams are fundamentally unsuitable as a pattern for a stable continuing institution. The suggestion is that team ministry is designed to release a variety of gifts in useful ways for the whole ministry of the local church. The assumption is that team members will then work with 'short, explosive bursts of creative energy, such as may be demanded by research to solve a defined problem.'

What makes this revisiting of *The Priest-like Task* so interesting for me is that at the time of its publication Carr was consultant to the East Ham team ministry when I was its team rector. He became consultant to Sheffield Cathedral chapter in the 1990s and in the last year has provided some consultancy to the Pendleton team ministry in Stretford, all three, I want to suggest, providing effective ministry to the parishes and Cathedral they serve.

East Ham

This was to be a new piece of team ministry, still very much in its early days as a model of ministerial practice, when I was asked to go there in 1975. The parish was at this stage of its development already large, some 36,000 people living within its boundaries. There were four distinct areas. In the north around Upton Park and its football ground, was the old parish of St Albans. Already seeing a growing Asian population the area had a rich ethnic mix. The local school my children attended had a wealth of different languages as mother tongues among the children. There was also a substantial Afro-Caribbean community. The church building had only recently been demolished and there was still a well-used church hall and a spare piece of land.

Close to East Ham's Town Hall was the enormous St Bartholomew's Church, seating 1200 and at one stage canvassed as a potential Cathedral for a new East End diocese. It cost more to put on the heating (and still freeze) than was taken in collections. This was the heart of East Ham with its local government offices, town centre, technical college and police station. In the south was the ancient Norman Church of St Mary Magdalene surrounded by allegedly the largest churchyard in England at some 12 acres. The community it served was still the nearest Newham came to suburbia, largely white and the property mostly owner occupied. In the south was Newham's docklands, then in terminal decline, with a small community of residents close to Beckton's gas works. Over the 13 years this area was to gain 20,000 new residents.

During its life the team grew to four team vicars, two non-stipendiary clergy, three Church Army officers, a reader, a community worker and a full-time parish administrator. Six new building developments were undertaken. At St Alban's the hall was reopened as a small church centre with 11 flats attached enabling the development to be funded. At St Bartholomew's the large church was demolished and replaced by a new substantial church centre in partnership with Newham Council, including day centre and luncheon club facilities for the elderly, a lounge and coffee bar open all day, meeting rooms, a medical centre with accommodation for a doctors' practice and 26 flats built as sheltered housing. Later the large former Rectory which was listed was to be converted into rooms for a thriving Asian Women's language and Social Work project, a Day Nursery and more flats. The Church Army Hartley Youth Centre underwent refurbishment and extension focusing on work with young unemployed. At St Mary's, in partnership with the local museum, the churchyard was turned into a nature reserve with a new interpretative centre built to provide access for local schools. In Beckton a new Church Centre was to be built with participation from all the denominations (including the Roman Catholics) and in partnership with The London Docklands Development Corporation. It was clearly a time of immense change, economically, socially and ecclesiastically and the team had to work with the laity in enabling this change to take place.

It wasn't easy. Managing the dynamics of rapid change never is, and the clergy particularly found themselves coping with the dynamics of loss of security both in church and community. Knocking down a church building is destroying one of the symbols of stability and changelessness for a community already undergoing massive change even if you replace it with something more useful. I suspect there was also the sense the team ministry was where the action was in church life, which could lead to a sense of powerlessness amongst the laity or a high number of ordinands. We had both.

The task was made easier by a very able team of clergy and lay people. When things did go wrong it was clear that the work of the whole team became disabled. The imagery of the connected body was very real to everyone involved and some members struggled with it having been trained to expect a sole charge responsibility rather than a team where mutual accountability and a share in an overall task for the team was a prerequisite.

Carr worked hard to ensure that there was a clear definition of task for the team ministry. No working institution can operate without a mutually agreed definition of the task and commitment to it. We accepted it and refined it on several occasions. Vivid memories remain of the two approaches to team ministry which Carr offered: the cake and column models. The cake was the slicing up of the work of the team into cake segments with the team rector working at the boundary between 'the cake and the world'. The column model had clearly defined pieces of work and areas of responsibility forming the individual columns with the team rector providing the linking slab across the whole edifice.

Carr was working hard at the same time in the Diocese to establish what he describes as the consultancy model of ministry (Carr, 1985: 14–18).

> Such a person has skills, but he chiefly uses what he feels is required in his role as consultant to offer interpretations to those with whom he is working. Using himself to try and discern what they are doing and what is happening to them, his particular skill is to be able to hold apart what is being put into him from what was already there. He uses himself as a measure and his commitment is to enable those with whom he is working to understand what is happening and then to take their own authority for acting. This he does by offering interpretations that are built upon the evidence both of what all may see and hear and of what he experiences as happening to him. He shares in himself the feelings of all but consistently interprets them by relating them mainly to a point of reference, namely the task'. (Carr, 1985: 15)

Carr offered this as a model of priesthood in the church but what his personal consultancy to the East Ham team offered was a clear working model for the role of the team rector. In East Ham, in the latter years of my stay there, there was a floating role for the team rector with no particular responsibility for any one church. The work was very much being under all yet over all, supporting and enabling the ministry of my colleagues and indeed the whole institutional system and at the same time working at the boundaries, interpreting the institution to the church and world outside. The accountability was to the team as a whole for this role and to the Bishop who gave both me and the other members of the team authority to exercise our ministries. Carr had encouraged me to attend the Tavistock Institute's Human Relations Conference at Leicester. Lasting a fortnight it created a temporary institution to explore the nature of authority, leadership and organization with an international membership drawn from many backgrounds. Together with the Conferences Carr provided for Chelmsford clergy at Clacton and another two Leicester events I was given the basic tools for understanding the processes of organizational behaviour. I would still regard this form of training as an essential tool for those working in teams just as I would regard the involvement of a consultant to the team ideally with some of this training in his or her background.

The criticisms revisited

Carr's first concern was the nature of authority in a team ministry. The licence given by the Bishop to a new team vicar, usually chosen by both the Bishop and the team rector, is 'to commit a share in the cure of souls of the parishioners under the leadership of the team rector in the said team ministry'. Often the licence will go on to designate a particular responsibility for a parish with the team. The nature and style of that leadership is critical and here Carr's consultancy model provides the most satisfactory approach towards team leadership. Authority to take on this role is given and received each time a new team member joins under the leadership of the team rector yet recognizing that every team member has an identified and critical responsibility within the satisfactory functioning of the whole institution. Carr used to underline the fact that if one part of the team became dysfunctional then the work of the whole team would be impaired. This helps to define the task of the team rector in enabling the team ministry as a whole to function effectively. In teams where there are at least two team vicars and probably other team members the issue of authority no longer seems to prevent the team's work.

Secondly, Carr carries these concerns about authority into perceived confusion among the laity. Defined geographical areas of responsibility and particular areas of expertise seem not to confuse lay people but rather release some who can feel that amongst the clergy there are skills that can both be shared with lay people and used by them. The Wythenshawe team ministry in Manchester has one team member with particular responsibility for links into the community of the area. This does not absolve the rest from this responsibility but gives him a coordinating and lead role on behalf of the team. Another has a liturgical expertise, which she uses in all the parishes of the team. Each has a clear local parish responsibility and the laity knows their vicar. But they also know and welcome the skills and colleagueship that other team members bring.

Thirdly, Carr expressed doubts about the way in which team members might work. He worried about 'short creative bursts of energy' focused on problem solving. Again I see no evidence of this in recent years. Licences for all team members for seven years and a membership of many teams of clergy who have had previous posts of sole responsibility and incumbent status has given a more strategic long-term feel to many team ministries. Carr recently consulted to an inner city team ministry in Salford whose planning was strategic and medium term and where there was no evidence of these 'bursts of energy' focused around problem solving.

Cathedral chapters

The new Cathedrals Measure visited something of a revolution into the governance of our Cathedrals. On the one hand the untrammelled power of Provosts and the often paralysing divisions of Dean and Chapters were in need of some urgent reform. The new Chapters with their elected members and Bishop's nominees have undoubtedly changed the dynamics of the old bodies but it would be surprising if the full-time ordained staff of the Cathedrals did not find an opportunity to meet and prepare the ground for such chapter meetings. My suspicion is that much of Carr's concerns about the difficulties of team ministries arose from some of the serious dysfunctional behaviour of some Cathedral chapters. How well Bristol Cathedral and Westminster Abbey have functioned under his leadership is probably more due to his skill in enabling a small group to work than in the inherent soundness of the structure. The Lincoln Cathedral saga illustrated these problems only too clearly.

Sheffield Cathedral chapter in the late 1990s was functioning with a Provost, two Residentiary Commissioners' Canons (one Pastoral, the other Canon Precentor), a part-time Residentiary who was also Director of Ordinands and the Archdeacon of Sheffield who was also a very part-time residentiary. A full-time administrator joined them towards the end of this period. Carr became the consultant to the chapter and urged the members to define the task of the Cathedral, identify areas of work – usually at a residential for the year ahead – and to allocate specific responsibilities within that work programme. Sheffield Cathedral also had a Parochial Church Council and a

Cathedral Council at this time and governance was uneasily shared between them and the chapter. The new Statutes in most Cathedrals have produced a large Cathedral Council with wide representation but limited powers and a chapter with power but still dominated by the Dean and Canons. The 'team ministry' aspect of Cathedral life is bound to reside in the non-statutory Cathedral team meetings which, because of the regularity of meeting and their powerful membership, will immediately be of considerable significance to Cathedral life.

Rather than simplifying the governance of Cathedrals the new measure has confused improved representation with effectiveness. The relationship between Cathedral and Diocesan Bishop remains confused. Issues of authority between the two have stayed obscure as a result of much lobbying by the Deans. Indeed any clarity about the responsibilities held by individual Canons and even the Dean are further obfuscated by periods of Residence for the Dean and Canons when 'who is in charge?' seems difficult to determine. It seems likely that there will have to be a further look at the way our Cathedrals are run. Successful though they may have been in recent years at attracting increased visitors and congregations, only a very few are not dependent on external subsidy from the Church Commissioners. York Minster's decision to charge for admission against the Archbishop's wishes indicates that issues of authority have not yet been properly resolved. In the end it seems that the degree of communication between Minster and Archbishop about the state of the Cathedral's finances was woeful.

The Bishop's staff meeting

'That is where the real power lies in the Diocese'. This is the widely held belief amongst those who have been observers of the structures of the Church of England. Yet this meeting exists nowhere in the legislative structure of the Church despite the fact that it should be modelling best practice for team ministries. It depends for its composition entirely on the whim of the Diocesan Bishop although all would include the dignitaries of the diocese, that is Suffragan/Area Bishops, Archdeacons, the Dean of the Cathedral and the Diocesan Secretary. I have now worked under four diocesan bishops in two dioceses; one a single Suffragan diocese, the other with three suffragans managing an informal area system.

Carr's criticisms of team ministries find little justification in this team ministry. Authority clearly resides in the Diocesan Bishop who in reality appoints all his staff although most find themselves inheriting their predecessor's appointments. The possible exception is the Dean

but the Crown seems reluctant to go down the road of an appointment
without the full support of the Diocesan Bishop after the problems at
Lincoln. In an Area system the incoming Diocesan has the option to
continue it or dismantle it reminding the occupying bishops and
archdeacons of the root of their authority. Each is clearly an extension
of the Diocesan Bishop's *episcope* and without a full and committed
working relationship their ministries will be doomed and ineffective.
Yet there are still problems.

In the single Suffragan Diocese the task of the Suffragan Bishop is
ill defined. With no defined area of pastoral oversight the exercise of
the episcopal role is seriously constrained. Some Diocesans give their
suffragans responsibility for ministry, which often means the oversight
of selection and training within the diocese, a job more usually
undertaken by a Diocesan Officer. An irregular diet of confirmations,
the occasional licensing and some teaching opportunities are usually
not enough to satisfy some of the very able men who have been
consecrated to the same episcopal ministry as their Diocesans. There
are a fair number of frustrated suffragan bishops who feel that their
jobs are by no means stretching them or using their gifts. At the same
time few Diocesan Bishops are prepared to give up their suffragans.
As national responsibilities increase, including membership of the
House of Lords, the knowledge that there is episcopal cover back
home becomes vital. Few could take the study leave and sabbaticals or
overseas work without the episcopal curate and sadly this is how many
are treated. In many such dioceses it is the Archdeacons who deal with
the appointments and the crisis pastoral care of the clergy. In a church
which still maintains differentials in pay the suffragan bishop is only
paid a few hundred pounds a year more than an Archdeacon and the
same as a Dean while the Diocesan Bishop is paid £3000 a year more.
This no doubt reflects the unconscious valuing of these two
expressions of episcopal ministry and only adds to the frustrations
of many suffragan bishops.

Yet for many Area Bishops the situation is very different. In many
cases they have responsibility for areas larger than some dioceses
making the appointments, undertaking the institutions and licensings
of new clergy, ordaining priests in their areas and sharing in the
ordinations of deacons. They become the first point of episcopal
oversight for the clergy and work with an archdeacon within an
episcopal area. Here it is the Archdeacon who may feel less fulfilled
than some of his or her colleagues but overall in the larger dioceses the
system seems to work fairly well. However for those Diocesans who
have no area responsibilities at all there is a danger that despite their
ultimate authority they can become distant and rather remote figures
for many of the clergy and laity. Recent appointments to two such

dioceses, Manchester and Chelmsford, of senior Diocesan Bishops already in their sixties with substantial national responsibilities and membership of the House of Lords would suggest that they are being seen as releasing senior bishops from the day-to-day burdens of diocesan episcopal ministry. The danger is that without careful and effective work through the Bishops staff meeting three or more mini dioceses can begin to emerge.

The final problematic area is the role of the Dean as a member of the Bishop's episcopal team. Archdeacons and suffragan bishops clearly share in the episcopal oversight of the Diocesan Bishop. Deans see themselves very often as in a separate organizational system, holding on to a fierce sense of independence from the episcopal system. The continued complaints that can be heard from many Deans about Bishops and their perceived privileged status and support are but one symptom. More difficult in some dioceses is the Dean's frequent absences from senior staff meetings and the feeling of irrelevancy of much of their meeting to their task and the work of the cathedral church. Inevitably a gulf can develop and the divisions that the Cathedrals Measure was intended to address can recur. The more enlightened among the Deans work to be involved with Diocesan life. Some chair the Diocesan Pastoral Committee; others are involved in other parts of the diocesan structures. This enables them to bridge the gulf that sometimes seems to exist between Cathedral and diocese and enables them to play a fuller part in the Bishop's staff meeting.

The Bishop's staff meeting is certainly the effective seat of governance in Anglican dioceses. Despite the importance of often overlarge Bishop's Councils and Synods, a small group often meeting twice a month for a substantial period of time is bound to develop a coherence and authority directly related to that of the Diocesan Bishop. Fantasies usually develop amongst the clergy about what goes on but here appointments are discussed, deployment arranged, policy and finance given an initial airing. Bearing in mind that all the Bishop's staff will be members of the Bishop's Council early policy discussions are bound to have a considerable bearing on the outcome of debates in more public arenas. The parallel between them and team ministries is obvious. Just as every team and Cathedral chapter need a consultant so should every Bishop's staff meeting use one. Without such external consultancy all dysfunctional behaviour that can develop in small groups will sooner or later be in evidence and the work damaged.

Conclusion

In 1978 Bruce Reed published *The Dynamics of Religion* which looked at the operation of the Church of England in a culture of dependency and Carr has continued to challenge the Bishops of the Church of England to examine the way they exercise their episcopacy in such a culture. Many bishops unfortunately revel in a culture of inappropriate dependency and fail to realize the serious damage that can be done to the effective working of their dioceses. Miller and Lawrence did some work for the Diocese of Chelmsford in 1973 much of which remains as important today as it was then:

> The image of the Diocesan Bishop that emerged from the parish interviews was of a shadowy figure, whose function was to authenticate what was happening in the parochial ministry and to be available as a kind of long-stop in times of crisis, or possibly a scapegoat in case of failure. There was little sense that parish priests were acting on the authority of the Bishop, as agents of the diocese. He was rather a figure to be kept off-stage, except when required for ceremonial occasions, and the possibility of his wanting to analyse and question the exercise of ministry in his diocese was kept at arm's length. If differences or conflicts occurred, his job was not to examine them but to smooth them away. (Miller, 1993: 114)

The consultancy model of ministry is as relevant to Bishops, Deans and team rectors as it was then. Perhaps it is now better understood thanks particularly to Carr's work. But if the teams in our churches are to grow and develop then we need to examine the way we work and the dangers of complacency.

References

Carr, W., *The Priest-like Task*, London, SPCK, 1985.
Miller, E., *From Dependency to Autonomy*, London, Free Association Books, 1993.
Reed, B., *The Dynamics of Religion: Process and Movement in Christian Churches*, London, DLT, 1978.

Chapter 6

Standing for Something

Francis Ward

Introduction

There is a game that is available from the Bodleian Library in Oxford called *Ex Libris*. The box contains a pack of cards and an old, polished, halfpenny bit. On each of the cards is a résumé of a novel and the author's dates, and on the other side of the card is the first and last lines of that novel. The person in the game who is the 'reader' throws the coin, declares whether it is heads or tails, and then reads out the résumé. Each player then attempts to write the first line of the novel if 'heads' were shown, or the last line if it were 'tails'. The reader collects in the literary attempts of the group and reads them out, including the real sentence from the card, and the players then vote for the sentence that they believe to be the correct one. People earn points when their sentence is chosen, or when they choose the true author, and thus the game goes on, with ever more subtle attempts to fox your opponents with ingenious attempts at characteristic literary styles. How does *Frankenstein* end, exactly? You look around the room, weighing up your erstwhile friends and their reading proclivities. How might you capture a particular Victorian gothic that will convince your readers that yours is the proper ending? A really skilful player is able to out-do the original. To sound more like Jane Austen than Jane Austen herself as you write the first sentence of *Pride and Prejudice* is success indeed.

How might a player treat, say, *The Priest-like Task*? To convince your adversaries, perhaps familiar with Wesley Carr's *oeuvre*, you would most certainly need to relay the distinctiveness of his style. The sentence would not be long, and you would need to capture that brusque flavour that means business, although, as a wheeze, you might soften the tone by hinting at a poetical text. And what of the words you would use? Key words would obviously be 'Anglican', 'sentience', 'interface', and, of course, 'task'. If you were really brave, but at the risk of laying it on too thick, you might try and weave in 'dependency' or 'dynamics'. For my money, though, the word 'stance' is your best bet. It is there, throughout his writings, and somehow it also brings the man to mind – his very presence, his definite approach to things, his substance.

It is a characteristic word, both of writing style and of the man. Throughout his public ministry over many years Wesley Carr has stood for something. He has taken up a stance on a particular way of being Anglican that values a certain understanding of the interaction of church and local community and which gives an underpinning to the role of the minister as a representative figure, available to the world beyond the church as people seek to manage their lives. It is a stance that has had enormous influence on the Church of England as Wesley Carr has been called upon to consult within dioceses, ministry teams and with individuals. Often you will come across parishes, priests and bishops who speak highly of his work and the consistent way in which he interprets the dynamics of religion in different and diverse contexts.

Standing for something

I want in this section briefly to recapitulate on the consistencies of Wesley Carr's work under three sub-headings, church and society, the religious figure and dynamics of religion. He has remained firm, standing his ground, throughout the changing times of the final quarter of the twentieth century and into this. Carr has argued for a(n Anglican) church that is flexible in response, yet true to its distinctive position in society, with clergy and pastors who fulfil particular public roles in enabling others to manage their dependency. To elaborate the dynamics that lie behind the needs and transferences that people bring, and the way in which the church and priest can respond, Carr draws upon the work of Bruce Reed and the Grubb Institute, and the object-relations psycho-analytical theory of the paediatrician D.W. Winnicott.

This characteristic stance, though, is not without problems, especially if one attempts to engage with Wesley Carr's work in the light of contemporary gender theory. I attempt a reading of *The Priest-like Task*, as perhaps the best-known of his books, raising questions about the way in which Carr constructs the 'stance' of his representative religious figure over against a sea of otherness that is dependent, confused, chaotic. Many gender theorists today argue that this is exactly how patriarchy perpetrates itself, by disowning its others and consigning them to silences and places where they are deprived of their dignity as subjects, unable to articulate their own experience from standpoints of different knowing. The 'priest' of Carr's conception is a male figure who is able to manage 'the world' because it has been rendered 'dependent'. Conversely, because it is dependent, it requires the dependable priest of Carr's writing. So we have in his work a particular pairing of 'stance' taken over against a sea of 'confused dependencies', where each requires the other. In Carr's hands, this is made to work very well to describe a characteristic 'Anglican' way of being church and offering ministry to the world. I would want to argue, however, that the stance that Carr defends so strongly is one which often fails to recognize its own dominance and the way in which it unconsciously abjects other voices and different standpoints. When gender is seen as important we perhaps begin to approximate more closely to the experience of many Anglican clergy who see their role, rather than primarily managing the dependency of the 'other', as seeking to understand the gendered nature of their own identity and attempting to empty that position of a sense of traditional dominance so that a true negotiation of difference may result. Instead of a stance requiring its dependants, its hangers-on, we then have a religious figure come of age who is able to honour different standpoints and 'change the subject' (see Fulkerson, 1994).

Church and society

In his writing on the church and its place in society, Carr (sometimes writing with others, as in *Say One For Me*) takes a stance that always encourages institutional and individual confidence in the face of secularization, and represents a refusal to succumb to the reductionist tendencies of church congregationalism or parochialism (BE: 1).[1] This is a determination to sustain for the church an effective presence at the primary interface with non-church people. He holds onto a notion of a national church, expressed through the parochial system, engaging and serving society in pragmatic ways. Angela Tilby talks of a responsibility for 'the soul of the nation' (SOFM: chapter 7). A church that stands for the English virtues of tolerance and acceptance.

And if we have inherited an established church, then this is '... not merely an Erastian error: it is a specific ecclesiology not necessarily of privilege but potentially of duty and ministry' (SOFM: 9). The establishment of the Church of England enables the church to serve society by its very availability throughout the land, a point Carr makes at the beginning of *The Priest-like Task*:

---

[1] Carr's works are abbreviated as follows: BE – *Brief Encounters*; TPT – *The Priest-like Task*; TPAT – *The Pastor as Theologian*; SOFM – *Say One For Me*.

> Even now, when the place of religion as an obviously cohesive force in society appears to have diminished, the stance of the Church of England in allowing all a claim on its ministry remains one of its distinctive marks. Aspects of this have been incorporated into the uniquely English establishment. (TPT: 11)

The structures and organization of the church enable an outward-looking ministry that can engage with people in the wider society who may not come to worship regularly, but nevertheless look to their parish church at times of need. As they come, seeking to manage transition times of vulnerability and dependency, the church offers tools of interpretation and meaning in its rituals and in the person of the priest.

The religious figure

The religious figure of the minister is of tremendous importance. The first port of call for someone coming to church needs to be a person of thoughtful holiness, with whom questions of meaning and of God can be explored, able to be wise and inclusive, with a loving approach to God's world. The religious figure of the priest (or minister, pastor, clergy) fulfils a representative role, able to deal sensitively and competently with people's largely unconscious and therefore inarticulate expectations. He needs to be able '... to hold to a total view of the institution, one's role and the task, and then at the same time to immerse oneself in a wide range of experience and feelings. This is the traditional stance for the priest, who is believed to be able to hold such a distance through prayer and sometimes by acting it out and going on retreat' (TPT: 34).

Often the priest will be on the receiving end of many different projected feelings and transferred emotions, and needs to be able to handle himself and the situation with wisdom and an understanding of the dynamics that are occurring. He will often find himself required to stand on behalf of others at a point where they are unable to stand themselves (TPT: 55).

> The pastor as local theologian has to embody this stance in himself as he holds the mystery of God present to the everyday lives of ordinary men and women, believer and unbeliever alike. (TPAT: 6)

In *The Pastor as Theologian* Carr offers a systematic grounding for this work, integrating practice with theology and the activity of prayer and worship. This is of use to the pastor who can often feel that he is standing on a beach surrounded by the ambiguities of the world that can threaten to inundate and overwhelm. To provide tools to enable the priest to manage himself and those who come with powerful experiences requiring help, Carr reinterprets Winnicott's psycho-dynamic approach as used by Bruce Reed in his influential *Dynamics of Religion.*

Dynamics of religion

Bruce Reed's thesis is that the church serves society by enabling individuals to manage their own dependency through a dynamic process of oscillation between regression (dependence) and mature intra-dependence that is corporately carried by the ritual of the church. So Reed writes, 'Religion is a social institution which provides a setting in ritual for the regulation of oscillation processes in a social grouping' (1978: 52).

Carr understands the church to exist within a prevailing social culture which can be described as 'dependent' and which brings specific expectations to bear on the church (TPT: 23). Another way of looking at some of the processes that occur is to use Winnicott's idea of a facilitating environment and good-enough parenting that enables the child to make use of transitional objects and phenomena as he or she grows to maturity. In *Playing and Reality* Winnicott describes how the baby will first use the breast, and then a fist or finger to suck, and then turn to a doll or a teddy bear as she or he grows to understand the 'not-me' and then continues to develop and grow in maturity eventually to be able to form relations with other people in life and to manage themselves in subjective and objective fields. Often those coming to the priest will bring with them their transitional objects, or even use God in this way, as Carr describes:

> It may seem incongruous, even blasphemous, to compare God with a teddy bear. But this exactly describes the experience that pastors report in their dealing with people. God is from time to time dragged from some-where and brought to the pastor for recognition and action. (TPAT: 23–24)

To be effective managers of these processes, the church and its religious figures need to understand what is presented to them, and also some of the internal dynamics of dependence, transference and counter-transference they may experience within themselves. Church and the pastor can best serve society by enabling growth to maturity, a maturity that is '... marked by the confident exercise of autonomy based upon satisfactory management of dependence' (TPAT: 177).

The Pastor as Theologian offers a synthesis of classic theological concepts with this psycho-dynamic approach. Carr frames the incarnation, for example, as relational, based upon various pairings: God and man; God and the world; man and man. He develops this by drawing upon object-relations theory, arguing the point that we are formed as we negotiate difference and accept the limitations imposed upon us by the other (TPAT: 61). Such negotiation is enabled by the doctrine of the incarnation which allows for a pattern of transference and counter-transference to be employed: 'Incarnation is God's statement of his willingness to be used in the confused human dynamics of transference' (TPAT: 74). Carr presents here a skilful and creative cross-fertilization of theology and psychology that offers a fruitful reinterpretation of the incarnation for the pastor who stands at the interface between an established church and the world coming to him, full of confusion and needing help in managing its vulnerability and dependence. Carr offers the pastor the means to interpret his experience theologically, a bulwark against the surging waves and shifting sands so that they need not feel quite as much at sea (TPAT: preface), but may sustain their stance with confidence.

The important matter of gender

Wesley Carr makes various disclaimers about gender, primarily understanding it in terms of the challenge to use inclusive language. In 1985 in the preface of TPT, Carr writes: 'In any writing today the question of gender presents acute discomfort. Since there is no simple term for both male and female in English, I use male forms with generic reference' (x). Four years later, he has shifted ground slightly, writing in the preface of TPAT:

> Questions of gender are unimportant in the context of this book, although I have tried to acknowledge them. A major problem, however, occurs when we speak of the individual. Some sentences cannot be rendered in the plural without changing the meaning, and the repetition of 'he and she' or neologisms like '(s)he' are both in their different ways burdensome. I have done my best within the constraints of language. (TPAT: xvii)

I would contend that questions of gender, far from being 'unimportant', permeate Wesley Carr's writing, and can be discerned in the unconscious workings of the imagery and language that he uses. His writing has a dynamic that shouts aloud of powerful transferences that are exactly to do with gender, and call for a different understanding of 'otherness' than that offered by the object-relations theory he relies upon.

Despite his disclaimer that he uses male forms with generic reference, the constant use of the male pronoun is correct, I believe, for Wesley Carr's 'priest' *is* male. This priest holds a stance that, as a representative of the established church, is dependable ('... dependence cannot be worked with unless the ministry provides dependability' (TPT: 66)) and heroic in a characteristically 'masculine' way. In order to be this hero figure, all the confusions and chaotic urges of Leviathan are projected away, onto the world out there, beyond the boundaries of the Church. Like Ulysses, the priest encounters many monsters and seductive sirens, yet remains secure within his ark from the maelstrom that threatens to devour.

But why is this to do with gender? Two leading feminist philosophers of religion, in different ways, have argued that we are trapped within a masculinist symbolic (a.k.a. patriarchy) that requires a split between the rational, autonomous subject self and its others. So Grace Jantzen draws upon psychoanalytical theory and the ways in which French feminism has responded to Freud and Lacan in her discussion of the gendered subject of the philosophy of religion. She writes:

> In fact, no topic in the philosophy of religion, traditional or feminist, remains unaffected once we recognize that we are not straightforward, rational, autonomous Cartesian egos, but are embodied, sexuate persons in a web of life, caught up in unconscious desires and fears. ... What is obvious is that the ideal of the rational, passionless man, becoming god-like in mastery and knowledge and exerting his dominance over all (m)others is a fantasy that tells us more about male psychosexual development than about godliness. Yet it is a dangerous and destructive fantasy, played out in masculinist symbolic structures – religion, law, science, economics – on the bodies of women, Blacks, lesbians and gay men, whoever threatens the fragile and fractured self. Nor is there any hope for improvement without changes in the symbolic order by which men and women are constituted as subjects. (1998: 43)

Carr does often recognize that the priest is not immune from 'unconscious desires and fears', yet the main focus of Jantzen's critique holds true, I think. Whenever Carr talks of the desires and fears of the priest it is to show how they can be managed and made to work in the interpretative task of effective ministry. I would argue that the stance that Carr's priest adopts is precisely about 'becoming god-like in mastery and knowledge', and that his whole thrust is to shore up the 'fragile and fractured self' that is the male subject threatened by the otherness of the world.

Pamela Sue Anderson differs from Jantzen in her appraisal of the place of rationality in the scheme of things. For Jantzen, rationality is definitely a tool of the master's house. For Anderson, although it has been used symbolically, if not actually, in the exclusion of femaleness (1998: 8), it is to be re-appropriated in the analysis of the basis of situated knowledges. But both agree that the methods of the patriarchal symbolic effectively disown all that is not rational and safe. In the light of Carr's use of the imagery of the sea, interestingly Anderson uses a feminist reading of a passage from Immanuel Kant in which Kant employs the stormy sea to represent the illusions which threaten and surround the land of truth:

> ... Kant uses the sea to represent the danger of false belief and illusion as contrasted with the true beliefs and secure reality of the island. The feminist objection to the latter contrast is that desire and disorder associated with water and fluidity are feared, while reason and order linked with stability and solidity are highly valued. (1998: xi)

The work of both of these feminist philosophers is instructive in an engagement with Wesley Carr's work and the way he believes gender to be both a 'discomfort' and 'unimportant'. Bearing in mind Anderson's comments on the way in which imagery of the sea was used by Kant (and has, indeed, been used and responded to by others since in a similar way, and see Irigaray's *Marine Lover*), let's turn again to the opening pages of TPAT. Wesley Carr was obviously captured by the sea and its power as he began to write. In the preface, we are given a picture of the author standing on the beach:

> One moment the sea is inviting and seductive; splashing around the fringes of the profound issues of life and death, we write our intentions in the sand, hoping that they will be washed away and not held to our account. The next moment we are caught in the current and washed out to sea. The horizon retreats beyond our reach and our feet cannot touch the bottom.

The book is written for those on the foreshore, and like *The Priest-like Task*, Carr is concerned to provide for the religious figurehead a deep and abiding anchor to hold onto against the storms of life.

A double reading of *The Priest-like Task*

Jantzen draws upon strategies developed by Derrida and Irigaray and develops what she describes as 'double reading', and I want now to turn to TPT to engage in some playful analysis of the gendered nature of Wesley Carr's writing. Jantzen calls it

... a sort of reading which on the one hand pays close attention to the text, but which, in that very attention, discloses a rupture in that text which requires a radically different reading of it, thus destabilizing it and in the undecidability thereby created opens the possibility of thinking otherwise. (1998: 61)

My hope is that, in the rupture that may open up in Wesley Carr's text, other subject positions, besides that of the stance of the priest, may enjoy some space.

One of the commonly recognized structures of the patriarchal symbolic is the binary – that any facet of experience has its corollary that defines it – a pairing system, if you will, of which Winnicott's object-relations is a sophisticated example. I propose to present my 'double reading' of TPT in two columns. The examples are so numerous of attributes either to the religious figure who stands firm, and conversely to the world and all its confusions that I have only examined the first 60 pages or so. (One of the few times when 'the world' is not presented as a realm of dependency and confusion is when the mayor comes wanting a civic service, and then it becomes a question of limiting power and mutual critique, although even then '... the mayor kneels along with everyone else' (TPT: 24).)

I have put in bold the phrases and words I have lifted from the text, and these describe either the qualities of dependability that are required, or the 'storms of life' against which the priest heroically makes a stand. My suggestions are in italics.

Standing for something against	'The storms of life'
Calm	**Turmoil of emotions (4)**
Contained and managed	**Pressures of living (4)**
Dependable, available but not remote (6)	**Many social problems (6)**
Give reassurance in holding the thin line between order	**and chaos (6)**
Rational	**Powerful feelings (7)**
English virtues of tolerance and acceptance (7)	**Racially and religiously mixed (7)**
Rational certainties	**Feelings and irrational hope (10)**
Calm and control	**Intense hopes invested (14)**
Rational (14)	**Profoundly emotional (14)**
Conscious and clear	**Usually unconscious (14)**
Disentangled (14)	**Welter of confusion (14)**

Standing for something against	'The storms of life'
Critical coherence (14)	*Chaos*
Feelings as a clue (15)	**Feelings very powerful, behaviour of the mob (15)**
Ability to hold onto the task in hand (15)	*Slipping through fingers*
Skill in interpreting (15)	*No answers*
Articulation (16)	*Speechless, nothing to say*
Continued commitment (16)	*No staying power*
All the time scrutinized (16)	*In the dark*
Heroic life	**Ordinary experiences of life (22)**
Control	**Unmanageable (22)**
Understood	**Incomprehensible (22)**
Established religion	**Folk religion (28ff)**
Resolution through **Interpretation (34)**	**Unresolved ambiguities (30)**
Peace and quiet through **Distance (33)**	**Demands (30)**
Coherence	**Confusion (30)**
Integrity (35)	**Such emotional turmoil (47)**
Balance	**Thrown off balance (36)**

This list of binaries is not exhaustive, and should be read light-heartedly, as a set of attributes that paint a picture, I think, of the 'priest' who becomes ever more sophisticated at managing his own emotions with coherence and clarity, the better to manage the emotions and turmoil of others/the World/the sea.

To my mind two major questions now need to be addressed in the final sections of this chapter. What, then, of the standpoints of 'others' as *subjects*, who are seen not merely as examples from the turmoil of the sea that threatens to overwhelm? How might their standpoints be honoured? What of the different ways in which they might see and know the world? If the subject positions of 'others' are honoured as standpoints of different knowing, then perhaps the representative religious figure has to learn to swim.

Second, what of the stance of the representative figure, the Anglican priest, who in Carr's construction, stands so heroically? In Anderson's hands, feminist standpoint epistemology encourages the knowing subject to move 'backward reflexively to examine [their] basic background beliefs' (1998: 76), in the recognition that all knowing is dependent upon often hidden and unexamined presuppositions which include our gender, our ethnicity, our class, our sexuality. The more dominant the position we carry in the world the less it behoves us to examine our own situatedness in these terms. Dominant subjects become very adept at disguising the preconceptions of knowledge that enable and perpetrate their dominance. What happens if 'the male priest' is a 'she', or is gay or black, unable or unwilling to be heroic and dominant in the traditional patriarchal way? Increasingly 'priests' bring with them different life experiences, and because of who they are, they know from different places, have different 'others' with whom to negotiate and different transferences upon her or him in ministry. For example, there is an increasing amount of evidence now, almost ten years in the Church of England since women were ordained to the priesthood, that female priests often hold the role differently, and would not interpret their ministry in 'stance' terms in quite the way Carr does.

Feminist standpoint epistemology

Anderson gives a very good account of standpoint epistemology, a well-used method of analysis of different subject positions, and I draw on her work to carry my perspective further in this direction. In an attempt to understand how the subject knows, Anderson argues that a less partial knowledge comes from the standpoint of the lives of others, '... from the lives of marginalized others who include all women and some men' (1998: 84). The ground of knowledge is strengthened in so far as it is able to incorporate in the knower a breadth and depth of situated perspective, and in so far as it refuses a flight into the dominant stance of the conventional subject who is 'culturally and historically disembodied' (1998: 85). The standpoint epistemologist would argue, furthermore, that the conventional subject of knowledge is blind, in the attempt to be coherent and consistent, to the fragmented nature of experience, as difference is repressed and strangeness excluded (1998: 86). To know from standpoints of difference means that the subject, as an agent of knowledge, is no longer unitary, but now immersed in the multiplicity and contradictions of life, including those of her own position:

> Internally she is contradictory in generating knowledge as outsiders within; also as an agent of knowledge this subject is not unitary but divided as subjects who are also objects of their own self-reflexivity (1998: 87).

The multiple standpoints of such a subject are permeated by desires: following Hegel's dialectic of master and slave, Anderson unfolds a dynamic of desire projected onto the other which, self-reflexively, becomes the means by which we recognize ourselves, mimetically, in the other, and are enabled to reinvent ourselves as other (1998: 90).

Complicated though this theoretical analysis may seem, it offers, I believe, an alternative scheme to understand the complexity of relationship between the self and other to that of Wesley Carr's heroic stance against a sea of troubles. If subjects, especially if the subject is an Anglican priest, can begin to understand that their knowing is dependent on all sorts of different social and cultural factors, which actually play a major part in forming their own subjectivity, then the heroic stance they may be tempted to adopt becomes less viable. Instead of projecting out all the dependencies and uncertainties and emotions they feel, consciously or unconsciously, to establish their coherent stance, the subject becomes more aware of how those very elements contribute to their own subjectivity as they know and interpret the contexts and situations in which they are and minister. Carr's insights into how counter-transference can be used goes some way in this process, but fails to recognize, I think, how the real and different experience of others can enrich the character of wisdom. The priest becomes someone who begins to think and understand from the subject positions of those marginalized (out in the world) by the church, and who can honour the different experience and interpretations that are embodied and known in the lives of poor people, gays and lesbians, Blacks and women much more effectively than now is often the case.

To my mind, the stance of the Anglican priest needs to be much more critically self-aware of the ways the role can fail to take account of the different perspectives and formative life stories of people of difference. There is a certain cultural dominance that pervades Anglican clergy and ecclesial structures that is too often oblivious of the ways in which it subsumes and discounts other knowledge, other standpoints. To become less concerned with the establishment of a particular stance which is strong enough to withstand the dependency culture in which the Church finds itself, and to begin to think from the lives of different others in society today, would be to make a start on dismantling that dominance and status that the Anglican establishment does so well.

Conclusion

Wesley Carr's contribution to the life of the Church of England over a number of decades has been great, especially in his ability to draw together psychoanalytical traditions and a systematic theological grounding in a creative synthesis. My response to his work frames itself into a *yes, but* … what about recent analysis that provides a deeper reading of the gendered nature of knowledge and of subjectivity? With psychoanalytical tools, many feminist theologians and writers today are turning the tables on the dominant images and structures of a 'masculinist symbolic' that can too easily be read in the pages of Wesley Carr's books. Can he any longer be permitted to get away with so much talk of 'stances' and dependency, as if all the world is hanging upon the dependable male priest?

References

Anderson, P. S. (1998) *A Feminist Philosophy of Religion*, Oxford, UK & Massachusetts, USA: Blackwell Publishers Inc.

Carr, W. (1985) *Brief Encounters: Pastoral Ministry through the Occasional Offices*, London: SPCK (BE).

Carr, W. (1985) *The Priest-like Task: A Model for Developing and Training the Church's Ministry*, London: SPCK (TPT).

Carr, W. (1989) *The Pastor as Theologian: The Integration of Pastoral Ministry, Theology and Discipleship*, London: SPCK (TPAT).

Carr, W. (1992) *Say One For Me: The Church of England in the Next Decade*, London: SPCK (SOFM).

Fulkerson, M. M. (1994) *Changing the Subject: Women's Discourses and Feminist Theology*, Minneapolis: Augsburg Fortress Publishers.

Irigaray, L. (1991) *Marine Lover of Friedrich Nietzsche*, trans. Gillian C. Gill, New York: Columbia University Press.

Jantzen, G. M. (1998) *Becoming Divine: Towards a Feminist Philosophy of Religion*, Manchester: Manchester University Press.

Reed, B. (1978) *Dynamics of Religion: Process and Movement in Christian Churches*, London: DLT.

Winnicott, D.W. [1971] (1999) *Playing and Reality*, New York & London: Routledge.

Chapter 7

More Tea Vicar?
Tasting and Testing the Truth

Alastair Redfern

The pastor in the parlour

The Anglican approach to Christianity is sometimes caricatured by the image of providing tea for the parish priest. Modern versions would imply not so much the formal Victorian setting of best china and even better behaviour, but a pastoral encounter. There is a great deal of significance in this picture of priest and parishioners sharing a cup and a conversation. It epitomizes the pastoral strengths of Anglican ministry – an engagement in an everyday setting, on the parishioners' territory: the priest representing something of the mystery of God and of the church catholic, the parishioner placing something of their life in that context.

Nonetheless, this pastoral encounter is often deeply collusive. Neither party is really at ease: the two kinds of territory merge uneasily, and the situation is resolved by a steady concentration upon the tea and other matters superficial. The Christian Gospel is generally implicit: both parties need to travel to church space for something more concrete and challenging.

I worked as a colleague of Wesley Carr's for ten years as part of the chapter at Bristol Cathedral. Among many things that Wesley taught me, was the fact that Christian truth has a public dimension: a depth and a breadth which often comes to challenge our too ready complacency and cosiness as we collude to encounter others over the mediating moment of a cup of tea in a context of apparent domesticity. The personal and the private is always broadened into something of wider and more public significance when the Gospel is allowed to intrude.

In this essay I propose to explore this issue of the public and challenging nature of the truth of the Christian Gospel for pastoral ministry, by examining the encounter of Jesus with the woman at the well in John 4: 1–42.

Now when Jesus learned that the Pharisees had heard, 'Jesus is making and baptizing more disciples than John' – although it was not Jesus himself but his disciples who baptized – he left Judea and started back to Galilee. But he had to go through Samaria. So he came to a Samaritan city Sychar, near the plot of ground that Jacob had given to his son Joseph. Jacob's well was there, and Jesus, tired out by his journey, was sitting by the well. It was about noon.

A Samaritan woman came to draw water, and Jesus said to her 'Give me a drink'. (His disciples had gone to the city to buy food.) The Samaritan woman said to him 'How is it that you, a Jew, ask a drink of me, a woman of Samaria?' (Jews do not share things in common with Samaritans.) Jesus answered her, 'If you knew the gift of God, and who it is that is saying to you 'Give me a drink,' you would have asked him, and he would have given you living water'. The woman said to him, 'Sir, you have no bucket, and the well is deep. Where do you get that living water? Are you greater than our ancestor Jacob, who gave us the well, and with his sons and his flocks drank from it?' Jesus said to her, 'Everyone who drinks of this water will be thirsty again, but those who drink of the water that I will give them will never be thirsty. The water that I will give will become in them a spring of water gushing up to eternal life'. The woman said to him, 'Sir, give me this water, so that I may never be thirsty or have to keep coming here to draw water'.

Jesus said to her, 'Go, call your husband, and come back'. The woman answered him, 'I have no husband'. Jesus said to her 'You are right in saying, 'I have no husband'; for you have had five husbands, and the one you have now is not your husband. What you have said is true!'. The woman said to him, 'Sir, I see that you are a prophet. Our ancestors worshiped on this mountain, but you say that the place where people must worship is in Jerusalem'. Jesus said to her, 'Woman, believe me, the hour is coming when you will worship the Father neither on this mountain nor in Jerusalem. You worship what you do not know; we worship what we know, for salvation is from the Jews. But the hour is coming, and is now here, when the true worshipers will worship the Father in spirit and truth'. The woman said to him, 'I know that Messiah is coming' (who is called Christ). 'When he comes, he will proclaim all things to us.' Jesus said to her, 'I am he, the one who is speaking to you'.

Just then his disciples came. They were astonished that he was speaking with a woman, but no one said, 'What do you want?' or, 'Why are you speaking with her?'. Then the woman left her water jar and went back to the city. She said to the people, 'Come and see a man who told me everything I have ever done! He cannot be the Messiah, can he?'. They left the city and were on their way to him.

Meanwhile the disciples were urging him, 'Rabbi, eat something'. But he said to them, 'I have food to eat that you do not know about'. So the disciples said to one another, 'Surely no one has brought him something to eat?'. Jesus said to them, 'My food is to do the will of him who sent me to complete his work. Do you not say 'Four months more, then comes the harvest'? But I tell you, look around you and see how the fields are ripe for harvesting. The reaper is already receiving wages and is gathering fruit for eternal life, so that sower and reaper may rejoice together. For here the saying holds true, 'One sows and another reaps'. I sent you to reap that for which you did not labour. Others have laboured, and you have entered into their labour'.

Many Samaritans from that city believed in him because of the woman's testimony, 'He told me everything I have ever done'. So when the Samaritans came to him, they asked him to stay with them; and he stayed there two days. And many more believed because of his word. They said to the woman, 'It is no longer because of what you said that we believe, for we have heard for ourselves, and we know that this is truly the Saviour of the world'. (N.R.S.V.)

Go and fetch the man you live with

Pastoral encounter is always a missionary enterprise: the truth of the Gospel can challenge and change those who engage with each other within the context of the kingdom activity of Jesus Christ.

Many in our culture, including some Christians, would query the suitability of scripture to inform pastoral encounter in the modern and post-modern worlds. The case has been classically articulated by Denis Nineham in terms of an unbridgeable cultural gap between the respective worlds of the biblical writers and today.[1]

However, the key 'culture' for Christian pastoral encounter is not the superstructure of ideologies and values of a particular time, but the fact that human nature – from creation to the present day, remains a constant factor: characterized by the 'fallen' (from highest human aspirations of perfection and immortality) marks of limitation, vulnerability, wickedness, inconsistency and a fundamental inability to properly connect instincts for love, goodness and beauty, with performance and engagement in the theatre of earthly existence.

Thus tradition, in the sense of the Biblical canon and Christian reflection upon it, remains a self-evidently relevant resource to human nature in our time as in any other. In this sense Christian pastoral encounter, drawing upon, and rooted in, this tradition, is located deep within the maelstrom of those conflicting devices and desires which characterize each individual, every family or group, and every tribe or nation.

---

[1] Nineham, D. E. (1976), *The Use and Abuse of the Bible: A Study of the Bible in an Age of Rapid Cultural Changes*, London, Macmillan. Cf Barton, J., '*Reflections on Cultural Relativism*' in *Theology* LXXXII/686 (March 1979), pp. 103–9 and LXXXII/687 (May 1979), pp. 191–9.

Any kind of contextual analysis, whether taking its markers from an honest and rigorous self-awareness or from an assessment of events in communities and between nations, will highlight the fact that the human situation is characterized by large elements of confusion, conflict and issues of boundaries. 'Go and fetch the man you live with' is a sign of this reality – as powerful in first-century Samaria as in twenty-first-century Surbiton.

How is it that you, a Jew, ask a drink of me, a woman of Samaria?

Here is the world of actual and potential confusion, conflict and issues of boundaries: focused in the relationships between women and men, and between Jews and Samaritans. The same issues will almost certainly be prominent in this week's news – wherever or whenever this piece is being read: gender; race; nationalism; religion – classic arenas for focusing confusion, conflict and problems of boundaries. Pastoral encounter transacts in this human reality.

You have had five husbands: the one you have now is not your husband

The woman is an icon of human nature – whatever the apparent cultural context. She has come to the well 'at about noon'. This was not the usual time to go and draw water. The time may indicate someone whose life-style had caused them to be ostracized – pushed to the margins of the life of the community. Similarly, she came alone. More certainly, her agreed track record of having had five husbands and now being shacked up with a man who was not her husband is a clear sign of someone whose life is rooted in confusion, conflict and issues of boundaries. A life-style not dissimilar to some Hollywood models in our own time. The human world is not evolving in terms of much improvement in moral or spiritual life. Whatever the apparent achievements of medicine and science, human nature remains doggedly trapped in a dynamic that seeks love and perfection for body and soul, and yet so often fails to achieve this deep-seated aim. There is conflict and confusion within each person, and between people. Pastoral encounter which ignores these issues of boundaries will easily collude in patterns of human cosiness, even to the extent of the pastor being tempted to end particularly difficult situations with a prayer calling down healing and hope – a spiritual equivalent of the cup of tea syndrome. Neither the prayer nor the tea is unimportant: but the Gospel commitment to truth requires confusion and conflict to be recognized, owned and faced directly and honestly. Only then can God's grace rather than Earl Grey become the remedy.

Compare this blunt truthfulness about the reality of human nature, with the tendency in much of the contemporary culture towards the kind of spin which owns failure in schools, the health service or public life with a minimalist recognition of that fact, smothered in a maximum effulgence about learning from mistakes, revising and improving systems, and thus being confident that a situation such as someone spending 24 hours on a trolley in a hospital corridor will never happen again. This predominant confidence in human progress and capability is not unique to contemporary culture, nor does it simply emanate from a post-Darwinian conviction that, in Huxley's famous phrase, 'when man fell, he fell upwards'[2] – rather, this spin-which-smothers-truth in all its starkness has been the style of much government and religious organization since time began. The vicar coming to share a cup of tea is merely a recent manifestation of a deep human temptation.

A Gospel hinged upon a man nailed to a cross invites a different degree of realism. Wesley Carr employs the phrase 'Tested by the Cross'.[3]

He left Judea – to go through Samaria

In this pastoral encounter we learn how the Christ handles the inevitable negotiation between the realism of the Gospel of God and the confusion and tenderness of human being.

First, he enters the woman's territory. Where she lives her life of confusion, conflict, issues of boundaries (chaos seeking order) and yet clings to the desire for stable, secure relationship (salvation) is the place where truth can be discerned. She lives with a strong instinct that life can be transformed. But, this was not an encounter simply on the woman's own terms. The place of encounter is not her home, but a space charged with spiritual significance: Jacob's well. The whole symbolism of water in the well is redolent with hints of cleansing (baptism), nourishing (Eucharist) and the spiritual struggle to accept these mysterious aids of grace when the more immediate task is so self-evidently about survival at a more basic level which seems to depend solely upon our own efforts. Here is the territory of what Wesley Carr has described in *Say One For Me*:[4] our need for a person

---

[2] Worrall, B. G. (1988), *The Making of the Modern Church*, London, SPCK, p. 76.
[3] Carr, A. W. (1992), *Tested by the Cross*, London, Fount.
[4] Carr, A. W. (1992), *Say One For Me*, London, SPCK.

and often a place of encounter whereby the deeper spiritual issues that
are forever welling up amidst our necessary strategies for survival can
be owned and explored. The pregnant conjunction of the bucket and a
heart that knows its need of living water. The well is deep. The task is
not easy: the woman knows this truth – Jesus does not deny it. This is
to be no cosy, social conversation. At this stage, no one seems to have
put the kettle on.

Jews do not share things in common with Samaritans

Many pastoral encounters operate at a superficial level. Any genuine
engagement between two people is often illusory: each party processes
what is offered by the other in such a way as to keep it comfortably
within their particular frame of reference: anything that fails to fit
causes conflict, confusion or downright rejection. Generally it is easier
to play this processing game than to risk going deeper into the well
which holds the truth: the outcome may bring challenge and change
which shatters preconceptions. To risk delving into the well of God's
truth is to risk the spiritual encounter which Wesley Carr calls *huper*:
acting and offering on behalf of. Being willing to be done to (passion
in its proper sense) for the sake of God, and hence for the sake of
others of His children.[5]

Carr writes,

> When we act on behalf of others and are used by them, wittingly or
> unwittingly, cost becomes important .... Yet bearing costs on behalf of
> others is Christ-like, and lies deep in the disciples' spirituality. As with
> God's work in Christ, the aim is not to relieve others of their
> responsibilities. The delicate task is to hold responsibility for what does
> not belong to us so that others may be able to resume or discover their
> responsibility within God's world.[6]

Thus, in the encounter of Jesus with the woman of Samaria, the
foundational exchanges establish the truth about their differences
(rather than the temptation to drive immediately towards common
ground). These differences are highlighted in sharp and simple
starkness: Jesus is thirsty: the woman has resources to give him a
drink. In theological terms, the Christian encounter commences with
an acknowledgement that the determining context is God's desire for
us to co-operate with Him and thus meets His needs – our

---

[5] Carr, A. W. (1989), *The Pastor as Theologian*, London, SPCK, pp. 161–2.
[6] Ibid.

reconciliation in Him through being joined together with Jesus Christ.

The woman responds in the same direct and open vein of truth. She acknowledges their differences: a Jew and a Gentile; a man and a woman. The boundary issues and their attendant confusions and conflicts are equally fundamental. The kettle has not been put on: potentially the gloves are off.

Now the spiritual agenda can come to the surface. The mysterious common ground is not tea, but something much more basic: needing water, for body and for soul. Here is the possibility of collaboration, the mutuality of needs and resources, and the deep resources of tradition in sacred stories and holy places.

Yet, Jesus does not dwell on this more overtly spiritual agenda. As soon as it is acknowledged, he goes in deeper in relation to the woman's everyday life. How often I am tempted to engage in a short burst of spiritual engagement and truth seeking, only to escape hurriedly into more tea and cakes. Truth is in a deep well: in the desert and in each of us. The issue must be pressed. In Wesley Carr's terms, the encounter is not a matter of instant or easy interpretation: it seems to presuppose sowing the seeds of a richer and more ongoing engagement, not with the pastor, but with the Gospel.

Thus the conversation about the five husbands and the live-in lover. Brutal honesty about the desire for love and secure, stable relationship (hence the concentration upon 'marriage') and yet the frequent falling short. Truth about every human nature in all its blunt confusion, conflict and struggles with boundaries. Every 'evolutionary' step has proved illusory: progress has not been 'upwards' in Huxley's sense: it has simply been continuously uneven. This should be no surprise to anyone steeped in the scriptural realism regarding the human condition.

True worshippers will worship the Father in spirit and in truth

Once again a robust recognition of the truth about the human condition exposes the next level of spiritual agenda. The woman is moved to begin to explore her own framework of 'worth-ship': partly drawing upon an elementary knowledge of her community's religious culture and partly acknowledging that a rival religious culture exists too. Confusion, conflict and issues of boundaries predominate in the spiritual life as much as in personal and social intercourse.

This encounter is a discussion. Jesus listens and hears what the woman is trying to say. He helps her to articulate her understanding of

truth in relation to worth-ship. This has involved an acknowledgement of
His needs alongside their common humanness and yet desire for the
springs of eternity. Further, He has provoked a challenging ownership of
the imperfections and struggles of this life, which has highlighted the
need for deeper resources and a larger vision to embrace the apparently
confusing and conflicting elements of existence. The pastor has
established the trust and common concern which leads to friendship,
but only in the course of doing so much more. The sharpness and depth
of the encounter risks potential enmity for the sake of a real sense of
connection and friendship.

Only at this stage, when common ground and trust have been
established in relation to the truth of the human condition (rather than
simply in terms of interpersonal relationships) is Jesus in a position to
offer that interpretative element which does not solve these struggles
and situations, but rather it puts them in the context of a faith which is
grounded not simply in a religious tradition of special places or
previous epiphanies, but rather in a more embracing and essentially
forward-looking trust in a Father who is known in spirit and in truth.

The uneven and often tragic struggle for domestic structures to
provide a salvation of secure and stable relationship is to be fulfilled
not in our efforts and achievements, but in the reality of a Father: one
who offers that paradoxical framework of intimacy and otherness,
which each human being needs so as to find a proper connection
between our uniqueness and our dependency. This is the area in which
Wesley Carr's use of people like Bion and Reed is so creative.

Moreover, this Father, this greater context of oneness and yet
individual identity, is known through the worth-ship given in spirit and
in truth.

I know that Messiah is coming

The climax of the encounter is that the woman recognizes the need for
a mediator – a Messiah. This deep spiritual insight about a Father who
can be known through the worth-ship given to him in spirit and in
truth, needs to be mediated, incarnated – so that connection can be
made with her in her territory, on her terms, in all its particularities:
the agencies involve her truth and her spirit, engaged with this greater
reality in which issues of confusion, conflict and boundaries are
subsumed, though never fully solved.

Besides coming to the point of recognizing this necessity, the
woman is able to see in the figure of Jesus Christ, the manifestation of
this Messiah – because of the process and pattern of the pastoral
encounter which she had experienced.

For me this reaction underlines the importance of Wesley Carr's work on the role of those in public ministerial office: needing to be willing to be placed on a pedestal so that the dynamic and the distance which allows the engagement of spirit and truth to take place, can happen.[7] The notion of the Messiah is a hint about the importance of role: one who risks more than a social or personal encounter. One who offers engagement and interpretation 'on behalf of' as well as alongside.

This role requires one who is confident and competent to go in deeper, risking hurt and further confusion (the method of being tested by the cross), since it is only through such truth-seeking that the spiritual transaction can be unfolded. There is a particular place for pastoral work by those who can risk standing in the place of the Messiah, and offering an interpretation which connects the ownership of human need with the munificence of the grace of the Father. The priest-like task is to operate on the boundaries of comprehension and of competence, and to offer engagement with a spirit and a truth that both allows and yet transcends human being – so that faith and hope remain, but the goal of love draws us ever beyond the present place, without obliterating its frustrating and often debilitating realities.

The disciples came: they were astonished that he was speaking with a woman

Those who seemed to be closest to Jesus, his companions on the journey, were perplexed by this encounter. Too often the institutionalization of the gifts of grace given to us through Jesus Christ becomes a means of erecting new boundaries – in terms of religion (Jew or Gentile), gender (women or men), or class (slaves or free). These become sources of conflict and confusion in their own right. The truth cannot be camouflaged by Christian fellowship or doctrine: the Father connects with a deeper and more fundamental humanness: a need and an aspiration which remain common to Christians and to non-Christians alike.[8] The church too, has a priest-like task which requires a willingness to risk operating on the boundaries where human experience and the Father's providential love can connect. This should dictate the style and content of Christian worship: a context in which a tradition and stories of past epiphanies can enervate the spirit and truth which we bring from the rough and

---

[7] Redfern, A. (1999), *Ministry and Priesthood*, London, DLT, pp. 116–21. Carr, A. W. (1992), *Say One For Me*, London, SPCK, pp. 40–7.

[8] Carr, A. W. (1989), *The Pastor as Theologian*, London, SPCK, p. 163.

tumble and joy of everyday living. In liturgical terms the dynamic is between a world of encounters that have been explored with a depth and honesty which exposes and enacts the need for confession and repentance: and interpretative comment and action (sermon and sacrament) which embraces this human incompleteness and enfolds it in the Father-like faithfulness of reliability, trust and mutual freedom – God and humankind converse over bread and wine: where spirit and truth are made manifest. The focus is confessional conversation and the sharing of a cup.

Come and see a man who told me everything

The woman leaves her water jar: sign of her old self-sufficient life. She is so moved by the profound encounter that she becomes a missionary herself. She is keen to tell others, and to invite them to risk coming out of the secure shells of their everyday existences to the borderland where confusions and conflicts can be placed in a dynamic with the work of one who stands in the place of the Messiah, who is willing to spend the time required for serious exploration (two days rather than forty minutes) and who becomes in Himself the reason for their new confidence and trust in the salvation of the world. He helps to make the reality of the Father present.

When the two days were over he went from that place

This type of pastoral encounter is limited. The rigorous engagement with truth and spirit climaxes in the offer of an interpretation in terms of the Father which is the trigger for new life to those who have been thus engaged. Each has received a larger vision, a bond of commonness or communion in their worth-ship, and an appreciation of the power and necessity of those things being incarnated: the key is the Lordship of Jesus.

The pastor withdraws. Two days is more than enough for this rigour of encounter. Much of human life is simply to be lived – creating confusion, conflict and issues of boundaries. Ministry to this texture of existence comes in moments, at particular points when truth can be pursued in terms of a very deep well. Hence the importance of role, of choosing moments, and of recognizing that to worship the Father in spirit and truth gives seeds for a sense of direction, but not a blueprint nor a guaranteed security from further failures. The work will always go on: for individuals, for pastors in public roles, for the churches as institutions and agents of such grace. The style and method is one which Wesley Carr has pinpointed with characteristic accuracy: it is a style and a method of brief encounters.[9]

Look around you: the fields are ripe for harvest

This work will never be completed in this earthly context. Each of us enters into an ever-shifting inheritance of sowers and reapers. The basic requirement is that disciples of Jesus must learn to read the signs around us: whether on the level of 'natural' life with its cycle of fertility and mortality (highlighted at moments of birth/baptism, marriage and death/funerals) or on the level of that spiritual discernment which perceives that we survive on a more mysterious diet than manufactured and purchased food. These signs are focused in the two great Christian sacraments, whereby the rhythms of cleansing and feeding are related not simply to the human processes which provide water, bread and wine, but also to the divine mysteries of life tested by a cross and found to be capable of bearing not just brokenness, but also new life – a life which is essentially corporate. This one Body is cleansed and nourished by the One Blood: such encounter and interpretation is the priest-like task for all of God's children.

We know that this is truly the saviour of the world

This piece has explored this life-giving mystery in terms of the pastoral encounter between Jesus and the woman of Samaria, drawing upon some of the insights I have appropriated from my own colleagueship with Wesley Carr. As a temperamentally pastoral person, who has always tended to put tea and harmony as an unspoken priority in every encounter, I have been challenged by Wesley's example and writings to face up to the fact that the Gospel so often seems to demand a more rigorous engagement with the truth that sets our spirits free. My only consolation is that between these essential moments of interpretation and enlightenment, there is plenty of space for more ordinary relationships, such as drinking tea.

The problems come when we fail to appreciate the differences and the vital dynamic between these two modes, and succumb to the temptation to stick with cosiness and trust that conflict and confusion will go away (or, even, be taken away). No such avoidance is possible:

---

[9] Carr, A. W. (1985), *Brief Encounters*, London, SPCK.

to make a Christian witness is to discern those encounters when we can be tested by the cross, and meet the One who acts and interprets on our behalf.

Meeting the pastor in the parlour is a perilous moment, but one pregnant with the possibilities of salvation.

Chapter 8

Occasional Offices:
Natural Sacraments of God's Grace

Christopher Moody

Introduction

I first read Wesley Carr's *Brief Encounters* returning to parochial
ministry after a six-year gap as a university chaplain. It was a
fortuitous moment. This was the first time that I had been a vicar in my
own right, and the fluid, fragmented nature of the context in a deprived
area of central London, gave me a lot of power to define what my own
pattern of ministry was to be. Looking around me, I could see within
the immediate area, lots of different ways in which the boundaries of
church were drawn with the local community. Reading Wesley Carr's
book confirmed an understanding, which I had already begun to
develop in chaplaincy, that my role as a priest, or minister of religion,
was not something which I automatically brought into the situation as
part of my property (in, as it were, an ecclesiastical black bag!), but
something I discovered, negotiated, and improvised in that particular
context, using the props and purposes which were entrusted to me
there. I had to learn what the local culture was first, the religious
language and symbolic means of expression, the other voices and
authorities present there, before I could begin to articulate my own
role with any confidence. Learning not to make prior assumptions,
putting myself in the position of *not* knowing until I had picked up
what clues I could in the situation, was not easy. But Wesley's book,
bringing concepts drawn from psychotherapy, group analysis and
social theory within a theological matrix, gave me an intellectual basis
from which to work and at the same time understand my own feelings.
It helped me to rediscover my integrity as a minister of the gospel, in a
challenging context of ethnic and cultural diversity, social tension and
division, in which it would have been easy to privilege the views and
experiences of one group of people at the expense of others.

Most of my learning was done in relation to the occasional offices,
particularly funerals. My first step in learning, I remember, was in
agreeing with the undertaker to allow a casket to remain open for a

service in church. This was my first introduction to the still well
organized ritual surrounding funerals in the black community.
Significant moments in our growth as a deliberately local rather than
eclectic congregation continued to be connected with the hosting of
particular funerals, some of them celebratory, some of them traumatic.
I became aware of how important churches can be as carriers of
'common religion'[1] and how, if this burden was refused by one church,
it often devolved upon another, not necessarily of the same
denomination. I also came to realize that the relationship with the
religion of people who are in our opinion 'unchurched' (our term, not
theirs) is always two way. The policies and attitudes prevalent in a local
church or denomination help to determine the residual attitudes and
expectations which they subsequently encounter as alien or strange.

Now I work in a different context, in a team ministry in a
prosperous, expanding market town of 21,000 people, where the
demands placed upon us as clergy for the occasional offices are that
much greater. Here, in a much more stable community, I have been
made aware of the pastoral repercussions caused by the variations in
attitude of previous vicars to the occasional offices, and the
importance of developing a policy across the team which is equally
accessible to resident families and newcomers. Part of the challenge
has been to limit the demands placed on the clergy's time, by
introducing the ministry of others such as lay visitors and office
volunteers, without compromising the perception of the availability of
the clergy for the occasional offices which is such an important part of
it.[2] But the tools Wesley's book gave me for analysing my own role
and context in ministry, still remain as useful as they did before.

I want in the following pages to look at some of these tools of
analysis, referring in passing to some of the changes that have
occurred in the context for ministry in the occasional offices in the 19
years since *Brief Encounters* was first published. In particular I want to
develop the understanding of the occasional offices as 'natural
sacraments', a term which is already part of the traditional
understanding of one of the occasional offices, namely marriage,
and which the work of anthropologists like Mary Douglas and Victor
Turner gives new content to.[3] In the course of this analysis I will
highlight the difficulty that occurs when a 'natural sacrament' is also a
sacrament 'of the Church', in the case of infant baptism.

---

[1] Carr, W. (1997) *Handbook of Pastoral Studies*, London, SPCK, pp. 209–10.
[2] Ibid., pp. 213–14.
[3] See Douglas, M. (1970) *Natural Symbols. Explorations in Cosmology*, London,
Cresset Press. Turner, V. (1969), *The Ritual Process*, London, RKP.

Change and definition: the relations between the occasional offices, 'common religion' and different models of the Church

Most of the anxiety within the Church about the occasional offices still focuses upon infant baptism. Should we allow it? What priority should we give it? How do we incorporate it within the worship and mission of the local church? This should occasion more reflection than it does. More change has taken place in the rituals surrounding marriage and death than of birth. Take funerals, for example. Funerals today have become much more 'personal' events than they were before, more in the character of memorial services than a rite of passage, an affirmation of continuity rather than an encounter with the four last things of death, hell, heaven and judgement. The minister's competence in this field is judged on how well they have been able to affirm the inidividual identity of the deceased and speak as if they know them (even if in the majority of cases they do not) rather than in a presentation of the Christian hope of resurrection. Meanwhile, new forms of mourning have developed around sudden and tragic deaths, communal grieving for celebrities and reaction to traumatic disasters like the Hillsborough Stadium disaster and the terrorist attack on New York on 9/11. Accommodation to these changes in pastoral practice has been made without much comment. Nor does there seem to have been much of a decline in the demand placed upon clergy for these services.

Or take marriage. It is fair to say that the decline of marriage, which looks today as if it is levelling off, has caused as much anxiety generally in society as it has in the Church. The Church has often been as much on the defensive from critics outside its boundaries for not doing enough to preserve the institution of marriage as it has been responsible for generating a debate itself. The acceptance of remarriage for the divorced, including the clergy themselves, has become general in most Christian denominations in a relatively short time, and the pattern for when a couple actually get married in the course of a relationship becomes more and more varied – so much so that it becomes almost redundant to talk about a pattern at all.

In contrast to weddings and funerals, the request for infant baptism represents the maintenance of a more traditional and conservative trend beneath all the changes that have occurred elsewhere. But it is still seen as being the most problematic. Why? Because it most directly affects the Church's own sense of mission and identity. In the case of death and marriage it is much easier for us to acknowledge, as a minister, that we are entering a field which is not entirely our own, whereas infant baptism immediately confronts us with accepting or rejecting people, on what, as we see it, is our own territory. In relation to infant baptism, we do not see ourselves as having the same freedom

in terms of purely pastoral concern and priorities as we do towards the
conduct of marriage and funerals precisely because we see baptism as
being a sacrament of belonging in a way that other occasional offices
are not.

The reasons for this have as much to do with changes in the Church
as in society in general. The Church has responded to a period of rapid
change, advance in education and questioning of traditional sources of
morality and authority by redefining its boundaries in a way it
conceives will be of benefit to its own life. In general this has meant a
move away from a communal and sacramental model of the
institutional Church as representing and pointing towards a wider
vision of reality and the world, towards a model of church as voluntary
association whose membership is primarily a matter of individual
choice and conversion. The justification for this has usually been in
terms of an appeal to early church practice and liturgical precedent,
quietly ignoring the differences in historical context and social
psychology between 'then' and 'now'. Our very ignorance of these
conditions gives us the ability to project back into Christian history
what we think we need as strategies for growth and survival today.
This is what Wesley Carr calls 'the re-pristinization of the Church'. It
gives us the ability to change our practice whilst playing down the
pressures in the immediate context which have led to this response in
the first place. But the pace of liturgical change in the past 40 years is
itself as much a symptom of our situation, as it is a cure. We should
not be surprised, then, when our attempts to re-define the rites and
practices of the Church, and what is the right use or abuse of them by
others, is met with a large measure of incomprehension and hostility.

Those who approach us for the occasional offices often do so with
an implicit understanding of what the Church stands for and implicit
appeal to a model of the Church which we may currently ignore or
play down. Even then, we have to admit we do not do this consistently
across the ocassional offices, but only selectively, using one model
when we feel directly challenged to do so in relation to the sacrament
of baptism, and another when we feel we are being called off our own
territory to do a funeral at a crematorium or host a marriage service in
church (recognizing, in this instance, that the couple themselves
minister the rite in the exchange of vows). Many ministers resent the
role they are invested with in the occasional offices. They feel that it is
something imposed on them from outside, something that they must
either choose to go along with or to resist. Many see it as an expression
of 'folk religion' which actually obscures their role as active agents of
the gospel. But this is to mistake the role that 'residual' or 'folk'
religion has to play in people's approach to the Church through the
occasional offices. For just as the notion of 'Church' is not a static one,

moving as it does between communal and associational definitions all the time, neither is that of religion either, in terms of the deeper values and beliefs which hold communities together beyond the ties of law, kinship and reciprocal obligation. In his *Handbook of Pastoral Studies*, Wesley has chosen the term 'common religion' to define this (see fn 1). It is the by no means organized arena of different beliefs about the meaning and purpose of life, traditions, customs, values and strategies, which affects in different ways those within congregations as well as those outside them.

Perhaps when British society was more homogeneous, and there was a closer identity between religion and social conformity, there was more reason to fear co-option to a set of values not entirely consistent with the interests of the gospel. But that is not the case now. The danger we face today is that we have too much freedom to define the pastoral and missionary task ourselves, without taking into account how Christian values are held more generally in society, or the effect that our local strategies for church growth and 'prioritizing mission' have in helping to form the preconceptions with which people approach us for our services. As John Taylor pointed out, any institution can be analysed under five headings: context, task, technology or tools, structure or organization, people or personnel.[4] All of these have to be held in balance, understanding how changes under one heading have repercussions and implications for the others. In the present situation a high priority is given to evangelism, defined in narrowly ecclesiastical terms as vital to the Church for its own survival. But if we assume that the 'missio dei' is not coterminous with the Church but the world, then the Church needs to be constantly rediscovering and reformulating its task 'within the purpose of God and his relation to the world'.[5] In the contemporary situation, when the internal agendas associated with structure and personnel are so strong, it is important to give equal validity to those needs and pressures expressed from outside which help to recall and revise our own task in ministry.

Incarnation, sacraments and the gospel narrative

In the occasional offices, as I have argued above, we recognize a difference in the role we play as ministers in each of these situations and operate a different notion of 'Church' in each case. In respect of requests for infant baptism, we feel an acute sense of role anxiety,

---

[4] Taylor, J.V. (1988) 'Conversion to the World', in G. Ecclestone (ed.), *The Parish Church?* London, Mowbrays, pp. 127–8.
[5] Ibid.

caught, as we see it, between the church's need for active membership, and the time we spend with families who wilfully will not accept our agenda. But the families who use the occasional offices make little or no distinction between the role of the minister in each case. He or she becomes the 'vicar who married us', 'the priest who baptized my baby' or 'the minister who did the service for my grandad'. Our performance of the role often affects our ability to be called upon in one case and effective in another. As Wesley Carr notes, the Church's doctrine of the minister's worthiness not affecting the sacrament has little meaning for those who approach us for the occasional offices.[6] Why the vicar who did such a lovely service for my husband when he died suddenly becomes difficult when we want our grandaughter christened is a mystery to them, not least because we have been operating with a different implicit understanding of the church and, perhaps therefore, of God's grace, in each case.

Re-reading Wesley's book after a gap of 15 years, the point that comes across most strongly is that the sacraments are not the Church's property. Theologically, we may see them as being so, especially when we treat the eucharist as the Church's 'family communion' and infant baptism as the means of entry into the Christian family for the baby and its parents. But they are also powerful symbolic complexes, capable of carrying multiple meanings, 'signals of transcendence' to use Peter Berger's term,[7] which remind us that we live the whole of our lives 'sub specie aeternitatis'. Each celebration of the sacrament is at the same time a particular interpretation of it. A sacrament is performed always in interaction with, or, to use the theological term, 'in fellowship with', those present, their hopes, their brokenness and their expectations. As Wesley Carr writes:

> If thinking about the sacraments and the occasional offices is brought into this frame of reference, we ... find that what we may presume to belong to the church and to be offered to people, in fact already belongs to them. These sacraments are not the the church's possession, but a facet of common human experience within God's creation, confirmed by the new creation in the resurrection.[8]

The only word I would change in that statement is the word 'confirmed'. I would replace it with the words 'interpreted' or 'transformed'. I think that gives a much clearer understanding of what

---

[6] Carr, A.W. (1985) *Brief Encounters: Pastoral Ministry through the Occasional Offices*, London, SPCK, pp. 53–4.

[7] See Berger, P.L. (1969) *A Rumor of Angels*, Garden City, NY, Doubleday.

[8] Carr, *Brief Encounters*, op. cit., p. 54.

is happening, or at least has the potential to do so, when the personal rituals surrounding birth, marriage and death are brought into the orbit of the Church via the introduction of one of its ministers. There is a balance to be struck between the general notions that divine reality is 'revealed' or 'embodied' in particular human situations and the particular responsibility we have as ministers for the whole narrative associated with Jesus as Lord. This is a matter of incarnational theology and how it is worked out in social terms. Sacraments, whether 'natural' or 'of the Church' are, above all, social realities, sacraments of community. As Rowan Williams argues, a theology of incarnation cannot be used simply to sacralize what already exists.

> 'Natural' systems of relation, family belonging, membership of a race or nation, provide the metaphors for the relations of Christians to each other and to their God; but this has less to do with some vision of natural analogies than with a claim to establish the *true* relationships are a distorted reflection.[9]

So there is a justified anxiety if all we are doing as ministers in the occasional offices is simply sanctifying what already exists. It is difficult, if not impossible, to observe the nature of the occasional offices as natural sacraments in separation from the role we already play in them as ministers of the gospel. The role of the minister in the occasional offices is far more dynamic than calling to mind what already exists. It always involves some form of transaction between ('broken' or 'distorted') human experience and the truth revealed in Jesus Christ and yet to be established fully, either in the Church or the world.

Taking this further, we would also have to recognize that there is a difference in the way that baptism and the eucharist, the 'two Sacraments ordained of Christ our Lord in the Gospel' (Article XXV) relate to the narrative concerning Jesus Christ, and the life of 'his' community; and the way we relate to God in the occasional offices, in what we might term the 'natural' sacraments of birth, marriage and death. This is not to weaken the point that 'the sacraments are not the church's possession' because we cannot define a moment when any of the sacraments can be found in a pristine form, even the 'dominical' sacraments of baptism and eucharist. They have always been something taken up into the life of the Church. They have always been contextualized in a particular moment and for a particular group of people. They have always been at the same time 'local' and 'universal'. Even the sacraments 'ordained by Christ our Lord' took up

---

[9] Williams, R. (2000) *On Christian Theology*, Oxford, Blackwells, p. 229.

what was already there, 'certain existing rituals and actions – water baptism, passover and a shared meal'. We can observe the process of them changing and taking shape within the pages of the New Testament. Furthermore, and this is my main point, they always derive the raw material for their meaning from a sacramental awareness which is, implicitly, already there. They are an 'interaction with' as well as a 'representation to' those who come together as the participants in the sacrament. They actively bring into communion those who are participants for the duration of the rite. From this derives their character as sacraments of care, an extension of the ministry of Christ, as well as a vehicle for teaching and belief about him.

Rite and ritual: the occasional offices as group processes

The interventions we are called to make as 'ministers of religion' in the case of birth, marriage and death are in the context of 'rites of passage' which are much more extensive than the service itself. John Taylor gives a lovely, and often quoted, example of this in his chapter for the Grubb Institute's book *The Parish Church?*.[10] He describes how in his last year as Bishop of Winchester he inadvertently offended his gardener who had invited him to the baptism of his son by not attending the party afterwards. He was not quite sure whether he had been invited or not. He comes to realize that, for the child's father, the invitation had not seemed necessary because the service in church and the party afterwards were to him all part of the same process:

> For him the drinking of the champagne and the cutting of the cake were just as much part of the ritual as the sprinkling of the water. That was for him a rather strange part, he could understand the rest. The point was that the Church has always assumed that Baptism is *its* ritual which it can dispense to those who seem qualified for it, but which it certainly has to explain. I came to see that what we are asked to perform is *their* ritual, and if we are prepared to do that as one of the still surviving rituals of our society, then we can claim the right to say, 'can we tell you what *we* see in this?' and to explain the deeper Christian understanding of that ritual. But I believe that unless we start with the reacceptance of it as their ritual, we have very little chance of conveying the Christian interpretation of it. And I think that the same modesty applies to all rites of passage which may still take place – the marriage, the funeral and others.

---

[10] Taylor, op. cit. p. 135.

When we look at the occasional offices in this way, we begin to see them as group processes in which it is vital that we perform our role well. We usually think of baptism as a choice that the parents make on behalf of their baby of attachment to the Church, and we do our best through what we say and how we conduct the service to explain what that might mean. But as far as the parents are concerned they have already made their choice in bringing the child into the world in the first place. What they want to do in most cases is to celebrate its safe arrival and 'its coming to God at the start of life's journey'.[11] Often, particular ceremony surrounds the arrival of a first child, because the couple are themselves entering a new role as parents. More and more today, as marriage is postponed until a later stage in the relationship, this will be the first time that they have gathered their friends and families together in a public acknowledgement of their relationship. The whole process is therefore fraught with uncertainty. Often a baptism comes towards the end of the process of settling down with a new baby, and celebrates the reintegration of the family after a period of stress and confusion. Frequently, the birth has been associated with moving to a new house and the dislocation that involves as well. The baptism is therefore very much an acknowledgement of a new start for everybody. The acceptance of the child by God through the rite expresses their acceptability as parents as well, both to the wider community of their friends and family, and to God.

Birth, marriage and death are all boundary experiences which confront us with our own ignorance, fear and the limits of our own power to bring about a happy future for ourselves and those closest to us – our child, our partner, our departed relative. In these periods we experience our own vulnerability and mortality, and the deeper questions about the meaning and value of human life. They are potentially dangerous, but also transformative moments, when unusual levels of dependency and trust are expressed and transitional figures like the priest, the counsellor, the undertaker, the doctor, the nurse, can for a time assume a tremendous importance. The charisma to deal with the situation appropriately is not something which is given automatically, but something derived from the powerful projections and expectations present within the situation itself, the previous history of contact that that family may have had with the institution that figure represents, and the ability that person has as a professional practitioner to engage that situation fully and appropriately.

---

[11] Wilcock, P. (2000) 'Mixed Blessings: Suburban Experiences' in M. Simmons (ed.), *Street Credo. Churches in the Community*, London, Lemos & Crane, p. 93.

If one takes John Taylor's point about the wider ritual process surrounding birth, marriage and death as being as important as the church rite itself, the ability of the priest to act will depend on how well they are able to 'read' the rest of the process and negotiate with the other powerful figures involved. This is all the more difficult when the process is so different in each case. Sometimes people come to the rite with a very well-organized family or cultural tradition behind them. Once that is known it becomes relatively easy to know how one might negotiate one's own role in the process. One can read the signs quite easily. But at other times, the tradition they come with, that is to say, what has been handed on to them to help them deal with the situation, may be very thin indeed. Part of what one is called to do in these cases is to help develop a liturgy which will help the participants order and handle their experience in a way which will move the process on. A good example of this is how one deals with the whole business of what music is acceptable as part of the ceremony – particularly in the case of marriages and funerals. Working out with a couple or the bereaved family what music is appropriate is one of the best ways to understand their values and how they draw the boundary between the sacred and the profane. In my experience of funerals, it is often the particular piece of music chosen which has been *the* moment of transition, of crossing over, for the bereaved as well as the wider congregation. What is capable of bearing meaning as a sacramental sign is not organized in the way one is led to expect from 'church' sacraments. Sometimes it can be a poem or a particular action undertaken by friends. It is impossible to determine beforehand what the point will be. But part of the role of the minister is to be a master of ceremonies, and orchestrate what is going on rather than impose a pattern on the proceedings which prevents that point ever being reached. The involvement of the minister is in its very nature, a therapeutic one, involving a diagnosis of the elements present in a particular occasion and the best way of bringing things to the surface so that they can be handled and dealt with appropriately.

These observations draw their inspiration heavily from V. W. Turner's book *The Ritual Process*, in particular the chapter entitled 'Liminality and Communitas'. Those at the centre of these rites of passage, the parents and baby, the couple to be married or the next of kin, are like neophytes. They are, for the period up to the rite and immediately following it, 'entities in transition, as yet without place or position'.[12] This description attaches particularly to the people at the centre of the rite, the baby, or the couple, or the the dead person

---

[12] Turner, op. cit., p. 103.

themselves, but it affects those in closest relationship to them as well. It is interesting, in this respect, that though the modern rite of infant baptism allows for the parents themselves to be 'sponsors' for their children, without choosing godparents, hardly anybody chooses this option. Though it would make perfect sense to do so, if, for instance, the parents themselves are the only practising Christians in a family, it still seems to go against the grain. As ministers we often dismiss the question 'who would we trust to help bring up our child if something should happen to us?' as an inferior criterion for choosing a godparent than explicit evidence of Christian belief and practice. But if we see the rite as connected with the process of birth as a liminal state not just for the baby but its parents as well, the question seems less alien to the rite's central concern. Turner goes on to write:

> '[the] neophytes in many *rites de passage* have to submit to an authority that is nothing less than that of the total community. This community is the repository of the whole gamut of the culture's values, norms, attitudes and relationships. Its representatives – *and these may vary from ritual to ritual* [my italics] – represent the generic authority of tradition.[13]

In rites of passage, that is, what concerns the natural human cycle of birth, pairing and death, the Church cannot be seen as being the sole repository of authority and tradition. The minister of religion is there as the representative of the total community and not just the Church. Even in a society as fragmented and specialized as our own, he or she takes on the mantle, *for the time that it takes for that process to occur only,* as the guardian, caretaker or host for something much wider than the particular teachings of the Church (dogmatics).

Many ministers are confused by the fact that the authority they are invested with for the duration of the rite, and the relationships they enjoy with the participants as a result, often do not seem to outlast the rite itself. But if we see it in these terms as a special time of liminality, then it becomes not strange but explicable. It is not only 'the neo-phytes' themselves but the ministers of the rite who are liminal figures, representing a deeper form of community and of human relatedness, than the 'normal' status relationships of 'place and posi-tion'. Simply to transfer his or her role, and with it a single set of status relationships, from one sphere to another – for example, the position he or she enjoys within the congregation itself to the boundaries with the local community as a whole – is bound to lead to mistakes and pastoral confusion. In these boundary conditions we are often lent a 'statusless status' which allows us to cross the normal barriers based

---

[13] Ibid.

on education, social background and ethnicity and even, to an extent, creed. But always with the proviso that this is a role which we must *negotiate* within the situation rather than assume.

The occasional offices as natural sacraments: performative signs of change rather than statements about what already exists

We may term the whole of the ritual process associated with rites of passage, and especially the rite itself, as a 'natural sacrament'. As such it is an effective sign of what it attempts to convey. But this is as much through the conditions associated with 'liminality' as it is by direct appeal to dominical command or scriptural authority. As Turner puts it:

> The wisdom (*mana*) that is imparted in sacred liminality is not just an aggregation of words and sentences; it has ontological value, it refashions the very being of the neophyte.[14]

Wesley Carr makes the same point when he writes:

> ... the notion of meaning is not solely a matter of the words spoken. Communication includes a range of other signals, of which the words are one set. The sensed attitude of the minister, the environment, the seriousness or otherwise with which the occasion is treated, all these are as much part of the meaning that people construct. *The key for the minister in such occasions is to realize that what is done is more significant than what is said* [my italics].[15]

In other words the sets of language and symbols used are performative rather than declarative. They do not describe and confirm a status which has already been reached, but enable people to enter and negotiate their way through a state of being which puts them in touch with the deepest sources of threat and meaning to human life.

I always intimate to couples requesting marriage that, whatever stage they have already reached in their relationship, even when they have already set up home and started a family together, they must expect to feel different as a result of the ceremony. It will not simply confirm what they have already been through together. In providing a different frame of reference, it will reinterpret that experience and introduce them to new dimensions of it. In funerals, perhaps because

---

[14] Ibid.
[15] Carr, *Handbook*, op. cit., p 214.

we are so aware of the importance of what has come to be termed 'the grieving process', we also understand, quite naturally, the importance a 'good' funeral will have in helping the family to move on. It is only in relation to baptism that we seem to have the most difficulty. This is partly because what is a 'natural' sacrament associated with birth is also sacrament of initiation into the visible community of the Church. But it is also because of a confusion between performative and declarative language.

In the case of adult initiation, either by confirmation reception or baptism, we have slipped into understanding the language of the rite in a declarative way, as the confirmation of a status which the individual has made a choice about, a public recognition of what they have already received through faith. Because it is so strongly identified with 'active' church membership and, therefore, an associational model of the Church (we have touched on the reasons for this already elsewhere), this faith is usually taken as a rational process of acceptance of Church teaching and dogma (albeit supernaturally aided). Though this is itself but one model of conversion, and by no means the dominant one in how most people come to faith, we then import it back into our thinking about infant baptism, reasoning that if, for obvious reasons, this process is not possible for the baby, then, at least in truncated form, it should be possible for the parents or godparents. The fact that we also dealing with what I have described here as the 'natural sacrament' of birth, and what that means as a group process for the whole family is allowed very little room in this discussion dominated, as it is, by a paradigm of adult initiation based on historical, liturgical research. In the 19 years since Wesley Carr's book was published, there has been a stronger theological emphasis on baptism as a constant dimension of the Church's worship and vocation of a 'saved' community. This is witnessed in the growing liturgical practice of renewal of baptismal vows. With this new emphasis has come a wider understanding that the Church *itself* is a sign and sacrament of the call of God in creation to community through Jesus Christ. As that emphasis grows, so new ways of relating the rite of infant baptism to Church membership and fellowship may become clear. In the meantime we can only assert the priority of grace. Our particular skill as ministers of the occasional offices is in relating the primary realities of birth, marriage and death to the narrative of God's love revealed in Jesus Christ. It is something we embody in how we act, as much as we contain it in what we say. Performed well, each of the occasional offices can be, as someone described infant baptism, a 'sacrament of God's embrace'.[16]

---

[16] Wilcock, op. cit., p. 93.

Chapter 9

Strong Feelings in a Polite Church

Emma Percy and Martyn Percy

Introduction

> In some of my conversations with Anglican theologians ... I have been struck by how much of the coherence of Anglicanism depends on good manners. This sounds, at face value, like an extraordinarily elitist statement. It is clearly not meant to be that. What I mean by manners is learning to speak well, behave well, and be able to conduct yourself with integrity in the midst of an argument ... It is often the case that in Anglicans' disputes about doctrine, order or faith, it is actually the means that matter more than the ends ... politeness, integrity, restraint, diplomacy, patience, a willingness to listen, and above all, not to be ill-mannered – these are the things that enable the Anglican Communion to cohere ... (Percy, 2000: 118–19).

There can be no question that enabling ecclesial polity depends, to some extent, on managing anger. In macro-theological disputes, such as those over the ordination of women, part of the strategy that enables unity can be centred on muzzling some of the more passionate voices in the debate. Extreme feelings, when voiced, can lead to extreme reactions. And extreme reactions, when allowed full vent, can make situations unstable. Nations fall apart; Communions fracture; families divide. Things said briefly in the heat of a moment can cause wounds that may take years to heal. What is uttered is not easily retracted.

It can be argued that many casual descriptions of Anglican polity are focused on its essentially peaceable and pastoral nature. For T.S. Eliot, the Church of England is the *via media* (Eliot, 1928: 14). It is a synthesis of tensions; a delicate infusion of polarities. It is partly protestant, partly catholic, partly evangelical and partly liberal. It is an Episcopally-led church, and yet also one where Synods govern, and also has a supreme governor who is a laywoman (the Queen). It is a church, as one former Archbishop of Canterbury so eloquently put it, which embodies 'passionate coolness'. There are causes and beliefs that it pursues with a righteous intensity. But the communication of such things can often be characterized by reticence, temperance and openness. Any such statements the church may make might be sharp and penetrating, but are often balanced by an instinctive pastoral reflex: to be soft and accommodating as well.

Good manners, then, is not a bad analogy for 'ideal' Anglican polity. In a church that sets out to accommodate many different peoples of every theological hue, there has to be a foundation – no matter how implicit – that enables the Communion to cohere across party lines, tribal borders and doctrinal differences. And just as this is true for macro-theological disputes, so is it also true for micro-ecclesial squabbles. Keeping the peace in a congregation that is at loggerheads over church fabric and fittings, or perhaps unable to agree on an appropriate resolution in a complex ethical debate, is a no less demanding task for a parish priest. Often, congregational unity in the midst of disputes can only be secured by finding a middle, open way, in which the voices of moderation and tolerance occupy the central ground and enable a church to move forwards. In such situations, the cultivation of 'good manners' can be seen to be essential; civility quietly blossoms where arguments once threatened to lay waste.

And yet there are several important pastoral and theological issues that surround this type of narration for a congregation, diocese, church or communion, and question its apparent wisdom. 'Good manners', for example, can be a form of quasi-pastoral *suppression* that does not allow true or strong feelings to emerge in the centre of an ecclesial community, and properly interrogate its 'settled' identity. This may rob the church of the opportunity to truly feel the pain of those who may already perceive themselves to be on the margins of the church, perhaps even disqualified, or who already feel silenced. 'Good manners' can also become a cipher for excluding the apparently undeserving, and perhaps labelling seemingly difficult insights as 'extreme voices'. The prophetic, the prescient, and those who protest, can all be ignored by a church that makes a virtue out of overly-valuing a peaceable grammar of exchange. Put another way, if the 'coolness' always triumphs over the 'passionate', then the church is effectively deaf in one ear.

We are also aware of some factors here that are, in all probability, gender-based. Ursula Le Guin makes a helpful distinction between 'mother' tongue' and 'father tongue'. The 'father tongue' is the language of power: 'spoken from above ... it goes one way ... no answer is expected or heard ...' (Le Guin, 1989: 149). The 'father-tongue' is the clinical language of the lecture theatre or the professions – it distances the emotions, passions and desires. In contrast, 'mother tongue' is the language of the home. It is, according to Le Guin, 'inaccurate, coarse, limited, trivial, banal ... earthbound, housebound, common speech, plebian, ordinary ...' (Le Guin, 1989: 149). But for

Le Guin, the 'mother-tongue' is also the language of connection and relationships; its power lies in uniting and binding, not dividing. It is Le Guin's contention that much public discourse, especially professional discourse within institutions, is a learned 'father-tongue' that deliberately marginalizes the realm of feelings and the scope of relationality. She argues that a recovery of 'mother-tongue' within public discourse is an essential step for the reconstitution of public life, where 'plain' speaking can reclaim its proper value (or currency) as bona fide expression.

Quite naturally therefore, there is the issue of anger itself, and of strong feelings. In the body of Christ, how are these feelings received, articulated and generated? Quite apart from appropriate 'righteous anger' (e.g., on matters of justice), how does a mature church receive and respond to aggression within itself, and to strong feelings such as anger, dismay, passion, rage or enthusiasm? For example, the issue of anger comes to a head in two different places in David Hare's play *Racing Demon* (1990). In the first case, the Bishop of Kingston states that the job of the Church of England (and especially a bishop), is 'preventing problems turning into issues' (p. 39). In this case, it is the suppression of anger that is paramount, even though it is clear that the underlying feelings are not being addressed. Clearly, the bishop simply hopes that the feelings will 'go away' in due course, and 'everything can return to normal'. But they don't. So second, and by the end of the play, some of the underlying anger about the church and its *via media* and accommodating tendencies simply erupts. A different bishop (Southwark), furious at his lack of power, and the inability of the church to make a decision, and do anything about the apparent incompetence of one of his clergy (Lionel), explodes with rage:

> In any other job you'd have been fired years ago. You're a joke, Lionel. You stand in the parish like some great fat wobbly girl's blouse. Crying for humanity. And doing absolutely nothing at all ... .you are the reason the whole church is dying. Immobile. Wracked. Turned inward. Caught in a cycle of decline ... a great vacillating pea-green half-set jelly ... you parade your so-called humility, until it becomes a disgusting kind of pride. Yes, we can all be right if we never actually *do* anything ... (Hare, 1990: 80).

Clearly, we don't want to defend the kind of outburst quoted above. But in this essay, we *do* want to argue that there is a right and proper place for anger and aggression and other strong feelings in ecclesial polity and pastoral praxis. We want to challenge the idea that the interests of the church are best served by the 'silencing of subjectivity'. In place of this, we want to explore how the rightful appropriation of anger and aggression can enable the work of the church, taking pastoral praxis away from the cerebral and peaceable, and into the arena of feelings and desires. We believe this to be important material for the church to be addressing at this time. At local, regional and national levels, there is often a marked inability to deal with feelings about the church and Christian life, hampering both the witness of the church as well as distorting its inner life. Rather like a good marital or parent-child relationship, learning to articulate and channel anger can be as important as learning to control it. It is often the case that in relation-ships where the expression of anger is denied its place, resentment festers and breeds, and true love is ultimately distorted. Strong feelings need to be acknowledged for relationships to flourish. If strong feelings on one or both sides have to be suppressed for the sake of a relationship, then it is rarely proper to speak of the relationship being mature or healthy. Indeed, some relationships that apparently present as being idyllic and peaceable (e.g., 'we never argue') can turn out to be pathologically problematic. Both parties, afraid of conflict and its consequences, deny their full truth to one another and themselves.

Of course, and in terms of ecclesial polity, it is sometimes the case that feelings about an issue are far from paramount. But equally, we are aware that feelings often need to be suppressed as a pre-condition for entering into any kind of debate or ecclesial process, and we suspect that this too can be unhealthy for the human and theological processes that make up so much of church life. In a festschrift such as this, an evaluation of strong feelings is timely and appropriate. Feelings such as anger can drive or distort ministry, and their impact upon human organization and process can be considerable. There can be no question that being cool, calm and collected is important in pastoral ministry. But sometimes, being angry, avuncular and ardent can also have its place in a mature church.

We can perhaps give one example by way of introduction. At a diocesan residential conference, all the Eucharistic worship had been organized so as not to give offence to any clergy with strong views. No woman priest was scheduled to celebrate Communion, but neither was any clergyman opposed to the ordination of women invited to celebrate. In this way, (perhaps understandably), the senior staff and conference organizers hoped to avoid an argument. Of course, the net effect of this policy was that the only people to celebrate Communion were men who approved of the ordination of women. But the women priests and those male priests who would habitually oppose them were far from happy with this apparently peaceable compromise. Silent anger simmered below the surface of an apparently happy and bubbly conference.

But one woman priest took an interesting initiative. Seeing that her own feelings and those of her colleagues were being 'checked' but never acknowledged, she arranged for the women priests to meet with the male priests who opposed the ordination of women. She argued that neither side could be happy with the enforced compromise, which created a sense of their being 'no argument'. Both sides had a very agreeable meeting over a few drinks, and began to see that proper expression to their true feelings – both their desires and hurts – was being denied. Both sides felt that their genuine, God-given anger (even though they didn't agree), was being muzzled by the hierarchy. Both sides felt that their subjectivity was being suppressed. In not allowing their anger and division to be publicly symbolized, (either by men refusing to receive communion from women priests, or women only receiving from men who recognized their priestly ministry), their actual feelings were being ignored. Both sides, even though they seldom met, and were angry with each other (at least sometimes), felt that it would have been more mature to allow differences and feelings to surface, and thus generate more dialogue, rather than devising a Eucharistic schedule that apparently found a compromise in which no-one was hurt. But in actual fact, all the schedule did was deny people the opportunity to express their hurt, leading to further accusations and pain. Both sides claimed that they were still being marginalized, in spite of assurances to the contrary. Both sides claimed that they were not really being listened to, and that the 'settlement' imposed upon them (for the kindest, nicest reasons – 'to minimize pain', etc.) failed to take account of their raw and strong feelings.

To take this argument further, we want to pursue two lines of enquiry. First, we want to explore some of the more promising feminist literature that deals with pastoral theology and praxis, and with the realm of feelings. And second, we want to look more generally at the ecclesial and theological issues surrounding the inculcation of strong feelings into the body of Christ, and the possible consequences of this, with some reference to black and liberation theologies. A brief conclusion will suggest some further areas for reflection.

Exploring strong feelings

'Gentle Jesus, meek and mild' is a prayer that many learnt to say as a child. It often went with the picture of Jesus cradling a lamb on his shoulder, and gentling children on his lap. To be sure, gentleness is a virtue to be cherished. But advocating such virtues can have its darker side. In the Church of England, and during the debate over the ordination of women, many women were informally counselled 'not to become too strident', to 'avoid militancy', and more besides. (Similar sentiments can be expressed within the Roman Catholic Church. See Steichen, 1992.) Pain and frustration were not to be expressed; the present and future poise of the polity depended on suppressing any kind of raw anger. Now, 'anger' and 'aggression' are terms that Christians tend to struggle with, or perhaps more often simply try and ignore. Gentleness and love that is detached and self-sacrificing have often been held up as the virtues that Christians should be striving for. Politeness is certainly an important part of the polity of the church, but often with little acknowledgement that the *form* and *patterning* of manners have normally been established by those in power, so that consciously and unconsciously their privileges are maintained. At the same time, we may need to appreciate that anger and aggression are often correlated with violence and chaos, and their intimate connection with love is therefore not acknowledged. The expression of passionate feelings, or perhaps of any feelings, is seen as a threat to the manners and politeness that maintain the coolness of rational faith. The danger, as Harrison and Robb point out, is that

> We need to recognize that where the evasion of feeling is widespread, anger does not go away or disappear. Rather, in interpersonal life it masks itself as boredom, ennui, low energy, or it expresses itself in passive-aggressive activity or in low moralistic self-righteousness and blaming. Anger denied subverts community. Anger expressed directly is a mode of taking the other seriously, of caring. The important point is that where feeling is evaded, where anger is hidden or goes unattended, masking itself, there the power of love, the power to act, to deepen relation, atrophies and dies (Harrison and Robb, 1985: 15).

Equally, aggression is almost always understood as negative, and often equated with violence. Yet feminist writers such as Kathleen Greider call for a proper reappraisal of aggression and its place. She points out that the Latin etymology of 'aggression' lies in the verb *aggredi*, meaning 'to move towards', and she uses an intriguing working definition that is significant for our discussion here. Greider sees aggression as a central part of human nature present from our earliest infancy. It is as important as love in the human capacity to survive and thrive.

> aggression is one primary expression of the life force, of the drive to survive and thrive, embodied in positive and negative movement toward and engagement with goals, persons, objects, and obstacles ... These two primary forces can be seen in infants who have at birth both the sentiment (love) to engage others and the force (aggression) especially through their ability to cry, to influence the powerful others around them to meet their needs ... (Greider, 1996: 126).

Thus for Greider, aggression and love are interrelated. They are both deeply connected to the importance of building and sustaining relationships that enable self and others to flourish:

> When functioning in this essential unity, aggression and love cannot be fully differentiated. However, an approximation of their particular contributions might be that love is 'desire' and aggression is 'movement'. ... Aggression enables love to move toward the thing desired, love enables aggression to desire the thing toward which it moves. Love has gumption in it, aggression has affection in it. Without this intermingling, love might be passive, aggression might be only self-serving; with this intermingling, aggression is more likely to be constructive, love is more likely to have backbone (Greider, 1996: 127).

This working definition of aggression alters our perception of the term. It relocates it as a neutral given in human and organizational relating that can be expressed positively and negatively. In its positive form it is about drive; about the activity that moves things forwards so that love and relationship might flourish. In its negative form, it reacts with violence to those things that appear to deny or destroy the self. Thus, 'aggression is used negatively when it is directed toward wasteful and/ or unconscious violence; aggression is used positively when it is directed toward the affirmation of life and well-being in both its personal and collective dimensions' (Greider, 1996: 129).

Greider's 'aggression' is what others might call 'assertion'. Celia Hahn writes that 'assertion means moving outside oneself, reaching out with vigour and initiative, acting on the world' (1994: 21). Hahn draws a clear distinction between aggression and assertion, seeing the former as negative; but Greider argues that sometimes it is the very strength of aggression that is needed. She reflects on the fact that on the rare occasions where aggression is defended, it is because it is utilized on behalf of others, or constitutes a creative push. So what is needed is a reappraisal of aggression for the sake of self, and the value of its destructive as well as constructive power:

> Yet there are some things that need to be destroyed, such as systems of oppression: is there no healthy and ethical way psychically to explore 'creative destruction'? (Greider, 1996: 133)

Arguably, what is needed here is an exploration of the issue of aggression, and a reflection on its relationship to love, and to the valuing of self. The overwhelming tendency for many who have achieved a role within the structures is to avoid behaviour that may unsettle the *status quo*, even though it may allow inequality to continue. And what is true for women in this regard can be true for all who are powerless: their aggression is ignored or vilified, because it questions the structures of power that currently stand. Hahn writes:

> According to a recent survey, white men believe that if others (women and minorities) win better positions, the men will lose out. If all power is arranged in pyramids, they are right. (Hahn, 1994: 22)

So in terms of ecclesial polity and pastoral praxis, the difficulty is this: the church is too used to defining all aggression as negative. Correspondingly, the church often fails to see the value of aggression or anger in the pursuit of just relations. Of course in retrospect we can acknowledge that freedoms for the oppressed have been won by aggressive behaviour, even when it has been militantly peaceful or pacifist: the Civil Rights movement in North America and the peaceful protests of Gandhi spring to mind. (On this, see Marsh, 1997.) But all too often churches and society collude in a fiction, believing that an end to slavery, the emancipation of women, and perhaps even the end of apartheid, could all have been achieved without the aggressive behaviour of militants. Typically, the church also fails to acknowledge the levels of inequality within itself. Many may still need to express or deploy aggressive behaviour in order for Kingdom values to be established.

So Greider is especially concerned with women's aggression, and how it has been suppressed:

> Almost always, women's aggression is ignored, mocked, or violently punished ... Women's aggression represents the potential or real loss of privilege and power resulting from the disturbance of dominating and subjugating social structures, and the repression of women's aggression may seek consciously and unconsciously to avoid or revenge any threats to the *status quo* ... (Greider, 1996: 133)

Greider also points out how women themselves often collude in this, especially those who are from white, educated backgrounds: 'Women of privilege do not regularly have a lot of conscious relationship with or access to the forms of everyday aggressiveness that lie between survival and fun' (p. 135). The overwhelming tendency for those who have achieved a role within the structures (as they now are) is to avoid behaviour that may unsettle the *status quo*, even though women may be conscious that it allows inequality to continue. And what is true for women is true for all who are powerless: their aggression is ignored or vilified because it questions the structures of power that prevail.

The inability to share power, the fear of loss of control, coupled to a mistrust of sharing, can therefore lead to a position in which others are distanced. Aggression is one way in which the distanced try to seek to re-establish the connection: it is part of the human desire driven by love to build up community. In seeking that aim it may well challenge and seek to destroy the structures and behaviour that prevents relationships from flourishing. The primary strength of assertive authority, claims Hahn, is 'the willingness to reach out with energy, take responsibility, and make things happen' (Hahn, 1994: 72ff). Where others might block this energy, aggression can be a necessary agent to assert the right of the relationship to flourish. To simply accept the denial of relationship is to devalue the other and the self.

Inculcation and incarnation

These observations lead us to reflect on the type of love within polity and praxis that we are beginning to describe. Love, in Christian terms, has too often been equated with a disinterested detached *agape*, which involves self-sacrifice. The sacrifice of Jesus on the cross has been held up as a paradigm for love but often interpreted as an example of suffering as an end in itself. Of course, self-giving which can be costly and sacrificial is at the heart of the gospel; yet it is a giving that is motivated by love and looks for mutuality. Jesus' sacrifice was not about diminishing self; it is about the cost of his radical inclusivity, as he sought to draw all people into relationship with himself and God. In understanding the Christian calling to be Christ-like and to love God and our neighbours as ourselves, we need to be clear that love is about the flourishing of the self and the other. This way of understanding love stresses mutuality, and this is not possible without a sense that the self is worth something.

The understanding of the mutuality of love and the danger of equating self-giving with self-sacrifice is at the heart of understanding the importance of acknowledging the strength of feeling that love contains. Harrison and Robb speak of 'the Power of anger in the work of love' and, like Greider's call to take aggression seriously, they declare that where anger is suppressed, love dies. Furthermore, when love is equated with self-sacrifice, (apparent) selfishness becomes the major sin. Yet in criticizing selfishness, it is easy to damage the necessary sense of self worth that is inherent in God's love for each of us. This way of seeing love can end up diminishing both the self and the other. As Brita Gill-Austern notes,

> self-denying love may lead to patterns of caretaking that cripple and inhibit another's initiative, and lead the caretaker into successive roles of rescuer, persecutor, and victim. The rescuer takes responsibility from another, implicitly calling into question the other's competence. The

rescuer is likely to slip, in short order, into the roles of persecutor and victim, lashing out in anger and then passing into hurt and self-pity when the person she rescues is insufficiently grateful. Finally, the caretaker feels used and abused and void of self. Self-sacrificial love turns to resentment of those who have exacted the sacrifice (Gill-Austern, 1996: 99).

But when mutuality is taken seriously, then one can begin to accept that aggression and anger are part of the drive towards creating community. As Harrison and Robb remind us, 'anger is a mode of connectedness to others, and it is always a vivid form of caring' (Harrison and Robb, 1985: 14).

So those who in their different ways have been oppressed and excluded from communities and denied access to power need to be allowed to work for their rights. This is not about selfishness or self-centeredness. We are quick in the church to label any desire for a voice in the power structures as egotistical, instead of acknowledging the *positive* desire for power: to change and alter things for the sake of justice. Those in liberation and black theology have much to teach us about the right use of anger and aggression in challenging the inequalities in our churches. And where these worlds come together for women, the power of the voice of protest of feeling can be very striking. Consider, for example, the speech of an ex-slave who called herself Sojourner Truth, who addressed the Ohio Women's Rights Convention on 28 May, 1851, with these words:

> May I say a few words? ... I am [for] woman's rights. I have as much muscle as any man, and can do as much work as any man. I have plowed and reaped and husked and chopped and mowed, and can any man do more than that? I have heard much about the sexes being equal; I can carry as much as any man, and can eat as much too, if I can get it. I am as strong as any man that is now. As for intellect, all I can say is, if a woman have a pint and a man a quart, why can't she have her little pint full? You need not be afraid to give us our rights for fear we will take too much, for we can't take more than our pint will hold. The poor men seem to be all in confusion, and don't know what to do ... I have heard the bible and have learned Eve cause man to sin. Well if a woman upset the world, do give her a chance to set it right side up again. The lady has spoken about Jesus, how he never spurned woman from him, and she is right ... And how came Jesus into the world? Through God ... and the woman who bore him. Man, where is your part? But man is in a tight place, the poor slave is on him, the woman is coming on him, and he is surely between a hawk and a buzzard ... (Arnold, 2000: 110).

The narratives that drive so much black, liberation and feminist theology have been amongst the most important theological and ecclesial developments in the last 50 years. Theology and the church, instead of describing life as it could be or should be, and engaging in dry, cerebral and contextually-detached thinking, have been forced to reckon with the living accounts of Christian witnesses who experience oppression at the hands of their brothers and sisters in the church. The implicitly excluded – women, ethnic minorities and the economically oppressed – have had their place in theology and the church restored not by learning the grammar of 'pure' theology, but by resisting it with their stories and experiences, which in turn has led to new hermeneutics. Thus for a black theologian such as Cornel West, it is the feelings of despair that white conservatives and liberals will not engage with: 'we must delve into the depths where neither liberals nor conservatives dare to tread, namely into the murky waters of despair' (West, 1993: 19). Similarly, for James Cone, another black theologian, liberation begins to take place only when the oppressors begin to hear the *story* of the oppressed, and enter into the experience of marginalization: 'the church is that people called into being by the power and love of God to share in his revolutionary activity for the liberation of man' (Cone and Wimore, 1999: 67). So for Cone, the refusal to hear the stories of the oppressed and enter into the realm of feeling and subjectivity becomes a denial of the gospel and of the incarnation:

> where there is black there is oppression; but blacks can be assured that where there is blackness, there is Christ who has taken on blackness so that what is evil in men's eyes might become good. Therefore Christ is black because he is oppressed and oppressed because he is black. And if the church is to join Christ by following his opening it too must go where suffering is and become black also ... (Cone and Wimore, 1999: 71).

To be sure, this type of theology, which is, at its simplest, a theology of solidarity, has its weaknesses as well as its strengths. But it is not our purpose here to elucidate any further on such matters. Our point is a simple one, namely to remind the church and its theologians that stories and experiences, which convey and reify strong feelings, and act as repositories for alternative narratives of memory, are a vital part of theology, and are important material for the church to inculcate and incarnate in its polity and pastoral praxis. In other words, the manifestation of aggression and anger have a theological significance and value, for behind the expression of feelings, most likely, will lie stories of oppression.

Aggression, then, is part of the economy of liberation theologies (i.e., black, feminist, gay, etc.), and is centred on the will to survive and flourish. It will be aroused where the self is being stifled, or communities are oppressed. Rightly used, it is the drive to challenge and change things for the good of all. Strong feelings are a sign of life and a pointer to the desire for growth. Yet too often, strong feelings are marginalized and demonized (Steichen, 1992). So the Church may well need to find ways of enabling these strong feelings to be explored and used constructively for the good of the whole.

Presently in the Church of England, the fear of conflict and aggression makes it very difficult to air strong feelings; the neuralgic anxiety is that the manifestation of feelings leads to the loss of poise in ecclesial polity. And yet we live in a world and within a church that are shaped by human failings, and if we truly love these institutions then we will inevitably be angry about the ways they fall short. So what we do with our strong feelings, and how we handle the aggression that moves for change, will depend on whether we can see them as a sign of life and growth, or whether we suppress them for fear they will rock the boat too hard:

> The moral question is not 'what do I feel?' but rather 'what do I do with what I feel?' Because this is not understood, contemporary Christianity is impaled between a subjectivist and sentimental piety that results from fear of strong feeling, especially strong negative feeling, and an objectivist, wooden piety that suppresses feelings under pretentious conceptual detachment. A feminist moral theology welcomes feeling for what it is – the basic ingredient in our relational transaction with the world (Harrison and Robb, 1985: 14).

Too often, aggression is seen as something that destroys: clearly, although it can be a drive for creative action, it does contain the power of destruction. So the church may need to reflect on whether there are things that need to be destroyed, and, as Greider says, look at the possibility of exploring healthy and ethical 'creative destruction'. (For a fuller perspective on feminist ethics, see Frazer *et al.*, 1992.) Inevitably, part of what aggression seeks to destroy is those structures that perpetuate inequality and that lead the voiceless to frustration, anger and aggression. These structures, often unconsciously, create privileges for those who have a voice, and within the Church of England this means mainly white, middle-class educated men. An air of reasonableness, of polite attention to the other, can often be the means of failing to acknowledge the strength and depth of feelings that might motivate a desire for change.

In the Church, the desire to avoid conflict both in parochial matters and in relationships in the diocese can often be a recipe for atrophy. When situations arise which cannot be ignored, the scale of feelings aroused can surprise and disappoint those who believe that if we all try to love each other, we will all agree. To truly love is to take seriously the desire to deepen relationships and work against all that limits and devalues human worth. Harrison and Robb put it like this:

> Radical love creates dangerous precedents and lofty expectations among human beings. Those in power believe such love to be 'unrealistic' because those touched by the power of such love tend to develop a reluctance to accept anything less than mutuality and self-respect, anything less than human dignity, anything less than authentic relatedness. It is for that reason that such persons become powerful threats to the *status quo* (1985: 19).

So discovering how to acknowledge and give voice to strong feelings – in ways that can enable radical working together for the growth of all – is a challenge that the Church needs to heed. In his ministry, Jesus listened to the voices of the marginalized all the time. Indeed, not only did he listen, but he assimilated such voices into his ministry, and often made the marginalized central, and placed those who were central on the periphery, thereby re-ordering society, forcing people to witness oppression and the response of the Kingdom of God to despair, anger and marginalization. So in the Church, we need to allow the experiences of the oppressed to challenge and shape the way we hold power and broker relationships. The churches need to learn continually from the veritable panoply of liberation theologies: that marginalized people should not simply be made welcome in the church, but that their anger and aggressive desire for justice might be allowed to reform the manners of the church. Learning to listen to narratives that convey strong, powerful feelings, rather than seeking to dismiss such stories as 'uncultured' or as 'bad manners', is a major and costly task for ecclesial polity and pastoral praxis. Ultimately, the aggression of those who seek justice may help the churches to move from a 'domesticated' valuing of crucifixion and suffering for its own sake, and work instead 'not to perpetuate crucifixions, but to bring an end to them in a world where they go on and on' (Harrison and Robb, 1985: 19).

Further reflections

We are conscious that an argument for a church in which feelings are allowed to be given their full vent is potentially dangerous and irresponsible. We are well aware that there is rightful place for reticence, and for the withholding of emotions. We understand that a temperate ecclesial polity can, to some extent, depend on finding a non-emotive language for expressing views and communicating across divisions. But we are also struck by how many churches, at local, regional and national level, deliberately disenfranchise and marginalize the proper expression of strong feelings. We find this not only to be poor ecclesial and pastoral practice, but also theologically weak and urbane, rendering the church into some kind of semi-detached realm, in which all the correct probity of manners and politeness are observed, but 'real' feelings are never mentioned or aired. This cannot be a proper reification of a strong incarnational theology, and neither can it make for the church being an especially genuine community of the redeemed. If one of the tasks of the church is to make it possible for people to truly face one another – and we think it is – then strong feelings must be properly addressed so that they can be appropriately located in the body of Christ, and not suppressed as part of some kind of artful process of subordination. As Harrison and Robb note,

> A chief evidence of the grace of God – which always comes to us in, with and through each other – is this power to struggle and to experience indignation. We should not make light of our power to rage against the dying of the light. It is the root of the power of love (1985: 21).

How, though, do we discern when anger is a legitimate call for justice, and when it is a petulant reaction to not getting one's way? Here we need to look at patterns of power and the motivation of anger. In the debate over the ordination of women, there is, perhaps, a clear difference between the aggression of those who have been calling for a right to be heard, and those who are angry because their (privileged) position has been shared with those they do not feel are competent to share it. Yet, the good news of the gospel is about the accessibility of God: the welcoming in of the religiously marginalized, and the breaking down of barriers. In our aggression and anger, we need to be clear how we are moving towards a vision of the Kingdom, and how we are motivated by the radical mutuality of love. The command to love God and to love our neighbour as ourselves ultimately defines the place of our aggression and anger. It demands action, and that action demands drive, which at times requires generative anger and aggression. The church needs to find a way of holding and utilizing the strong feelings that are part of human loving, remembering, as Harrison and Robb put it, that

> The important point is that where feeling is evaded, where anger is hidden or goes unattended, masking itself, there the power of love, the power to act, to deepen relation, atrophies and dies (Harrison and Robb, 1985: 15).

The task for the Church, therefore, is not to find ways that suppress or block out strong feelings of anger or hurt and the aggression it arouses, but to help discern how to channel the energy they bring into the work of the gospel. This means listening to the experiences that lead to aggression and anger, and seeing them as far as possible from the perspective of those with less power. It means humility on the part of those who hold power, and an acknowledgment of the fear of losing power and control. It means a new way of looking at power relationships that takes the gospel seriously in their equalizing and levelling. The ever-graceful Magnificat reminds us that the gospel message is *not* the same to all: the proud are to be brought low, and the lowly will be lifted up.

We are aware that these reflections belong to a wider debate that needs to be continued. In an Anglican Communion where feelings 'run high' on certain issues (i.e., on gender, sexuality, order and authority, not to mention race), the development of a theology and polity that is receptive to strong feelings would be timely. What cannot continue, we suspect, is the prevailing climate that is encountered at many local and regional levels, where those who want to express strong feelings are denied a proper platform for their voice and their place in the church. We remember that part of the ministry of Jesus involved the expression of anger, and was occasionally constituted in acts of wilful aggression. It is hard to imagine some of Christ's words being spoken in anything other than simmering rage. (See for example Lk. 19:45, Mt. 21:12–13, Mk. 11:15–19, Jn. 2:13–17; Lk. 11:42–44, Mt. 23:1–39.) There can be a *creative* rage – the kind of rage that the poets and the prophets speak of – which is markedly impolite, but utterly godly. It is this that we seek to restore to the church, for its polity and pastoral praxis, and for its maturity and health. Without it, there is only the pretence of politeness, and the bland veneer of civility. In contrast, we want communion to be authentic and deeper, and this can only happen when strong feelings have their proper place in the life of the church restored. Then we can truly face one another, and learn the full mutuality of loving our neighbour as ourselves, in spite of difference, and perhaps because of it.

Bibliography

Arnold, J., *History: A Very Short Introduction*, Oxford, Oxford University Press, 2000.

Cone, J. and Wimore, G., *Black Theology: A Documentary History*, Maryknoll, Orbis, 1999.

Eliot, T. S., *Essays on Style and Content*, London, Faber, 1928.

Frazer, E., Hornsby, J. and Lovibond, S., *Ethics: A Feminist Reader*, Oxford, Blackwell, 1992.

Gill-Austern, B., 'Love Understood as Self-sacrifice and Self-Denial: What Does it Do to Women?' in Moessner, J. (ed.), *Through the Eyes of Women: Insights for Pastoral Care*, Minneapolis, Fortress Press, 1996.

Greider, K., 'Too Militant? Aggression, Gender, and the Construction of Justice', in Moessner, J. (ed), *Through the Eyes of Women: Insights for Pastoral Care*, Minneapolis, Fortress Press, 1996.

Hahn, C., *Growing in Authority, Relinquishing Control: A New Approach to Faithful Leadership*, Washington, Alban, 1994.

Hare, D., *Racing Demon*, London, Faber & Faber, 1990.

Harrison, B. and Robb, C., *Making the Connections: Essays in Feminist Social Ethics*, Boston, Beacon Press, 1985.

Le Guin, U., *Dancing at the Edge of the World: Words, Women, Places*, New York, Grove Books, 1989.

Marsh, C., *God's Long Summer: Stories of Faith and Civil Rights*, Princeton, Princeton University Press, 1997.

Percy, M., 'On Sacrificing Purity?' in Markham, I. and Jobling, J. *Theological Liberalism*, London, SPCK, 2000.

Steichen, D., *Ungodly Rage: The Hidden Face of Catholic Feminism*, San Francisco, Ignatius Press, 1992.

West, C., *Race Matters*, New York, HarperCollins, 1993.

PART THREE
THEOLOGY, CHURCH
AND WORLD

Chapter 10

Spirituality and the Mass Media

Angela Tilby

Life today is media-saturated. The vague word media for all its inherent difficulties, best describes the general context in which the Churches in all parts of the world now live.[1]

The mass media as the context of pastoral theology

Wesley Carr is not the first Christian theologian to consider the subject of the mass media. But his contribution is of unique interest because he writes as a *pastoral* theologian. His primary interest is neither communication nor hermeneutics but the context of the entire pastoral task; the context in which ministers preach, teach and nurture individuals, both those involved in congregational life and those whose connection with the church is more fleeting. He has consistently attempted in his writing and teaching to raise awareness of the theological dimensions of pastoral theology and help ministers to reflect critically on their own practice. By such reflection he hopes that ministers will become reflective practitioners, genuinely learning from their experiences and integrating theory and knowledge with feelings and attitudes. This is the wisdom to which his writings call us, a wisdom which is inseparable from spiritual awareness and growth.

Wesley's interest in the mass media goes back to a period in the 1980s when he was Dean of Bristol and an inspector of the Church of England's theological colleges and courses. Under the auspices of a media project based at New College, Edinburgh, he worked over a period of two years with 55 trainee ministers, considering the impact of the media on four main areas of their ministerial formation: preaching, pastoring, spirituality and leadership. The result was a book, *Ministry and the Media*.

I can well remember the startling impact this book had on me. It 'spoke to my condition' as nothing else had. Although it was clearly

---

[1] Wesley Carr, *Ministry and the Media*, London, SPCK, 1990, preface.

written for ministers and those engaged in the training of ministers it described with penetrating accuracy and insight the world I lived and worked in as a television producer for the BBC. He recognized the opportunities and conflicts that the mass media represent and he avoided the typical polarized responses of condemnation and over-enthusiasm. He also showed an awareness of something that had long puzzled me, an attitude of edginess and defensiveness that I found in myself and my media colleagues when faced with scrutiny from those 'outside'. I thus began to understand my own context, and to reflect on it theologically. His insights have continued to be helpful, as I have changed roles, entered the ordained ministry of the Church of England and become involved myself in the formation and training of ministers.

The mass media as the new cathedral?

My interests now as a teacher are in understanding the Christian spiritual tradition and exploring the nature of contemporary spirituality. The dialogue I have had with Wesley's writings over a number of years has been about how living in a media-saturated world affects our sense of self and of God. My reflections in this essay have been prompted chiefly by the book *Ministry and the Media*.[2] – I shall also consider briefly towards the end of this essay one of the insights of *Manifold Wisdom*, his exploration of New Age spirituality.[3] But first, as an introduction to his thinking on the topic of the media, I shall look at an article he wrote for the Jesuit journal *The Way*, 'The Mass Media as The New Cathedral?'[4]

Wesley prefaces this article with a provocative quotation from James Curran: 'The modern mass media in Britain now perform many of the integrative functions of the Church in the Middle Ages'.[5] To illustrate the point Wesley compares the role of the medieval cathedral with that of television and radio today, to show in what sense media can be seen to have displaced the Church in performing many of the 'integrative functions' in society. He argues that there are three particular areas in which modern media can be compared with ancient cathedrals. These are pilgrimage, art and teaching.

---

[2] Wesley Carr, *Ministry and the Media*, London, SPCK, 1990.

[3] Wesley Carr, *Manifold Wisdom,* London, SPCK, 1991.

[4] Wesley Carr, 'The Mass Media as the New Cathedral?', *The Way*, Volume 31, No. 2, April 1991 (Media and Communication), 105–14.

[5] James Curran, 'Communication, power and social order', in *Culture, Society and the Media*, ed. Michael Gurgevitch *et al.*, London, Methuen, 1982.

Pilgrimage

He first describes the sense in which the medieval cathedral was a place of pilgrimage: a sacred place, the goal of a special journey. It was not a place for most people to live in or stay in, but a place to be visited. Once there the pilgrim received an overwhelming impression of reflective space. Mediaeval cathedrals were (and are) huge. They must have been even more impressive when there were no buildings remotely comparable in size and splendour. Once within the cathedral the pilgrim was able to recognize and receive something of his or her own individuality. This sense of self-in-space was tempered by the hugeness of the environment. At the same time as speaking of the significance of the individual pilgrim, the cathedral challenged that individuality with a sense of the transcendence of God.

How do the modern media act as a focus of pilgrimage? Wesley suggests that although people do not literally travel to radio and television, they make a similar 'journey' by switching on to reconnect with a wider life than that of their own. They listen to the news or the Archers or turn on the television. In this way people punctuate their individual impressions of the day by 'visiting' a place of collective consciousness. (The term 'visit' is used specifically, of course, of browsing on various web sites, but at the time Wesley was writing, the Internet had not assumed the cultural significance it has today.) The point he is making is that by 'visiting' media the individual meets with the collective; the private self reconnects with communal life. That is not to suggest any agreed understanding between individual and collective. It is more a question of getting in touch with the events and atmosphere of the day or the week in order to relocate oneself within the wider community.

Cathedrals and media both tend to confirm the individuality of the pilgrim. (I think Wesley may have exaggerated the aloneness of the medieval pilgrim to make his point. Chaucer's Canterbury pilgrims seem to have been a rather gregarious lot.) As he sees it, though, the pilgrim in the medieval cathedral is alone in a sea of space and form. It is from that aloneness that he or she connects with communal life. The pilgrim's individuality is also developed by the building itself. Its dimensions are a constant reminder of the transcendence of God. And this is where a major difference emerges between the integrative functions performed by the cathedral and that performed by television. The television viewer zaps across channels, a lone pilgrim visiting a succession of worlds. But instead of reminding the media pilgrim of others and God, modern mass media reinforce a belief in individual autonomy which is actually at odds with the fact that we do not have ultimate control over what there is to watch, buy, consume or do.

Art

With his second area of comparison, that of art, Wesley writes of the vivid colours of the medieval cathedral and the contrast within of darkness and light. The cathedral reveals that the individual's story is set within a wider narrative, which is provided both by the Biblical stories illustrated in glass, fresco and stone and by a sacred cosmology provided by the shape and layout of the building. The pilgrim to a cathedral does not, in fact, make the journey wholly alone. The medieval cathedral in its time would have been a busy, social place, the nave offering space for trade and gossip. So the static art of the walls and windows reflected the life lived below and gave it meaning. It proclaimed that the pilgrim was part of the communion of saints, both here on earth and in heaven. Cathedrals were, of course, major patrons of the arts, and the arts provided meaning and interpretation for the individual's life.

It is not hard, in this area, to make the link with mass media. In our age, television and radio are perhaps the most significant patrons of the popular arts. They also produce the themes, images and stories that express our social mythologies. As I see it, following Wesley, they provide us with heroes and heroines and patterns of dysfunction and flourishing that nurture our search for significance. Again, they provide our cosmological framework by exploring the natural world, science, space, and history. Wildlife and archaeological programmes are enormously popular, because they locate us in space and time, and tell us where we have come from and where we might be going. They reinforce the collective science-derived myth of our origins and threaten us with the possibility of judgement, either in environmental disaster or cosmic accident.

Teaching

In the third area of comparison, Wesley explores the role of the cathedral as a centre of teaching and learning. The cathedral contained the bishop's chair, the *cathedra*, which gave it its distinctive name. It held together a coherent image of the world as shaped by scripture and Christian truth. In a similar way, the mass media are the source of most of the information we have about the world around us. The media provide us with our image of the world and allow us to hold together some of the unbearable polarities of our experience. They tell us that the world is vast and dangerous, but they also transmit reassurance through familiar formulas and friendly personalities. The cathedral testifies to the struggle of good and evil on a cosmic scale; the media to conflicts and tension on a global scale. The cathedral mediates reality through its images of saints and gargoyles; the media through familiar loved and hated personalities. The mass media encourage us to trust their presenters and anchor-men and women. They also tell us whom to distrust. They build stereotypes and replicate them. They feed public suspicion and provoke witch-hunts: asylum seekers, paedophiles, terrorists – the media reflect, enhance and trumpet back our fears. But, as Wesley points out, they are not wholly successful or consistent in 'teaching' us trust and distrust. Just as cathedrals were and are often resented for their power, visibility and success, so the mass media, in the enormous impact they make on our lives, evoke a degree of distrust and scepticism.

The spiritual issue: the media within us

Having looked at these three areas, before drawing out some implications for our sense of self and God, I want to emphasize a point which is implied by Carr's 'The Mass Media as The New Cathedral?' but is much more fully made in *Ministry and the Media*. This is that we need to suspend our tendency to see the media as a phenomenon that can be appraised as though we were outsiders. We are simply not capable of making objective judgements for or against the mass media. This is the trap that Christians, among others, often fall into, either by uncritically joining the clamour of dissent against the media or by attempting to utilize the techniques of media without really understanding their social and spiritual significance.

The issue is not the content of individual programmes or even of the whole range of programmes, so much as the processes which media generate in us. We need to come to an understanding, which will be more than a purely intellectual matter, that the media are changing not only our landscape, but also us: they are *within* us as well as around us. Wesley asks us to recognize that, in spite of the illusions that we have some control not only over our external choices but our interior dispositions, we are all in profound ways *formed* by the mass media. The media are not *out there* but in our minds, our hearts, our ministries and our prayers.

Context is the key word here. Wesley Carr sees the mass media primarily as a holding context, a container of meanings, for the whole of society. The mass media are a major part, perhaps the major part, of our social and spiritual environment. They are where we live, mature, change and die. This is true whether or not we approve of them. It is true even if we do not happen to own a television set or use a computer. The media provoke their own dissent, unbelief and protest.

The unfamiliar landscape

So, what does all this mean for contemporary spirituality? I hesitate at this point because I have to declare that I find Wesley's writings on media are far from being his most accessible contributions to contemporary theology. Compared with *Brief Encounters,* his writings on the media, especially *Ministry and the Media,* are dense and difficult. I used to set certain chapters of *Ministry and the Media* as reading for a module on communication that I taught for the St Albans Diocesan Ministry Course. Most students found it heavy going and in the end I decided it simply was not written clearly enough to be of much use to these trainee ministers. I have since wondered whether there might have been not only a *resistance* from the students to what Wesley was trying to say, but a difficulty which Wesley himself faced in trying to describe our social and spiritual landscape, as it were, from a wholly unfamiliar perspective.

It is very difficult to describe what you are part of without falling into the illusion of 'apartness'. This is particularly complicated with the mass media, because their appeal and success are based on the fact that they nurture the illusion of apartness: of individuality without transcendence, of choice without the need for negotiation. So I struggle with Wesley's writings and I am not always confident that I have understood him. I am also aware that what I draw out of his work may well not be what he put in or intended others to discover. After all, I began my interest in his writings by reading my own concerns into a book that was not directly addressing them. As a BBC producer I found his rather pedestrian book written for ministers and trainee ministers uplifting and spiritually liberating. Perhaps it does not matter in the end whether I have got him right or wrong. Both of us are aware that, in a media saturated world, 'meaning' is not handed down from on high, nor imposed by one upon another, so much as negotiated, mediated within the spaces that exist between ourselves and others. So here are some of the fruits of that internal negotiation.

Reflective space

Spirituality cannot happen at all without reflective space. Retreat conductors, preachers and spiritual directors are always bemoaning the lack of such space in contemporary life. Usually they recommend setting aside some special protected time for silence and quiet, and finding a physical space set aside for this purpose. Yet for many people that discipline has a note of artificiality about it. It becomes one more task to fit in, one more achievement that can be ticked off, separating the super-pious from the ordinary struggling believer. (How exhausted, not to say defeated, one feels when confronted by book titles which pronounce that mystical prayer or meditation or contemplation is for *everyone*.) When people do set aside a physical space for prayer and insist on special time, the practice can be quite awkward for others to live with and difficult for the practitioner to explain. The potential for genuinely opening up the imagination is rather limited when reflective time and space have to be carved out under this kind of pressure.

The mass media offer a new kind of reflective space that may be more effective in nurturing spiritual awareness than the traditional methods. The person who comes home from work and flops down in front of the television is, probably without recognizing it, in a state of willed and longed-for surrender. S/he is receptive, possibly for the first time in 24 hours. As a viewer or net surfer s/he can open up new worlds with the zap of a channel controller or the click of a mouse. S/he has freedom to linger or to move on. Television and the Internet have opened up massive possibilities for the roving imagination. The main reason for this, I believe, is that in our society this kind of apparently aimless, exploratory viewing has become a genuine leisure activity. It is not a hobby, which is purposeful; it is not like sport, which does you good; it does not make social demands. It is genuine down time, waste time. It is one of the most precious commodities available for individuals in contemporary society.

For this very reason the reflective space for individuals offered by the mass media should be seen as a place of spiritual potential. Wesley Carr himself recognized in *Ministry and the Media* that the contemporary viewer/surfer is in a situation of potential transformation not unlike that of Ignatius Loyola after the battle of Pamplona.[6] Ignatius, convalescing from his wounds, entertained himself by skimming through an array of novels and lives of the saints. In this bored, but vulnerable state of mind he began to observe his reactions to different kinds of reading matter and to discern which stories opened up his imagination, and which, even if superficially appealing, seemed to leave him unsatisfied. A period of tedious boredom provided the reflective space that turned out to be the seedbed of Ignatius's *Spiritual Exercises*.

I find it interesting in this respect to reflect that the earliest origins of Christian spirituality in the third and fourth centuries were not in domestic space and time carved out in the presence of less committed others, but in the radical ascetic movement which followed the era of

---

[6] *Ministry and the Media*, 19.

persecution, when large numbers of individuals abandoned their social obligations by fleeing to the deserts of Egypt and Palestine. A featureless repetitive landscape was the chosen background of their quest, punctuated by the relentless contrasts of the desert night and day. Both place and time were suspended. The desert was the background in which individuals faced both their desires and their temptations, and discovered rules for the discernment of spirits.

It may sound bizarre, but I think it is at least possible, that the seeds of personal spirituality might be nurtured for many people by apparently aimless channel-hopping. The viewer suspends time and space and is temporarily unattached to any particular place or context. Yet the variegated display of the screen exposes both superficial desires and deeper longings, and brings to light genuine temptations. With such richness available, addictions become obvious, harmful obsessions surface as easily as inspiration. There are, of course, nutters and saints on the Internet and on television just as there were in the desert. The spiritual life usually begins with a desperate awareness of distractions. Some early ascetics became lost either physically or spiritually in the desert, victims of their own lusts and narcissistic fixations. And yet others survived and achieved an earthed holiness which was neither individualistic nor over-severe. The purpose of the whole spiritual experiment was to find God, fight temptation, and in the process learn to discern spirits.

The opportunities and dangers for the development of the spiritual life are no less complex in the rich desert of contemporary mass media. Whether they can also provide the kind of wisdom needed for the discernment of spirits is another question.

Participation

The second point I draw from Wesley Carr's analysis concerns spiritual participation. While the mainstream institutional churches find themselves drawing their active members from a smaller and smaller constituency, the mass media offer other, more inclusive, points of participation. These are moments of collective celebration, grief and aspiration. These moments, some of which occur in an annual cycle, others of which arise as the result of crime or accident, are ritualized through the media. The New Year, St Valentine's Day, Mothering Sunday, the London Marathon, the World Cup, the beginning of the school year, Hallowe'en, Remembrance Sunday and Christmas are points in the annual calendar which the media celebrate. There was an interesting discussion at a meeting of the Church of England's Liturgical Commission over whether the Church should draw up a media-based *Temporale* or seasonal cycle, based on the different characteristics of the twelve months of the year. So January would be about New Year (sales, diets), February about love (St Valentine), March would be Spring (new life and growth), April would bring the secular into coincidence with Easter etc. The suggestion was not taken up by the compilers of the Church of England's new service book *Common Worship*, but the fact that the discussion occurred at all shows the impact of the mass media on the Church's thinking about corporate spirituality.

Alongside this is what has become known as the 'Diana factor'. The death of Princess Diana united the nation in a weird collective grief which was also a moment of profound protest against the monarchy and the establishment. Wesley Carr's writings on media were written long before this event, of course, but the event bore out the truth of his insights. He himself, as Dean of Westminster, was much involved in negotiating the precise details of the funeral service in Westminster Abbey. The event itself was a media event and yet it drew thousands of people, as if in pilgrimage, from all over the country, who were content to sleep out on the streets in the hope of catching a glimpse of the funeral cortege. They would have seen more at home, but this was an occasion when the media event and the actual event reinforced each other. The crowds were febrile, emotional; there was a sense of destiny or revolution in the air. Gone was the British stiff upper lip, the stoic dignity of tradition was represented by the military and religious functionaries, but not by the immediate participants, nor by the crowds. Even the Prime Minister, Tony Blair, managed to ham up his reading from 1 Corinthians 13. And the strangest moment for those inside Westminster Abbey was when the relay of the bitter eulogy by Earl Spencer provoked a wave of applause from the crowds outside, a wave which rippled through from outside into the abbey itself, like the sound of the sea or a long roll of thunder.

Reflecting on that moment afterwards, it seemed a powerful example of how the media enables us to form a collective moment of spiritual awareness that is marked by emotional outpouring. People in the streets were singing, praying, weeping, joining in unself-consciously with the Lord's Prayer and the hymns. It was clear to those involved in the event that many were not only grieving for Princess Diana, but were suddenly overwhelmed with grief for their own dead. The presence of media enables us to watch ourselves in grief and has brought emotions to the surface that were once con-sidered indecent. The individuals on the street were those who were prepared to lose their individuality in a collective outpouring of sorrow and anger, which was then mediated back though the cameras to wider society. The casual, conscious waved hand from the streets to those back home signified the unity between viewer and participant which the media enabled. We were all there. Except, of course, the dissenters, who were there too, but in the sense that their absence was deliberate. After the event we heard from those who had avoided the funeral and refused to watch the television pictures, finding the whole event vulgar, annoying or cloyingly sentimental. Yet their protest would have been impossible and meaningless had the media event not been so prominent.

With hindsight, however, it is curious how ephemeral the feelings expressed by this event, and perhaps others like it, proved to be. The emotions generated did not last. The spiritual outpouring died down leaving, perhaps, a slight sense of shame. We should be aware that some forms of public spirituality may well be ephemeral in their effects, precisely because of the media context in which they occur. There is a genuine yearning for public rituals which can authentically express collective feelings. The media cannot provide the resources for this expression without drawing on the resources of Christian tradition, albeit mediated through popular culture. The funeral service for Princess Diana was a strangely effective, (and at the time affective) blend of the Book of Common Prayer, the English choral tradition, popular nationalism, romantic song, the King James Bible, and the exotic mysticism of John Tavener's *Song for Athene*. And yet the event was of the moment, the feelings did not last.

I find an important contrast here with traditional forms of collective spirituality, such as Morning Prayer and Evensong. In such forms of worship, expression is not enough. The worship also includes didactic and formative elements, and it is these which make worship transformative, not only in the present but in the long term. It is interesting how far contemporary liturgical revision has elevated expression and emotion at the expense of formation. In doing so it reveals a perhaps uncritical acceptance of the influence of our media environment. It has been a deliberate policy of many revisers to cut back on the use of scripture and the habit of consecutive psalmody in order to allow for flexibility and spontaneity. This inevitably means that such worship does not have the same transformative potential. It may well meet the needs of the occasional churchgoer, but it is not clear how far it will nurture Christian character in the long term. A more boring and stable diet may still be required.

It is encouraging, though, that the longing for a collective expression of spiritual feeling is still met by the churches, both in traditional ways at Christmas and Remembrance, and by various forms of charismatic worship. We should note, though, that for many, worship is now incompatible with duty. There is a conflict between the traditional aim of long-term spiritual growth under the impact of the

Scriptures, and the desire for spontaneous self-expression, inspired (or not) by the Holy Spirit. Communal worship is successful in a media context if it engages the emotions and calls on the artistic resources of a pluralistic culture. So churches are left in a dilemma over how to conduct worship. Is the aim to give expression to feelings or to nurture commitment? Are both possible, or do the two aims simply fight one another?

I find in the men and women coming into ministerial training that there is both an expectation that communal worship will deliver a spiritual high, and also a sense of loss and frustration with the more pedestrian forms of communal worship that are usually the norm at training institutions. Yet as students become more familiar with a less emotional style of worship they sometimes express a slight sense of shame rather similar to that expressed after the mourning for Princess Diana died down. The shame expressed by the students is that they were once so taken up with what they have come to see as rather indulgent patterns of corporate worship. Some, of course, do not make the transition and go into ministry with a determination to generate and replicate the highs, a recipe for the sectarianism and emotional shallowness which characterizes many so-called successful churches.

It is easy for traditionalist worshippers like myself to be dismissive of the kind of spiritual participation which the media help to generate. Yet I am not wholly unfamiliar with media-inspired worship. I worked for a time on *Songs of Praise* and I admire its ability to act as a vehicle of popular spirituality. I would like to think that such formats not only inspire in the short term, but can be a way in to a more grounded spirituality for people who at first find more traditional approaches inaccessible. They are also undeniably forming us as a spiritually diverse community, rooted in the dialogue between tradition and shared popular culture.

Autonomy and grace

My third area of reflection concerns the spiritual implications of the media's sense of power and autonomy, a sense which, as Wesley observes and I have already noted, is actually at odds with the facts. The mass media suggest that the individual possesses the power of choice. Life is a series of apparently free personal decisions. Yet the flood of information which besieges individuals means that people have had to learn skills of screening out unwanted information. The consequence of this is that their personal preferences are sharpened, and the illusion of personal control over the media environment is reinforced. But the screening-out mechanisms become so well developed that change, development and exploration can be very difficult. This leaves a problem about how mistakes are to be acknowledged and new approaches assimilated. This is a problematic context in which to make sense of sin, repentance and forgiveness.

I think it was when I came across Wesley's reflections about personal autonomy that I first began to understand my own context as a media practitioner. The media so emphasize individual autonomy that they generate a notion of the self as independent and self-determining. This is at odds with the facts, because in reality we are not at all autonomous. We are more and more dependent on technology. Our lives are more and more pressured by factors outside ourselves. Yet we shelter under the illusion that we are in control and admire those who seem invulnerable.

The illusion of invulnerability is part of the psychological armour which journalists and television performers and executives rely on. I found among my media colleagues, particularly those who worked in television, a set of characteristic ways of behaving which seem to make them immune to some aspects of spiritual growth and awareness. Television people need to be adept observers. They need to be able to read the surfaces of things. They have antennae for picking up the public mood, the shifting political allegiances within the television world, the fall and rise of particular stars, the coming styles and genres. I often found a permanent prickliness in the face of criticism. This was not only in my colleagues; I found the same defensiveness in myself. Challenge suggests response and response requires participation. Yet to remain in control, the observer needs to be outside the frame, manipulating the pieces within. Inside BBC Television, temper tantrums were frequent as the need for control led to frequent arguments. My friends in radio seemed to have normal private lives, personal interests and a sense of humour, but my television colleagues seemed to have very little capacity for introspection and almost no sense of irony. They were capable of immense charm when they needed to win someone over, but relationships did not develop. The charm displayed today could be freezing indifference tomorrow. They did not smile much, either.

Radio, of course, is an incomplete medium. The listener provides the pictures. But television looks as though it is complete, sound and vision come together and image takes priority over interpretation. It is hardly surprising that narcissistic personalities are attracted to work in television. And even those who are not primarily narcissists sometimes adopt narcissistic defences in order to survive. One of the characteristics of narcissism is the illusion of invulnerability. Narcissists never age, and, though often inconsistent, they never really change or develop.

So, at the same time as the mass media present us with the illusion of individual choice, they conceal the context in which we make our choices. The media can tell us a great deal, but not tell the truth about themselves, which is, of course, that their real focus is not individual but collective. They encourage conformity by what appears to be personal flattery. The global advertising campaigns, which enable a product to be presented across a range of cultures through a wordless montage of instantly recognizable images, are an obvious example of this. But there are other more subtle ways in which individuals are collectivized and stereotyped through the media. The *Guardian* reader, the Radio Four listener, the person who prefers Five Live are real and active consumers in the minds of the editors and programme makers. The media do not always open new windows as much as present us with a hall of mirrors. I now realize that the edginess and defensiveness I found in myself and in others when I worked in television was something to do with disguising from ourselves what we were really about. The projections we made on to the audiences would have been intolerable if we had accepted them as being true of ourselves. We needed the illusion of invulnerability.

Our contemporary sense of self is mediated through images. Yet these images are rarely shown in any time sequence which would allow for perspective. It is impossible to trace change or transition. In fact almost the reverse is true. The mistakes and flaws of the individual self are fixed in time. Prince Charles is still the little boy who once asked for a cherry brandy; Myra Hindley died as the hard faced peroxide blonde she was at the time of her trial. The media do not allow for growth and development, nor do they permit forgiveness. It is almost impossible to learn from a mistake and move on, because the image of the self is fixed forever.

It is as a consequence of this that a confessional style of television has emerged which gives individuals a chance to admit their sins in public. This is compelling viewing. Whole evenings are given over to testimonies about diet and weight loss. Stars give moving interviews about their addictions and past abusive relationships. But the most noticeable feature of these media confessions is that they do not involve either forgiveness or restitution. The revelation of damage is thought to be enough. The confession itself is taken to be an act of courage and to be inherently purifying.

This is particularly interesting because it reinforces the often-expressed view that we are moving from a guilt culture to a shame culture. It also gives weight to a remark made to me by the Orthodox theologian and teacher George Bebawi, a colleague in the Cambridge Theological Federation. Having lived for many years in Egypt he is often asked about the impact of Islam on the West. He believes that in spiritual terms the impact of Islam is minimal. The important rival to Christianity is, in fact, Buddhism. Buddhist psychology and philosophy, at least in the popularized form in which they are often presented, do appear to interact rather aptly with the fractured sense of self which the media reflect back to us. Buddhism resonates with contemporary religious agnosticism and can feed the desire for control over our inner and outer environment. The non-self doctrine, so crucial to Theravadan Buddhism, meets the emptiness of the inner self and encourages the individual to 'go with the flow'. In such a model of the self, forgiveness is inappropriate. There is no such thing as sin, rather a lack of wisdom which can be corrected through increased awareness.

Wesley addresses these issues directly in his book on New Age spirituality, *Manifold Wisdom*.[7] He recognizes that the traditional Christian 'solution' to the problem of the self does not entirely match the dilemma with which our context confronts us. The Christian self is in the image of God; it is flawed by sin, but restored in Christ. There is a story to absorb, a transformation to occur. Yet the sense of self that comes through media is both more rigid and therefore more fragile than in traditional Christian accounts, which allow for both brokenness and healing. Wesley suggests that these changes in our self-understanding, influenced by the New Age movement as by popular Buddhism, could give rise to new expressions of what is wrong with us, in which the focus is more on incompetence, lack of wisdom and failure to learn, rather than on transgression and guilt. On the other hand, Christianity cannot abandon its investment in the vulnerable self. It is after all the vulnerability of Christ on the cross which effects God's salvation of the world.

There seems to be a painful discrepancy between the empowered view of the self which the mass media appear to offer us, and the partial and conforming stereotypes with which they actually need to operate. The media have sharpened the distinction between the private and the public sense of self. The spiritual struggle for many, not least for those in training for the Church's ministry, is to manage these different and competing selves. Many suffer from a lack of self-esteem, a fear of criticism and a sense that the rift between the public and the private self is too wide to be explored safely. The private self is often experienced as frighteningly empty, while the public self can seem worryingly inauthentic.

This is not an entirely new struggle. Spiritual experience has often begun with a sense of fragmentation, a homesickness for authenticity.

---

[7] Wesley Carr, *Manifold Wisdom*, London, SPCK, 1991: 106–7, 122–8.

The quest of the fourth and fifth century ascetics was for oneness, integrity. The monk, '*monachos*', is one who imitates the unity of God by learning to become one. Yet oneness, as the desert ascetics painfully discovered, involves the renunciation of autonomy. We need to come home to ourselves and to recognize that our choices are actually quite limited. In spite of our delusions, we are actually vulnerable and it is in our vulnerability that our Saviour God meets us. In this recognition are the seeds of humility, one of the most important, and most permanently counter-cultural, of the Christian virtues.

Conclusion

It will be obvious from what I have written that I owe Wesley Carr a great deal. I have learnt much from his observations and his analysis. He has enabled me to give attention to the systems and structures of society and the part our multiple contexts play in shaping our individual lives. But I have also learnt from the way his mind works and from his character as a Christian and as a priest.

I see in his attempt to understand our media context an engagement with that most often neglected, but vital element of the Christian spiritual tradition mentioned above, the virtue of humility. This is shown in his refusal to begin from a stance of judgement. A small, but significant, example of his non-judgemental attitude with regard to the mass media is his frequent choice of the phrase 'media-saturated' to describe our society, rather than the more obvious, but more condemnatory 'media-dominated'. To use the phrase 'media-dominated' would not only start from a negative judgement, it would make a possibly false assumption that the media *do* actually dominate our experience, in the sense of controlling it. Given the negativity often felt towards the mass media, this seems premature. At another level, Wesley knows that true wisdom comes from true understanding. We open ourselves to judgement if we indulge in pronouncements on the media *before* we have tried to make sense of them. Understanding involves self-examination. We need to acknowledge that we are not outside the media but inside it, just as it is inside us. A stance of humility actually brings illumination about ourselves that we could not otherwise attain.

As well as humility and wisdom, another, related, spiritual virtue I find in Wesley's thinking is his adoption of what in Christian spirituality is described as *apatheia*, detachment. This suggests a genuine intellectual asceticism, which is immensely refreshing and necessary because 'the Meeja' do indeed evoke strong opinions; not only outrage, but violent enthusiasm, hilarity, scorn, bad temper, delight. The media make us emotional while Christian asceticism requires a certain distancing from our drives and passions in order to get a handle on *what exactly it is* that drives us. This is a task which can never be completed because we can never comprehend precisely what it is that drives and compels us. But the Christian ascetic tradition suggests that the attempt to understand is worthwhile in that it keeps us aware of our limitations and thus open to the possibility of a transcendent God.

From this detachment comes a freedom to act, or not, in response to our circumstances. Since he became Dean of Westminster, Wesley Carr's relationship with the media has not always been easy. His first few years were overshadowed by the difficult decision he had to make to act on the results of investigations into the financial arrangements of his Director of Music, Dr Martin Neary. I greatly admired his discipline and reticence when he came under fire from the media at the instigation of Neary's supporters. He was similarly stoical when faced with public outrage at his refusal of the request to give the poet Cecil Day-Lewis a place in Poet's Corner. No doubt he paid a heavy cost on both these occasions. It is much easier to enter the fray defensively than to remain silent, even if it does not help in the long term. On the other hand Wesley has used the interpretative expertise he has gained in this area in the liturgies he has overseen at Westminster Abbey. I have already written about Princess Diana's funeral, but he also dealt admirably with the Queen Mother's funeral and the moving memorial service for the victims of September 11th.

Most of all I am grateful for his example in allying his natural scepticism not to a destructive and bitter cynicism, but to Christian hope. He is a realist, he knows we are all self-deluded sinners, and also that Christians have no choice but to go on trying to pray and believe and live half-decent lives. In making the attempt to understand our media context, we might reach the degree of self-awareness and self-acceptance which the Biblical tradition describes as humility, and even recover a vision of the transcendent, 'the fear of the Lord', which the Bible sees as the beginning of wisdom.

Chapter 11

Gospel Values and Modern Bioethics

Robin Gill

Despite his first name and forebears Wesley Carr is quintessentially Anglican. He takes Bible very seriously, but not literally, he engages closely with the secular social sciences, while remaining distinctively theological, and he consistently searches for continuities between rationality and faith especially in pastoral areas. Indeed, he concludes his *Handbook of Pastoral Studies* with the following conviction:

> It is ... essential that pastors are familiar with the nature of the therapeutic approach. They will also discover that they have to work out their pastoral theology within that world without surrendering to it.[1]

This paper is written from a very similar conviction. As it happens an earlier version was also first given at a seminar chaired by Wesley in the Deanery at Westminster Abbey. My focus is specifically upon the distinctive contribution that a pastoral theologian might bring to modern bioethics.

Many of the pioneers of modern bioethics were hospital chaplains, church leaders or academic theologians. In the 1960s the American theologian Paul Ramsey, and later William F. May, anticipated many of the issues that have now become commonplace in bioethics. In Britain Bob Lambourne and his successors at Birmingham, followed by Gordon Dunstan at London, were instrumental in nurturing an interest in ethical and pastoral issues in medicine. In addition, a number of experienced hospital chaplains, such as Norman Autton at St George's Hospital, London, and church leaders, such as John Habgood and Ted Shotter, were also key pioneers.

Yet within a generation the discipline – variously termed medical ethics, bioethics, biomedical ethics, health care ethics, or ethics in medicine – became largely secularized. In part this was because secular philosophers and academic lawyers – such as Ian Kennedy in

---

[1] Wesley Carr, *Handbook of Pastoral Studies*, London, SPCK, 1997: 235.

London, John Harris in Manchester, Sheila McLean in Glasgow and
Peter Singer, first in Australia and now in the United States – became
leading voices in bioethics. They offered distinctive legal and
philosophical skills that brought new clarity to the developing
discipline. However, it was also because they seemed to bring a more
neutral basis for bioethics within a society that increasingly perceived
itself as pluralistic. Precisely because it had become less acceptable to
identify Britain, let alone the whole of the West, as 'Christian',
bioethics needed to be moulded in a more neutral direction. However
well intentioned the work of the pioneer bioethicists from the
churches, the discipline clearly needed to be relevant to doctors,
nurses and patients whatever their religious or ideological
commitments. More than that, in areas of sharp controversy involving
medical practice (despite frequent protestations from English Law
Lords that they are not experts in medical ethics), the judicial system
has increasingly become the final arbiter. In a pluralistic society
judges rather than bishops, and lawyers rather than theologians, may
now be considered to be the most appropriate arbiters.

This pattern of secularization can be viewed in quite different ways
within Christian ethics. On one understanding of secularization it is yet
another example of the marginalization of religion in modern society.
It is part of a larger process involving the gradual erosion of religious
beliefs, practices and institutions in the Western world. Temporarily
theologians and church leaders in the 1960s thought that they had
discovered an area – namely bioethics – in which they could uniquely
contribute even within a largely secular society. Yet secular ethicists
have now appropriated even this area for themselves. Moreover, this
secular appropriation has taken place both in Britain/Europe and in the
United States. There is no so-called European exceptionalism apparent
here. Secular philosophy and academic law, and not theology, now
dominate public bioethics throughout the Western world, even in the
United States (despite continuing high levels of private religious
commitment there).

A quite different understanding of secularization argues that it is the
social function of churches to mould society at large in a more
Christian direction. Once a particular change has been reliably
initiated, churches can then return to their central function of worship
and prayer. Just as there were a number of Christians who were
instrumental in establishing the welfare state and the national health
service in Britain in the 1940s, so there were also Christians who
pioneered bioethics in the 1960s. But, once their work was achieved, it
was crucial that people of other forms of religious and secular faith
also became 'owners'. It was no longer necessary – or perhaps even
desirable – to claim that the welfare state, the national health service or

bioethics were dependent upon Christian precepts. Instead, they are all projects that owed much to the intervention of Christians in the first place, but which now are *sui generis*.

A good illustration of these alternative understandings of secularization is the different ways that Christian ethicists have reacted to Tom Beauchamp and James Childress' influential *Principles of Biomedical Ethics*.[2] Many Christian ethicists today are critical of the approach championed by Beauchamp and Childress – arguing that it marginalizes Christian belief, privileges secular moral reasoning, and offers four arbitrary 'principles' for bioethics (autonomy, justice, non-maleficence and beneficence) with inadequate meta-ethical justification. For them this is a clear example of secularization in the first sense. Despite the fact that Childress still sees himself as a Christian ethicist, they argue that he makes little attempt in his joint textbook with the secular philosopher Beauchamp to articulate (let alone defend) a distinctively Christian perspective. Instead he has in effect capitulated to the secularist.

In contrast, other Christian ethicists argue that this misunderstands the Beauchamp/Childress approach and unnecessarily polarizes secular and religious ethicists concerned with issues in health care. Adopting the second understanding of secularization, they applaud this attempt to find a basis for bioethics that secular and religious people can use alike within a pluralistic society. They believe that it would be counter-productive to argue for an explicitly Christian version of bioethics within such a society. Instead, a combination of Childress' implicit Christian perspective and Beauchamp's principled utilitarianism allows bioethics to be genuinely inclusive and to mould the moral perceptions of health care workers and patients regardless of creed.

This brief account of bioethics misses an obvious piece of evidence, namely that, despite the apparent triumph of secular philosophers and academic lawyers, theologians are still regularly included in the membership of national ethics committees concerned with science and medicine both in Britain and in the United States. Sometimes they are given the broader title of 'religious ethicist' but at other times the term 'theologian' is still used and (in Britain at least) it is in some instances a bishop who is included on such committees. At present, at least, there even seems to be some pressure on national ethics committees to be inclusive in this way.

Again, those holding these variant understandings of secularization are likely to interpret this evidence quite differently. Holders of the

---

[2] Tom L. Beauchamp and James F. Childress, *Principles of Biomedical Ethics*, New York, Oxford University Press, 4th edn, 1994.

first approach may well see this as an attempt by secular bodies to appear to be inclusive but without their making any serious concessions to the religiously committed. As long as it is just one religious ethicist who is included on a particular committee (as is usually the case), then there is little prospect that she/he will much affect the predominant secular discourse. More than that, there may be an implicit bargain that the religious ethicist adopts the secular discourse herself, or, if she does not, that she uses religious language simply to identify the idiosyncratic beliefs of variant religious minorities – in effect a sociological rather than theological use of distinctively religious language. Ironically, it may be sensitivity as much towards the beliefs of Jehovah's Witnesses as towards those of mainstream practising Jews, Christians or Muslims that such a religious ethicist is expected to represent as a member of such a committee.

Holders of the second approach to secularization may well view this evidence differently. For them it perhaps represents a significant retreat from an ideologically secular understanding of bioethics. Two rather different interpretations of 'secular' are present here. On one, bioethics needs to be secular in order to be inclusive within a pluralist society, but, on the other, bioethics becomes secular in order to eliminate specifically religious interpretations. The former includes both religion and non-religion, whereas the latter excludes religion. It is, of course, the former that is likely to appeal to followers of the second approach to secularization. So, for them, the presence of a religious ethicist on a national ethics committee can be welcomed as a genuine attempt to be inclusive. This is not simply a sop to religious minorities but a recognition that a pluralistic society includes both those who are religious and those who are not.

In the past two decades two philosophers who have done more than most to expose the inadequacy of a purely secular approach to moral issues are Alasdair MacIntyre and Charles Taylor. In their seminal books, *After Virtue* and *Sources of the Self*,[3] both published in the 1980s, they helped to advance the insight that, not only do religious minorities need to be respected if pluralistic society is to be genuinely inclusive, but that a number of crucial, but supposedly secular, moral notions have religious roots and may even make full sense only when these roots are explicitly acknowledged. This applies to bioethics just as much as it does to any other area of ethics.

---

[3] Alasdair McIntyre, *After Virtue: A Study in Moral Theory*, London, Duckworth, 2nd edn, 1985 and Charles Taylor, *Sources of the Self: The Making of the Modern Identity*, Cambridge MA, Harvard University Press, 1989.

Using insights also from John Hare's remarkable book *The Moral Gap*[4] I have argued elsewhere[5] that three specific moral gaps can be identified in purely secular accounts of ethics: the gap between theoretical and actual moral communities; the gap between personal resonance and a shared understanding of cosmic order; and the gap between moral demands and human propensity to selfishness.

Alasdair MacIntyre's *After Virtue* helps to identify the first of these gaps. There is a tension in his writing between his negative assessment of the incommensurate individualism that he believes lies at the heart of much post-Enlightenment moral philosophy and his positive endorsement of moral traditions carried within living (characteristically religious) communities. The tension can be illustrated by juxtaposing two quotations from the final chapter of *After Virtue*. In the first he offers the following summary:

> My own conclusion is very clear. It is that on the one hand we still, in spite of the efforts of three centuries of moral philosophy and one of sociology, lack any coherent rationally defensible statement of a liberal individualist point of view; and that on the other hand, the Aristotelian tradition can be restated in a way that restores intelligibility and rationality to our moral and social attitudes and commitments.[6]

MacIntyre's negative thesis here is that 'the liberal individualist point of view' lacks both coherence (for example, it is unable to resolve specific moral dilemmas such as abortion) and rational defensibility. His positive point, enshrined in the very title of the book, is that the Aristotelian tradition of virtues carried in moral communities might be able to re-establish such coherence and defensibility. Or, more accurately, it might be able to do so if only we really could identify suitable and persuasive forms of moral community in the modern world. It is this point that leads him to reach the famous conclusion to *After Virtue*:

> What matters at this stage is the construction of local forms of community within which civility and the intellectual and moral life can be sustained through the new dark ages which are already upon us. And if the tradition of the virtues was able to survive the horrors of the last dark ages, we are not entirely without grounds for hope. This time however the barbarians are not waiting beyond the frontiers; they have already been governing us

---

[4] John E. Hare, *The Moral Gap: Kantian Ethics, Human Limits and God's Assistance*, Oxford, Calendon Press, 1996.

[5] William Schweiker (ed.), *The Blackwell Companion to Religious Ethics*, Oxford, Blackwell, 2003.

[6] MacIntyre, *After Virtue*, p. 259.

for quite some time. And it is our lack of consciousness of this that constitutes part of our predicament. We are waiting not for a Godot, but for another – and doubtless very different – St. Benedict.[7]

Having deconstructed the universal claims of moral philosophy, MacIntyre is finally able to see only fragmented and changing moral communities in the Western world. He does see the need for new forms of moral community, but offers little hope that it is actually still possible for any particular moral community to gain widespread acceptance. At most, presumably, a series of fragmented communities can bring their virtues to modern medicine, but without any expectation that everyone can accept them. This is the first moral gap: the gap in the modern world between theoretical and actual moral communities.

The Beauchamp and Childress approach to bioethics attempts to stave off this fragmentation by offering principles that can be justified by people drawn from a variety of moral communities and holding quite different meta-ethical positions. In later editions of the work the authors have also attempted to show that their approach is compatible with a virtue ethic approach to bioethics. At best this seems to be a truce. As long as these principles can be upheld by different groups in medicine, albeit for very different reasons and, in addition, buffered by lawmakers, then they can be used to foster ethical discussion. Yet these principles, lacking support in any overall moral community or even in a series of communities that share some common culture, remain vulnerable.

Charles Taylor identifies a second major moral gap here: the gap today between what he terms 'personal resonance' and some shared 'cosmic order of meanings'. He is reluctantly convinced that in the modern world it is now 'personal resonance' that has replaced any shared 'cosmic order of meanings':

> This is a major gap … We are now in an age in which a publicly accessible cosmic order of meanings is an impossibility. The only way we can explore the order in which we are set with an aim to defining moral sources is through this part of personal resonance. This is true not only of epiphanic art but of other efforts, in philosophy, in criticism, which attempt the same search. This work, though it obviously fails of any epiphanic quality, falls into the same category … The philosopher or critic tinkers around and shapes images through which he can or another *might* one day do so. The artist is like the race-car driver, and we are the mechanics in the pit; except that in this case, the mechanics usually have

---

[7] MacIntyre, *After Virtue*, p. 263.

four thumbs, and they have only a hazy grasp of the wiring, much less than the drivers have. The point of this analogy is that we delude ourselves if we think that philosophical or critical language for these matters is somehow more hard-edged and more free from personal index than that of poets or novelists. The subject doesn't permit language which escapes personal resonance.[8]

To apply this analysis to bioethics, it is painfully obvious that in ethical discussions about health care today we cannot even agree upon a notion of 'health': for some it is concerned narrowly with an absence of disease (itself a term with cultural variants), whereas for others it is concerned with wider well-being (a term with meta-ethical variants) and for others still with physical, mental and spiritual health (now with metaphysical variants).

Within a detailed discussion of Kantian ethics in his book *The Moral Gap*, John Hare suggests a third major moral gap: the gap between moral demands and human propensity to selfishness. He argues that this gap arises within Kant's understanding of morality from a high moral demand for individuals combined with his belief that everyone has a propensity not to follow this demand. The high moral demand that all people should always behave morally in ways that are universalizable is in clear tension with their propensity to selfishness. Thus Kant (and indeed Hare) 'holds that humans have an original predisposition to the good, overlaid with an innate but imputable propensity to evil, which can be overcome only by a revolution of the will which itself requires what he calls a "divine supplement" '.[9] This gap is particularly acute precisely because Kant believed that 'ought' implies 'can': if it is not the case that people can live by the moral demand, then it cannot be the case that they ought to do so. In his book Hare concedes that this gap can be narrowed either by reducing the moral imperative (perhaps moral demands need not be regarded as universalizable) or by exaggerating natural propensities (perhaps humans really are not selfish after all). Both of these strategies have also been used at times in bioethics: if the moral demands in bioethics are sufficiently low then we should be able to attain them, or if we can assume that all health care professionals and patients will act selflessly then we can keep the demands high. Hare is finally unconvinced by such strategies and states modestly:

Suppose all the arguments in the book worked, what would the book have accomplished? Would it, for example, have proved the Christian doctrines

---

[8] Taylor, *Sources of the Self*, p. 512.
[9] Hare, *Moral Gap*, p. 35.

about God's work in our salvation? Not at all. All it would have shown is that *if* we keep morality as demanding as Kant says it is, *and if* we want to concede what Kant says about our natural propensity not to live by it, *and if* we want at the same time to reject these traditional Christian traditions, then we will have to find some substitute for them.[10]

In summary form, then, modern bioethics seems to present at least three moral gaps: the gap between theoretical and actual moral communities; the gap between personal resonance and a shared understanding of cosmic order, and the gap between moral demands and human propensity to selfishness. Yet there also seems to be an increasing divide between those theologians who make sharply particularist claims to address these 'moral gaps' and those who see only relative differences between Christian and secular thought. John Hare himself is aware that some Christians will be critical of his own defence of the supposedly 'secular' Kant. The divide was apparent in the earliest phase of bioethics – as the differences between Paul Ramsey and James Gustafson illustrate – but have become more pronounced today. Christian bioethicists such as James Childress, Gordon Dunstan and Alastair Campbell, as well as pastoral theologians such as Wesley Carr, contrast sharply with others such as Stanley Hauerwas and Gilbert Meilaender. Tristram Englehardt's work has been particularly important in analysing the issues involved in the divide.

In seeking to explore the distinctive contribution that a pastoral theologian might bring to modern bioethics I have been increasingly drawn to the healing stories in the Synoptic Gospels. These stories, after all, represent the most abundant biblical resource on healing and seem to lie close to the centre of Jesus' own ministry. In the context of modern bioethics, however, it is possible that the 'miraculous' features of these stories are less relevant than the virtues that shape them. It may also be anachronistic to jump from practices in these stories to modern medical practice. Following Howard Clark Kee and Gerd Theissen,[11] I believe that the Synoptic healing stories should be understood in a first-century context before they are applied carefully to the twenty-first century. And, following John Pilch's[12] biblical research using insights from medical anthropology, I am largely persuaded that these stories may have more to do with 'healing' than

---

[10] Hare, *Moral Gap*, p. 37.

[11] Howard Clark Kee, *Medicine, Miracle and Magic in New Testament Times*, Cambridge, Cambridge University Press, 1986 and Gerd Theissen, *The Miracle Stories of the Early Christian Tradition*, Edinburgh T & T Clark, and Philadelphia, Fortress Press, 1983.

[12] John Pilch, *Healing in the New Testament: Insights from Medical and Mediterranean Anthropology*, Minneapolis, Fortress Press, 2000.

with 'cure' in the modern sense. Instead, using a method derived from qualitative research in the social sciences, I have sought to identify an ideal typology of virtues that shape the Synoptic healing stories as follows.

Four virtues occur most regularly within these stories. Compassion is the first of these, not because it is more frequent than the others but because it often comes at the beginning of a story. Occasionally the healing stories directly recount that Jesus was moved by compassion before healing someone. More often it is those to be healed or their friends/relatives who ask Jesus to show mercy or compassion. Sometimes the latter beg Jesus to respond. Compassion is also an important element within parables such as the merciful servant, the good Samaritan and the prodigal son, and is given by Mark as the initiating point for the feeding of both the four and the five thousand.

Care is a second distinctive virtue. This takes several forms. The most common of these forms is personal touching. An important part of many healing stories is Jesus touching the one to be healed, including touching those already labelled in the story as being 'unclean'. Many commentators identify this as ritual, even magical, action. However, from a perspective of healing, it may be viewed in more personal terms as the healer reaching out to care for the one who is to be healed but who has already been rejected by others as unclean. Another common form that care takes in the healing stories is anger. Sometimes Jesus appears to be angry at the illness or disability itself, sometimes Jesus 'sternly' warns those who have been healed not to tell others, but more often Jesus' anger is directed at religious authorities who place their principles (especially about keeping the Sabbath) before helping the one who could be healed. Care in this double sense – Jesus caring through personal contact with the vulnerable and unclean and Jesus passionately caring that they should be healed – is a strong feature of these stories.

Faith is a third distinctive virtue. Jesus often notes the faith of those to be healed or of their friends/relatives, and, conversely, can do little to help when there is an absence of faith. A recurrent conclusion he draws is that 'your faith has made you well'. On two occasions – the centurion's servant and Canaanite woman – he particularly commends the faith of those who are not Jewish.

Reticence is a fourth virtue shaping the healing stories. A frequent end to healing stories in Mark, but also in places in Matthew (see especially Matt 8 and 9) and Luke, is a command (in one place 'repeatedly') to the person healed to tell no-one. Not surprisingly this feature has puzzled many biblical commentators. Even though Wrede's notion of the so-called Messianic secret is now largely discounted, its shadow still remains in many commentaries. Viewed from a

perspective of healing it may appear rather differently. There are
frequent mentions in the Synoptic stories of the amazement of the
crowds at the healings and alongside some of these are other indications
that Jesus was anxious to withdraw from the crowds. Viewed as
miraculous 'signs' – an occasional observation in the Synoptic Gospels
but far more explicit in the Fourth Gospel – Jesus' healings could
appear simply to be a dramatic demonstration of who he really was. Yet
viewed as the healer reaching out to the ill and disabled with
compassion, care and faith, a command to reticence is perhaps less
surprising. It is the one concerned to demonstrate miraculous signs who
needs crowds, not the one who is most concerned to heal the
vulnerable. There may also be another reason for reticence in the
healing stories, namely the related virtue of humility. There are direct
and indirect references in a number of the healing stories to 'power' and
'authority', set in a wider framework of teaching about the Kingdom of
God. The healer who is conscious that it is finally God's power/rule that
is at work in healing has good cause to feel personally humble.

Set in a wider context of religious ethics, all four of these virtues –
compassion, care, faith and restraint – could be claimed by Judaism,
Christianity and Islam alike. These virtues characterize Jesus as a Jew.
According to Kee and Theissen it is only their setting in a wider
apocalyptic context within the Synoptic Gospels that differentiates
them from contemporary Judaism. Again, although healing is not such
a strong feature of the Qu'ran, these four virtues are very characteristic
of the Qu'ran's sense of how good Muslims should behave: almost
every Sura begins with 'In the name of God, the Merciful, Compas-
sionate'; followers of Jesus are specifically commended for their
'kindness' and compassion; care for the poor and vulnerable,
especially through giving alms, is a clear requirement for Muslims;
faith is evident throughout the Qu'ran; and humility is required of
those who remember that it is God who created them.

The virtue of compassion makes possible a double critique: of much
secular bioethics for not making compassion sufficiently explicit and
of a number of Christian versions of bioethics for failing to place
compassion before principles. Compassion, properly understood, is an
essential starting point for bioethics even within a pluralistic society.
Within the Synoptic healing stories compassion is not simply about
feeling sorry for the vulnerable, nor is it even just about empathy, a
preparedness to identify with the vulnerable. Rather, compassion is
both a response to the vulnerable and a determination to help them.[13]

---

[13] For a fine theological analysis of compassion see Oliver Davies, *A Theology of
Compassion*, London, SCM Press, 2001.

In the Synoptic stories the vulnerable beg and cry for mercy and Jesus responds and acts. In many of the stories it is compassion/mercy that initiates the process of healing.

Within secular bioethics a proper attention to the role of compassion may help to narrow the moral gap between personal resonance and a shared understanding of cosmic order. Even within a pluralistic society there may in reality be more common ground on compassion than is sometimes supposed. It is notoriously difficult to find agreement on common goods within a pluralistic society (as critics of natural law have often maintained), but it may be somewhat easier to agree upon common ills. So even if people cannot agree about what constitutes 'well being', most might agree about what generally constitutes illness or disability and that, other things being equal, it is desirable to find ways of reducing or eliminating them. Of course there will still be some areas where agreement remains elusive – for example, whether blindness constitutes a disability within blind families – but these areas are vastly outnumbered in modern society by areas of general agreement. Whether this agreement is entirely the result of cultural determinants or whether it is based, at least in part, in human nature need not be resolved here. It is sufficient that there is general agreement that it is desirable to reduce or eliminate illness and disability. Here there does seem, even within a pluralistic society, to be a general agreement that is not simply the result of personal resonance.

Compassion as a virtue is, however, more than a general agreement that it is desirable to reduce or eliminate illness and disability. It is both a response to the ill and disabled and a determination to help them. An approach to bioethics based only upon the four Beauchamp and Childress principles might miss this. The four principles are, to use an analogy, more akin to principles governing *ius in bello* than *ius ad bellum*. That is to say, they suggest criteria to be considered carefully within the context of medical intervention, but they do not denote what drives and motivates that intervention in the first place. Behind the principles there is an implicit assumption that medical professionals should indeed respond to the ill and disabled and be determined to do their very best to help them.

The term 'care' is already widely used in secular medical contexts, for example in the term health care itself, in community care and care assistants. It has been seen that in the Synoptic stories Jesus both cared through personal contact with the vulnerable and unclean and passionately cared that they should be healed. Both of these senses remain in these secular uses of the term 'care'. The health care professional is permitted and even expected to risk personal (but not intimate) contact with those who are ill and has a duty to do everything appropriate to cure them (if possible) or to reduce their pain or discomfort (if not). Care, properly understood, involves a range of core personal values, including competence, integrity, responsibility and confidentiality. Total patient care may also involve advocacy on behalf of the vulnerable and non-competent patient.

Care, properly understood, is particularly demanding and highlights the gap between moral demands and human propensity to selfishness. In secular care one method adopted to ensure that adequate care is provided to patients is to produce written codes of professional practice and another is to have regular and systematic audits of actual practice. However, such methods fall short of ensuring care, because care, properly understood, involves a personal relationship between a carer and a (conscious) patient. Written codifications and the written track records essential to audit, although important and certainly not to be denigrated, nevertheless tend to set out or test the minimum conditions for professional practice rather than the personal and passionate care characterized in the Synoptic healing stories. Nonetheless there remain important features of secular medicine today which explicitly (and many more implicitly) contain care in the latter sense and which help to reduce the moral gap here. The hospice movement will be used as an example here. It is, however, an example that raises the question whether such a movement could have arisen without having religiously committed founders.

What about faith in bioethics today? Particularly important here is the growing empirical evidence that there is a connection between religious belonging and health.[14] This suggests that religious belonging is a significant (but often ignored) independent variable in promoting physical and psychological health. Of course there is still much debate about the causal factors involved here, yet it does seem that people with strong religious affiliations are more likely than others to have a sense of purpose in life and to be altruistic[15] and it is possible, in turn, that such motivation may have important implications for physical and psychological health.

There are two obvious problems with this evidence. The first is that, from a theological perspective, it suggests a rather instrumental understanding of faith: faith is treated as something that is beneficial for health rather than as a virtue that is good in itself. It is extremely important to state very carefully that this is not the intention here. Rather it may be an indication that well-being at different levels may

---

[14] See Byron R. Johnson's very comprehensive review, *Objective Hope: Assessing the Effectiveness of Faith-Based Organizations: A Review of the Literature*, Philadelphia, Center for Research on Religion and Urban Civil Society, University of Pennsylvania, 2002.

[15] See my *Churchgoing and Christian Ethics*, Cambridge, Cambridge University Press, 1999.

be inter-connected. The second problem here is that the evidence is based upon a very generalized understanding of 'faith': many different forms of religious (or perhaps even secular) faith, some mutually contradictory, may be beneficial for motivation/health. In response it may be noted that faith in the Synoptic healing stories is itself quite varied: sometimes it refers to the faith of the person to be healed; sometimes it is the faith of the relatives or friends; sometimes it appears to be faith in Jesus as healer; sometimes it seems to be faith in God; sometimes faith appears to be belief; sometimes it seems rather to be trust; sometimes it is the faith of fellow Jews; sometimes that of Gentiles. To rephrase MacIntyre, the question 'Whose faith? What faith?' is surprisingly relevant even in the Synoptic Gospels.

Accordingly, the relationship of faith to healing can be analysed at a number of levels. The most basic of these is that of faith in the healing relationship. Without at least some trust in the medical professional – or, better, a mutual confidence between patient and professional – then healing may well be imperilled. Faith in the form of trust (but not always mutual confidence) was often present in the paternalistic medical practice, itself dependent upon patient compliance, of a previous generation. Within a context today that highlights patient autonomy and rights (without corresponding responsibilities) this trust may be weakened. The healing relationship understood in terms of mutual confidence offers a model of faith which respects both patient and professional autonomies and seeks to relate the two to each other.

The second level is concerned with the implicit assumptions of the healer herself. Paul Halmos' seminal book *The Faith of the Counsellors*[16] noted that secular counsellors tend to depict their role in 'scientific' terms and, in the process, ignore value-commitments that are also fundamental to good counselling. Writing from a secular perspective himself, Halmos even suggested that it is the Judaeo-Christian virtue of care or *agape* which is the (usually unacknowledged) *sine qua non* of effective counselling. It might be argued that a very similar case can be made within medical practice more generally.

The third level concerns specifically religious faith. Set within the context of the other two levels, faith in this sense can be seen as belonging to a continuum within the healing process. While healing is still possible without this level being made explicit, elements of it are likely to be implicit within many healing contexts. It is also at this level that the moral gap between the demand of moral duty and human propensity to selfishness can be narrowed. For the medical professional, especially when grounded in a worshipping community,

---

[16] Paul Halmos, *The Faith of the Counsellors*, London, Constable, 1965.

faith in this third sense offers a powerful source of motivation to act selflessly. For the patient such a community can also narrow the gap between personal resonance and a shared understanding of cosmic order. Even if an understanding of cosmic order is not shared by both the healer and the one who is to be healed, it can be explicitly shared by one or the other party with a worshipping community (especially a community that has regular intercessions for the ill and needy).

Finally there is reticence or humility within modern bioethics. In a context of exaggerated claims made in the name of medical (especially genetic) science and seemingly unlimited patient demand, this fourth virtue is particularly apposite today. Within medicine humility in a moral sense is to be distinguished from etiquette. In terms of etiquette it is good manners not to boast about being able to do something even when there are grounds for believing that it can be done. However, as a moral term humility involves a proper recognition both of personal frailty and of the role of others in achieving something. For the medical professional there is a constant temptation to claim too much authority and knowledge (a temptation in which patients themselves frequently conspire). At a theological level the temptation is to 'play God'. A recurrent pattern in the Synoptic Gospels involves excessive pressure upon Jesus from crowds seeking healing and Jesus himself withdrawing from these crowds and warning those healed to tell no-one. With the exception of instructions to John the Baptist's disciples, it is only in the Fourth Gospel that miracles unambiguously become 'signs' of Jesus' own divine status. Viewed from a theological perspective the medical professional has very clear reasons for not taking all the credit for any particular act of healing.

In a need- rather than demand-led health service, patient reticence is a crucial ingredient. To work properly such a health service does require patients to realize that there are others who are in need and possibly in greater need than themselves. For example, a system of rationing or prioritizing that is not simply based upon a patient's social status or ability to pay does require a shared sense of equity and fairness. The secular economist Amartya Sen's notion of 'equality of basic capability' is important here – especially his contention that moral perception is inextricably involved in an adequate under-standing of equality and inequality in the world. An equality of basic capability, whether applied to the health service or more widely to society at large, involves qualitative issues and not simply a quantitative provision to satisfy basic needs. Douglas Hicks[17] argues

---

[17] Douglas A. Hicks, *Inequality and Christian Ethics*, Cambridge, Cambridge University Press, 2000.

that, once this is acknowledged, Christian ethics can contribute at three distinctive levels. First, it provides a moral vision and justification for how inequality matters and why public response is needed. Then it can offer moral examples of Christians who have actively striven against inequality. And, thirdly, Christian ethics provides a particularly compelling moral call to action: at best, Christian communities can transform lives and behaviour towards a greater equality of capability.

It is evident that Hicks belongs to the group of those Christian ethicists who avoid particularist claims for the discipline and who look instead for continuities with secular ethics. His three distinctively Christian levels are important for the 'moral gaps', but he avoids making strong claims about them – a proper sense of restraint is relevant here too. Religious communities can reduce the moral gap between theoretical and actual moral communities but their capacity to do so can easily be exaggerated. At best such communities offer a shared understanding of cosmic order which may still resonate with implicit assumptions about equity and fairness in wider society (especially on health care issues). Yet the fact that these assumptions tend to be implicit rather than explicit remains a matter of concern given human propensity to selfishness.

Properly understood, I believe that the four distinctively religious virtues of compassion, care, faith and humility complement rather than conflict with the four bioethics principles of autonomy, justice, non-maleficence and beneficence. It is right that compassion should impel medical professionals to care for those in need and that, in turn, care should involve both caring about and caring for those who become patients. A proper understanding of the relationship between medical professionals and their patients also requires them to pay attention to non-maleficence, beneficence and the autonomy of these patients – and, in turn, for patients also to respect their autonomy. Faith is involved in some sense in the healing relationship between both parties and, for some, also between them and God. Justice is also an essential consideration in the broader context of health in society at large. And finally humility should restrain both medical professionals from making exaggerated claims and patients from making selfish demands.

Chapter 12

God and Caesar, Then and Now

Tom Wright

'Render unto Caesar,' declared Jesus, 'the things that are Caesar's; and unto God the things that are God's.'[1] That famously cryptic comment serves not only as a title for this article but as a reminder of the question-mark that hangs over life in an established church, not least in that most established of churches, Westminster Abbey. Having served under Wesley Carr and experienced the joys and puzzles, the stresses and opportunities which the intermingling of church and state produce, I am delighted to offer these reflections in gratitude for his brave leadership and wise collegiality.

How, today, should we approach the question of God and Caesar – of Christ, church, crown and state? To answer, I shall first outline some current assumptions, and suggest that they are currently challenged from within contemporary culture itself. Then I shall suggest that the biblical basis for the topic is more solid and multi-faceted than normally imagined. Finally, I shall argue for a way of understanding church, state and crown in our own day.

The legacy of the Enlightenment

I begin by drawing attention to three influential features of Enlightenment thought which are taken for granted today. The first is the assumption of a split-level world in which 'religion' and 'faith' belong upstairs and 'society' and 'politics' belong downstairs. This assumption has effectively privatized religion and faith on the one hand, and on the other has emancipated politics from divine control or influence. God lives upstairs (many of the Enlightenment philosophers were Deists) and doesn't bother about what goes on downstairs. Our modern word 'state' is itself an Enlightenment invention, designating a self-operating system, free from religious influence. Thus even to phrase the question in terms of 'church and state' may run the risk of deciding things in advance.

---

[1] Mark 12:17 and parallels.

Many today assume this split-level world as the norm. Indeed, when
people hear Jesus' 'God-and-Caesar' line from Mark 12, they assume
that it affirms and legitimates this divide. That is why many assume,
further, that any link between church and state must be ill-conceived.
Surely, they think, we are now a *secular* society? Surely a church-state
link belongs with witchcraft and superstition, with Crusades and
prince-bishops? Surely – one of the favourite lines in Enlightenment
rhetoric – it's *mediaeval*?[2]

Well, it is and it isn't. This brings us to the second Enlightenment
assumption often taken for granted today: that political beliefs and
attitudes come in two packages, and that everyone has to choose one
or the other. There is the package of the Right: rigid social structures,
hierarchy, law and order, a tough-minded work ethic and a strong view
of national identity. Then there is the package of the Left: freedom and
revolution, overthrowing hierarchies, blurring old lines, doing things
in new ways. It is assumed that, with local variations, you are basically
in one camp or the other, and that many other decisions are determined
by it. In America many assume that if you believe in God and the
Bible you are also opposed to gun control and in favour of the death
penalty – or that if you believe in abolishing the death penalty and
introducing gun control you probably doubt the incarnation and the
bodily resurrection of Jesus. The packages vary from one country to
another, but it is assumed that political beliefs line up on one side or
the other and that a recognizable package will be held in common on
either side. It is also often assumed (this, too, was part of
Enlightenment rhetoric) that the church, and belief in God, are part
of the right-wing package. The more democratic, let alone
revolutionary, you become, the less you will have to do with God.

Things are not that easy, but old assumptions stick hard. The very
idea of Left and Right dates only to the French Revolution. Those who
have discovered in our own day that Jesus announced the Kingdom of
God, and that Paul spoke of Jesus as the world's true Lord, often
assume that this implies some variation on today's left-wing package,
just as for generations people who have discovered that Paul insists on
obeying 'the powers that be' have assumed that this implies some kind
of right-wing package. This too is anachronistic; but it explains why
many today look at the combination of God, church, crown and state
and declare that it's all part of a right-wing conspiracy and must be got
rid of; or, if they understand the New Testament as supporting a left-
wing package, that God and the church are hopelessly compromised

---

[2] See Bradley, note 24 below, p. 143.

by having anything at all to do with crown and state and must be set free at once.[3]

The third influential Enlightenment assumption, which affects how people see the other two as well, is the belief in progress. History (it is believed) reached a climax in Europe in the eighteenth century; humanity's calling ever since has been to implement this achievement. If recalcitrant elements in earlier worldviews have proved harder to shift than the early revolutionaries had imagined, they must be mocked or shamed into giving themselves up. Surely, we are told, 'in this day and age' certain things are inappropriate? Surely 'now that we live in the twenty-first century' it's time to get rid of some types of social organization or constitution? The assumption here is that everyone 'really' knows that the undoubted advances in science and technology have made older religious and political beliefs redundant, banishing God upstairs on the one hand and redefining politics into Left and Right, with a strong inclination towards some kind of egalitarian, one-level social democracy.

The Enlightenment agenda is, of course, far more complicated than this, but I hope these three aspects are recognizable. The achievement of the Enlightenment was to shape the way people think and feel so thoroughly that many today unquestioningly assume these radical innovations. This is simply part of 'living in the modern world'.

But just when the Enlightenment empire sits back and surveys its achievement, the Goths and Vandals are at the gates. Postmodernity, growing up within the western world over the last generation, has challenged every aspect of the Enlightenment package. Things are again more complex than we can explore here; I simply sketch, in reverse order, some of the effects of the current revolution against the modernist assumptions.[4]

Belief in progress has been under attack, not least politically. 'Progress' has often been associated with the Left, but in the more radical post-war Left, especially in France, 'progress' itself has been accused of being a covert excuse for imperial domination. The word *developed*, and its little sister, *under-developed*, encapsulate the position now under threat from postcolonialism. Belief in 'progress' has enabled western modernists to trample over much of the world in

---

[3] See, for example, the essays edited by Richard A. Horsley in the two volumes *Paul and Empire* and *Paul and Politics* (Harrisburg, PA: Trinity Press International, 1997 and 2000).

[4] On the postmodern turn see my book *The Myth of the Millennium* (London: SPCK, 1999), and for example, Brian Walsh and Richard Middleton, *Truth is Stranger than it Used to Be* (London: SPCK, 1998).

search of wealth and power, just as belief in 'Roman justice' excused
Caesar's first-century imperialism.

Likewise, belief in our own political right-and-left alternatives as a
one-size-fits-all map is hard to sustain. Western parliamentary-style
democracy is only one of several options that different societies find
appropriate. 'Democracy' means something different in the UK from
what it means in America and the different European countries. We
whose histories include rotten boroughs and beer-for-votes rallies
should not be surprised at how difficult it is to stage one-person-one-
vote elections in many parts of the world today. Fewer people voted in
the last UK General Election than in the 'Big Brother' TV series. We
are not in a wonderful position from which to offer the rest of the
world a permanent political solution. Anyway, the Enlightenment
didn't only produce democracies. It also produced Napoleon,
Bismarck, Mussolini, Hitler and Stalin.

In particular, the western world has become disillusioned with
secular modernism, the child of Enlightenment Deism. We may have
banished the older image of God upstairs, leaving him there to
mumble in his beard while we run the world by ourselves, but theology
like nature abhors a vacuum, and new gods have been bubbling up
from below to replace the absentee landlord. New Age movements,
Druids, Shamans, crystals and horoscopes: the 'religion' section in any
bookshop will reveal that 'spirituality' is big business. The spiritual
starvation diet offered by secularism made people so hungry that they
now eat anything. People are rediscovering their awareness of
something or someone they call God, or 'the divine', not least in
and through symbols, rituals and stories. People speak eagerly of
'mystery', 'magic', or 'other dimensions' – all things which the
Enlightenment tried to ban as mumbo-jumbo and superstition. Some
still try to enforce that ban, but mystery has come back to our lives,
and we like it and won't be put off. The question now facing us is:
How should we put God and the world back together again after an
artificial divorce of two centuries? That we must do so is increasingly
apparent. And all this means that the cultural assumptions within
which the God/church/crown/state debates have traditionally been
conducted have been eroded.

The kingdoms of the world and the kingdom of God

This brings us to the foundational question: what does the New
Testament say on the whole subject? Above the High Altar in
Westminster Abbey are inscribed words from Revelation 11:15: 'The
Kingdom of this world is become the Kingdom of our God and of his

Christ.'[5] This is typical of what the New Testament declares: God is king, and the kingdoms of the world are thereby demoted. The crucified and risen Jesus of Nazareth is God's Messiah, Lord of the world; he is already reigning at God's right hand; he will reappear to complete this rule by abolishing all enemies, including sin and death themselves.[6]

This early Christian belief goes back, through Jesus himself, to the ancient Jewish world. Throughout that world, both Jewish and Christian, the assumptions of the Enlightenment simply do not hold. God and the world are not separated by an ugly ditch; the political options are not polarized along the lines of authority versus revolution; and, though history does indeed move towards a great climax and then out to implement this in the world, this has nothing to do with automatic progress and everything to do with sacrifice, vocation and the strange purposes of the living God.

The story of how this works out is far too long to tell here. In many periods of Christian history the Israelite monarchy was invoked as the model for Christian kings and queens; but in the Old Testament itself kingship is ambiguous, and hardly supports a triumphalist use. In any case, the really formative period for Jewish political thinking, the period which set the tone for the New Testament, was during and after the Babylonian exile. Jeremiah urged the exiles to seek the welfare of Babylon, and to pray to God for it.[7] God, he declared, had raised up his servant Nebuchadnezzar, king of Babylon, and given him authority over all the nations.[8] Second Isaiah spoke of the pagan Persian Cyrus as God's anointed, who would rescue the exiles and send them home.[9] The exiles rebuilt Jerusalem and the Temple under the ambivalent auspices of pagan rulers. Despite some prophetic hopes, no Davidic king emerged to create a new, independent kingdom. Instead, Jewish writers from the exile to Jesus and beyond wrestle with the ambiguities of living as God's people under non-Jewish rule. Two books stand out.

Daniel tells stories of Jews who refuse to compromise with paganism. When they are vindicated by God, however, they (like Joseph under Pharaoh) are promoted to positions of service within the pagan kingdom. Jews may face martyrdom (not least because they refuse to privatize their faith), but they are committed to being good

---

[5] Actually, the inscribed text has made the 'kingdoms' plural; in the Greek the word is singular, and only occurs once in the sentence (literally, 'the kingdom of this world is become of our lord and of his Messiah').

[6] The classic statement is in 1 Corinthians 15:20–28.

[7] Jeremiah 29:7.

[8] Jeremiah 27:4–8.

[9] Isaiah 45:1–7; cf. 2 Chronicles 36:22f.; Ezra 1:1–4.

citizens even under a regime at best penultimate and at worst blasphemous. Of course, there comes a time when the true God will judge the
pagans, and then God's people must get out and run.[10] There will
come a time when all regimes, including the one within which Daniel
is a loyal civil servant, will give way to the kingdom that God will set
up, which can never be shaken.[11] Combining apocalyptic visions of
God's coming kingdom and public service within the present one
appears shocking to the Enlightenment mindset. But something like
this is what we find in the New Testament and the early church.

The Wisdom of Solomon offers a stern warning to pagan kings and
rulers. They have been appointed to their high office by the living
God, but he will judge them for what they do and fail to do. They
therefore need Wisdom, who has been active throughout Israel's
traditions, and who (we gradually discover) is more or less an *alter ego*
for God himself.[12] This is not the *absent* God of Enlightenment
Deism; it is the wise, guiding, judging, rescuing God of the biblical
tradition. This God does not divide the world between Right and Left,
authority and revolution. Both of those are too brightly lit, too
unambiguous, to be ultimately useful in guiding our steps in the right
paths. Wisdom herself proposes a different way.

Some Jews, of course, took more extreme positions. Some sought to
ape the pagan kings; the Hasmonean dynasty went that route, as did
Herod and his sons. Equally, there was a long tradition of revolt, from
the Maccabees to Bar-Kochba, sometimes using the slogan 'No King
but God'.[13] But when Jesus of Nazareth announced that God's
kingdom was breaking in, he seems not to have meant it in that sense.
What was he talking about? How did Jesus' vision of God's kingdom
stand in relation to the kingdoms of the world?

From the start, Jesus' proclamation of God's kingdom was fighting
talk.[14] Everybody knew that God's kingdom didn't refer to a place,
perhaps a place called 'heaven', where God ruled and to which God's
people would be gathered, well away from the wicked world, at the
end of their lives. Only a Deist could think like that. God's kingdom,
said Jesus, was coming, and people should pray for it to come, *on
earth as in heaven*; and here he was, on earth, making it happen before
people's very eyes. When Herod heard, he was angry; he was King of

---

[10] Isaiah 52:11–12; cf. 48:20; Jeremiah 50:8; 51:6, 45; Zech 2:6, 7.

[11] Daniel 2; 7; 9.

[12] Wisdom 6:1–11.

[13] On these Jewish movements, see *The New Testament and the People of God*
(London: SPCK, 1992), Part III.

[14] On Jesus and the Kingdom, see *Jesus and the Victory of God* (London: SPCK,
1996) and *The Challenge of Jesus* (London: SPCK, 2000).

the Jews, and rival claimants tended not to live long. When the Chief Priests heard, they knew that it meant a challenge to their power base, the Temple. If Caesar had heard, he would have reacted similarly. What none of them could figure out, and what even Jesus' closest associates had difficulty understanding, was what *kind* of a challenge Jesus intended to pose: what sort of a kingdom he was advancing, and what kind of a king he considered himself to be.

The answers begin to emerge when Jesus arrives in Jerusalem and symbolically purges the Temple, pointing ahead to its imminent destruction. This precipitates a string of debates, in which Jesus is virtually on trial, like someone being interviewed by a hostile media knowing that any verbal slip might prove fatal. Mark 11 and 12 offer a sequence of these debates, all of them politically and theologically freighted. This is where we find the trick question, and the opaque answer, about the tribute penny, about Caesar and God. It is not an isolated 'political' comment in an otherwise nonpolitical sequence of thought. It fits exactly where it is.[15]

Tax revolts against Rome were nothing new. A large-scale one had taken place during Jesus' boyhood, and had been crushed with typical Roman brutality. Saying, 'Yes, pay the tax,' would be to say 'I'm not serious about God's kingdom.' But to incite people not to pay would at once incur trouble.[16]

Jesus gets his interlocutors to produce a coin, tacitly admitting that they kept the hated coinage, with its blasphemous inscription and its (to a Jew) illegal image, a portrait of Caesar himself. Whose is it? he asks. Caesar's, they answer. Well then, says Jesus, *you'd better pay back Caesar in his own coin* – and pay God back in *his* own coin!

The closest echoes to this double command are found in 1 Maccabees 2:68. Mattathias is telling his sons, especially Judas, to get ready for revolution. 'Pay back to the Gentiles what is due to them,' he says, 'and keep the law's commands'. Paying back the Gentiles was not meant to refer to money. I am sure that some of Jesus' hearers would have picked up that revolutionary hint. Because he was standing there looking at a coin, his surface meaning was, of course, that the tax had to be paid; but underneath was the strong hint that Caesar's regime was a blasphemous nonsense and that one day God would overthrow it.

The setting and the saying show decisively, against what is so frequently asserted by both Right and Left within the Enlightenment tradition, that Jesus did not mean it as indicating a separation between the spheres of Caesar and God, with each taking responsibility for a

---

[15] On the passage, see *Jesus and the Victory of God*, 502–7.

[16] Indeed, Luke (23:2) indicates that this charge was levelled at Jesus before Pilate.

distinct part of the world. Even at the surface level, the saying must
have meant that God claimed the whole of life, including questions
about taxes. Of course, Jesus acknowledges, you may have to pay
taxes to the pagans, just as Jews in exile had to pray to God for the
welfare of Babylon; but that doesn't mean that God is only concerned
with a different, 'spiritual' world. God is present in the ambiguity,
summoning people to an allegiance which transcended but certainly
included the position they found themselves in vis-à-vis the occupying
power.

Jesus' death can itself be seen as Jesus' own offering, simultaneously, of what was due to Caesar (crucifixion was what Caesar did
to rebel kings) and what was due to God. Mark at least may have that
in mind; certainly the primary meaning of his crucifixion narrative is
what we would call 'political', though it is also theological and
personal as well. Once again, the Enlightenment categories are simply
unable to cope with the meanings the writers intend us to discover in
their narratives, let alone the meanings which the central character, it
seems, intended his followers to discern in his death. The death of
Jesus brings to a head the ambiguous character of the Israelite
monarchy from Saul and David right on through history. Calvary and
Easter become the focal points of the apocalyptic and wisdom
traditions, and hence of second-Temple Judaism's political theology:
God's new world is born, claiming the kingdoms of the world as its
own, because their central and most powerful weapon, death itself, has
now been broken.[17]

Most of the fixed points in our knowledge of the early Christians are
stories of persecution and martyrdom, as God's gospel and Caesar's
gospel came into conflict.[18] Think of the aged Polycarp, on trial for his
life. The Roman governor applies two tests: first, you must blaspheme
or curse Jesus Christ; second, you must swear 'by the Genius of the
Emperor'. No loyal Christian could do either. Polycarp's answer is a
specific rebuttal: 'I've served him for eighty-six years, and he's never
done me any wrong; how can I blaspheme my King who saved me?'
Caesar claimed to be King and Saviour; Polycarp is giving Jesus titles
claimed by Caesar. But then, against our expectations, Polycarp
proposes to explain to the governor what Christianity actually is. He
respects his office, since 'we have been taught to render honour to the
rulers and authorities who are appointed by God.' Even when Polycarp
is on trial for his life, he is content to say, like Jesus before Pilate in
John 19:11, that God has appointed the pagan governor who is about to

---

[17] On the political significance of the defeat of death see chs 12 and 19 of my *The
Resurrection of the Son of God* (London: SPCK, 2003).
[18] For details, see *The New Testament and the People of God*, ch. 11.

pass sentence. This is puzzling to us, but it would have made sense to the authors of Daniel, Wisdom, Mark, or John.[19] Or, for that matter, to Paul or Peter.

Polycarp's double point (Jesus, not Caesar, is Lord, King and Saviour, but God has also appointed people, however unfit, as authorities in the world) is echoed in the epistles. 1 Peter 2:9 declares that Christians form a royal priesthood. Well, then, we conclude, they owe no loyalty to any other royalty or priesthood. On the contrary, says Peter (2:13–17): you must respect the rulers; fear God, honour the Emperor. So, we conclude, he's saying that earthly rulers are always right. Not so; the next paragraph (2:18–25) discusses what to do, not when justice is done, but when injustice is done, resulting in suffering. Most of the letter is about suffering and possible martyrdom. Daniel would have understood, though the ambiguity would confuse the superficial and over-bright lights of Enlightenment political analysis.

The centre of early Christian reflection remains Paul. It is often supposed that Paul's only political comment is Romans 13:1–7, where he states that God has ordained 'the powers that be'; but this just shows how far our traditions have taken us away from reality. There is no space to explore this in detail, but in almost every letter Paul demonstrates that Jesus is Lord, and that Caesar isn't; that the 'gospel' of Jesus upstages the 'gospel' of Caesar; that the true salvation is achieved through Jesus, not Caesar; that the world needs God's justice, not Roman justice; and, with great irony, that the cross, a hated symbol of Roman rule, had been transformed into the life-giving symbol of God's self-giving love. Paul's central arguments constitute a massive outflanking movement against the imperial rhetoric of his day (emperor-worship was the fastest-growing religion of the time).[20]

So why did Paul write Romans 13?[21] Because of the whole tradition of Jewish monotheism and political thought to which he was heir. God does not want anarchy. Nor, of course, do we. It's fine to point out the wickedness of earthly rulers, but when someone

---

[19] Polycarp adds, interestingly, the phrase 'as long as it isn't to our harm': we render honour, as long as that honour is not damaging to us. Where this modification to Romans 13 came from, and what precisely is meant by it, are matters of debate.

[20] See, especially, my 'Paul and Caesar: A New Reading of Romans,' in *A Royal Priesthood: The Use of the Bible Ethically and Politically*, ed. C. Bartholemew (Carlisle: Paternoster), 173–93. This is a lightly revised version of my 'A Fresh Perspective on Paul?', *Bulletin of the John Rylands Library* 83, no. 1, 21–39. See too N.T. Wright, 'Paul's Gospel and Caesar's Empire', in *Paul and Politics: Ekklesia, Israel, Imperium, Interpretation. Essays in Honor of Krister Stendahl*, ed. Richard A. Horsley, 160–83. Harrisburg, PA: Trinity Press International, 2000.

[21] On this, see especially my *Romans* (New Interpreter's Bible, Vol. X, 393–770), 715–23.

steals my car I want justice. It's all very well to say that people in power are self-seeking, but if nobody is in power the bullies and the burglars have it all their own way, and the weak and helpless suffer most. God doesn't want that. God has therefore instituted rulers and authorities (even at the obvious risk that most of them don't acknowledge him and only have a shaky idea of what justice actually is), in order to bring to his world such order as is possible until the day when the rule of Jesus himself is complete on earth as in heaven. This is the Christian version of the political viewpoint we find in Daniel, Wisdom and other Jewish texts. Romans 13 is not, then, a carte blanche for rulers to do what they like. Paul is not setting rulers on a high pedestal, above criticism. Instead, he is reminding them that they have been instituted by God and remain responsible to him for the authority they bear.

The final book of the New Testament, of course, has its own point of view. Just as Ephesians 6 indicates that there is still a battle to be fought against the wicked powers, so Revelation 13 paints an apocalyptic picture of an empire that has gone so bad that the only word to be spoken is one of judgement. God will judge blasphemous wickedness, especially when it uses violence against the helpless. That is part of the means by which the kingdom of this world is becoming the kingdom of our lord and his Messiah. But nothing in the Jewish tradition within which the book must be interpreted indicates that this indicates a blanket condemnation of all rulers and authorities, or a refusal to give them the honour of being God's agents, however misguided and dangerous on occasion they may be. Rather, what the early Christians offer is inaugurated eschatology: like the Israelites under their monarchy, chafing at its imperfections and looking for the fulfilment still to come, the followers of Jesus are to live under the rulers of the world, believing them to be appointed by God but not believing that that makes them perfect or that they do not need to be held accountable. On the contrary. Because they are God's servants they may well need to be reminded of their duty, however dangerous and uncomfortable a task that may be. The stories of Paul in Acts suggest that he sometimes did just that.[22]

There is no space here to speak of the time between the suffering church in the third century and the church of Enlightenment modernism. One of the major achievements of Enlightenment rhetoric was to pour scorn on this long period, from the settlement of Constantine right through to the eighteenth century, as a hopeless compromise, maybe even 'the fall of the church'. The very word

---

[22] For example, Acts 16:35–39; 23:3–5.

'Christendom' has become a sneer. But, though there is a vital point
to be made about the dangers of assuming too ready an identification
between the cause of the gospel and the cause of any particular
country, nation or state (a danger which the Enlightenment has not
helped us to avoid), this criticism is trivial and superficial, and fails
to take into account the long, complex and by no means
compromised tradition of serious Christian political thought
throughout the millennium and a half from 300 AD to 1800 AD.[23]
It is false to suggest that from Constantine onwards the church was
muzzled, forced to do what its political masters told it. Of course
that happened sometimes – just as it does today, even in countries
where, as in the United States, non-establishment is much vaunted.
There were also many times when the church was able to confront
and challenge the state and crown directly. Establishment and
martyrdom are closer than we might suppose. Think of Becket. But
for our present purposes we skip over all this and more, and arrive at
our present British institution of monarchy and its supposedly
Christian meaning. How can the biblical theology of rulers and
authorites be reinterpreted appropriately in this setting?

The angled mirror

The New Testament offers a theology of rulers and authorities as
appointed by God. This places a huge weight of responsibility on the
authorities which many modern democratic rulers cheerfully ignore.
What is striking about the British monarchy, and some others that still
remain, is that they openly acknowledge and indeed celebrate this
responsibility.[24]

Earthly rule is a kind of sacrament. Dangerous to say; more
dangerous to ignore. Sacraments can be abused and turned into
sympathetic magic, an attempt to tap into God's power and life
without paying the price of obedient loyalty. That is what protestants
and rationalists have always objected to. But abuse does not destroy
the proper use. Proper sacraments – action, drama, symbol and ritual
on the one hand, words and prayers which tell God's story and invoke

---

[23] See particularly Oliver O'Donovan, *The Desire of the Nations* (Cambridge:
CUP, 1996); Oliver O'Donovan and Joan Lockwood O'Donovan, *From Irenaeus to
Grotius: A Sourcebook in Christian Political Thought* (Grand Rapids: Eerdmans,
1999).

[24] In what follows I am indebted (not without some disagreements) to Ian
Bradley's striking new book, *God Save the Queen: The Spiritual Dimension of
Monarchy* (London: Darton, Longman and Todd, 2002).

his presence and power on the other – are neither magical nor empty. Monarchy, like all sacraments, needs to be held within a strong theology of the ascended Jesus, Lord and King of the whole world, the one who has all authority.

All human power-systems are subject to Christian critique. All power can become idolatrous. Every knee shall bow at Jesus' name, and we must never tire of saying so. But there is another side to the story. Today's cheap-and-chattering republicanism owes nothing to the Christian critique of human power, and everything to the sneer of the cynic, noting the price of everything but ignoring its value. Monarchy at its best is a symbolic reminder that the power-games of this world do not stand alone, but in a curious and many-sided relation to a transfiguring love and power which exists in a different dimension. In a constitution like that of Great Britain, monarchy is meant to be an angled mirror in which we see around the dark corner to that other dimension of reality, and realize the provisionality of all earthly power. Woe betide a monarchy that merely mirrors a society back to itself, or that becomes an idol instead of a mirror. The monarchy we have had for the last 50 years, however, has done its best to avoid those dangers, and to reflect and embody the self-giving love which calls mere power to account. Let us not be naive. But let us be appropriately cynical about cynicism itself.

What about the constitutional questions we face today? We are in danger of doing to our national institutions what developers in the 1960s did with our ancient buildings. They tore down wonderful structures that had survived centuries of fire, flood and bombs, and they put up concrete and glass monstrosities, reflecting the soul-less secularism that created them. We now have agencies to stop that kind of thing; but our human institutions have no protection against the same unwelcome attention. Of course traditions and institutions must develop. But to tear them down because 'we live in the modern world' or because they are deemed inappropriate 'in this day and age' is to capitulate to an outworn ideology. There is nothing inevitable about a 'progress' towards flat secularist republics. Do we really want a French-style, or American-style, Presidency? Why do so many of our friends and neighbours envy us?

A Swiss doctor once said, 'British doctors don't know what tonsils are for, so they take them out; I don't know what tonsils are for, so I leave them in.' I think we *do* know, or are perhaps starting to rediscover, what monarchy is for. Monarchy is a reminder that the justice and mercy which rulers must practise are not their possession, but come from elsewhere; they are part of the God-given created order. Nations and states that have shed symbols which speak of responsibility to God have often become totalitarian. Of course, republics too can have such symbols. The United States maintains several, despite its official separation of church and state.

I am not suggesting that the present form of the British monarchy is necessarily ideal for the next century and beyond. That is an open question. But it is hard to deny, on Christian premises, that it is vital for the health of a nation and society to have such symbols, and the accompanying rituals with, yes, all their sacramental overtones. Since we have such a symbol, let us not be so foolish as to throw it away, especially when we have nothing else in mind to replace it. Before you cut down an oak tree without knowing what to plant in its place, ask yourself what you are about to lose, and whether you could ever get it back. Before you throw away real royalty, and turn our living heritage into a theme park of themselves, ask yourself if you would choose the obvious alternatives. Grey politicians standing for one last election; glitzy media stars improvising their own soap operas – neither can compete with what we already have. The stability and morale of Britain and many parts of the world (we should not underestimate the importance of the Commonwealth, or the extent to which it is held together by personal allegiance to the Crown) may be at stake.

What then about the interlinking of church, state and crown? The word 'establishment', granted, is a millstone around our necks. It has heavy and negative overtones. But the reality is very different. Away from the sneering world of the journalists, out in the country where it counts, the Church of England is still looked to by all kinds of people, from Lords Lieutenant to town councillors to groups of gypsies, not only to preach the gospel and minister the sacraments, but to be an honest broker, to hold the ring, to provide stability, focus and hope. Some sneer at 'implicit religion' and the inarticulate faith which, for instance, turns up at an Advent Carol Service but can't say why. I don't sneer at it; I want to work with it and nurture it, to take every spark of faith and help it, in its own time, to become a flame. Establishment means, among other things, that the church is there for everybody. Of course that sometimes means that nobody bothers, it also means that much of the society regards the church as its own. To cut the link, to insist that the church is only there for the fully paid up members, would be to send a signal to the rest of our world that we were pulling up the drawbridge, that we were no longer there for them.

Arguments for disestablishment regularly make points which cancel one another out. Establishment, say some, means a powerful church; the gospel is about weakness, not power; therefore Establishment must go. Establishment, say others, means the church is ruled by the state; the gospel is about the powerful rule of Jesus Christ; therefore we should not abandon Establishment. You can't have it both ways. Either we are dangerously powerful or we are dangerously weak. The truth, as usual, is more complex.

The main motive for disestablishment, in the press and elsewhere, is the old secularist agenda. Many are offended that the Enlightenment has not had its way with every area of society. When people argue that we live in a religiously plural society, they usually don't want to take those religions seriously; they are just repeating another bit of Enlightenment rhetoric, that there are so many religions that they are all equally irrelevant. In fact, though of course non-Christian faiths must be taken seriously, they still only represent a tiny minority of people in this country.[25] The evidence suggests that many Jewish and Muslim leaders communities are happier to have Christianity as the established religion than to live in a secularized state. The Jews in particular know what that might mean.[26]

There are, of course, different models of Establishment. The Scottish one is not the same as the English; we might profitably explore the differences.[27] I assume, as well, that Establishment ought to find ways of including, at whatever level, the other Christian churches – though I regard as disingenous the anti-Establishment polemic from some Roman Catholic journalists, who conveniently forget the 'concordat' arrangements that still obtain, officially or unofficially, in many Roman Catholic countries.[28] As we move towards increased mutual understanding, co-operation and sharing of a common life, I would hope that more flexibility might emerge on the axis between ecumenism and Establishment.

---

[25] Since I wrote the first draft of this chapter, the census figures for 2001 were published, showing that a remarkable 71.7% of the UK consider themselves in some sense Christian. The next figure down is 2.7% (Muslims).

[26] It is often said that a future coronation might be a 'multi-faith' event. But it is by no means clear whether what the Christian church has understood to be the meaning of coronation (including, for example, anointing) over the last thousand and more years would be something that any of the 'other faiths' would want to endorse. If it means that the religious and spiritual significance of the coronation would be reduced to having various religious bodies all saying prayers in their own way and to their own deities, this would simply be a late victory for the Enlightenment's downgrading of all religions to 'what people do with their solitude', and would not honour either the other religions themselves or Christianity. On the spiritual significance of coronation see Bradley, *God Save the Queen*, ch. 4.

[27] In Scotland, the monarch is not 'supreme head of the church'.

[28] The classic ones being in France under Napoleon (1801) and in Italy (the 'Lateran Treaty') of 1929. Both were, of course, subsequently modified, but *de facto* arrangements still obtain. The question of the Act of Succession, which is endlessly raised at this point in the discussion, is more complex than it seems. Would the Roman Catholic church be prepared to give up its insistence that children of mixed marriages be brought up as Roman Catholics.

The Establishment may well develop, then, but I see no reason to dismantle it. The negative signals sent by disestablishment would be profound, and unhelpful to both church and world. Do we really want the major turning-points in our national life to be conducted without prayer, and solemn seeking of God's blessing? Do we want leaders and rulers who will pledge themselves, not to ideals of justice and mercy which come ultimately from God, but simply to whatever the people may want? It is obviously not of the essence of the church that it should be established. The early church wasn't, and most churches are not today. But I believe it is of the *bene esse* of the church in England that it should continue to be established, while allowing for flexibility and development. Let us not capitulate to the tired, flatland world of secularism and modernism. Let us go on, learning from past mistakes but also building on existing strengths, confident that our God has not led us up a blind alley these last thousand and more years, but that the gospel of his kingdom can and will guide and transform our national life as well as our personal lives for generations to come.

Chapter 13

Theology as Queen or Servant[1]

Duncan B. Forrester

In this paper I intend to argue that truth is essentially something done, lived, loved and enacted. Theology as a subject concerned with truth is involved in practice and practices. It is not primarily a theoretical discipline. Relevant here is Kierkegaard's statement that 'It is impossible for a professor of theology to be saved!' Theology is to be lived rather than talked – or lectured – about in a detached way. Thus it follows that theology is not only or primarily concerned with ideas, or with the mind, but with the whole person, and thus with *formation*, with the orientation, the commitment, the practices, the relationships and the feelings of the whole person in community. And I want also to suggest that theology should not be ashamed to renounce academic or other status and seek what service (or *ministry*) it might offer to the church and to the world both directly (for theology is a form of ministry), and through its role in formation and dialogue with other forms of ministry. All of this relates to themes that pervade Wesley Carr's distinguished contribution to theology, and particularly practical theology, and to the understanding of ministry. I am thinking here especially of Wesley's books *The Priest-like Task* (1985), *Brief Encounters: Pastoral Ministry through the Occasional Offices* (1985), *Ministry and the Media* – (1990), and especially his *The Pastor as Theologian: The Integration of Pastoral Ministry, Theology and Discipleship* (1989). This paper is largely a contribution to the debate about theology and ministry that Wesley has so ably opened up.

Theology as the queen of the sciences

Christian theology has, of course, origins that go back to the very beginnings of the Christian faith. Prior to the Middle Ages, theology was studied by scholars and monks, mainly in monastic settings. It was

---

[1] Some parts of this paper are developed from material in my *Truthful Action: Explorations in Practical Theology.* Edinburgh: T. & T. Clark, 2000.

reflection on faith, in Anselm's terms *'fides quaerens intellectum'*, faith seeking to understand itself, the critical exploration, appropriation and commending of faith. The ultimate goal of this study was the beatific vision, fellowship with God, wisdom, and at a more mundane level, the equipping of clergy and the people of God for their tasks. In as far as faith involved discipleship, and was an orientation, a formation, of the whole person rather than a simple act of intellectual assent, theology was understood as a practical matter. Contemplation could not be separated from action, particularly pastoral action, any more than faith could be separated from the Church, the community of faith.

In the Middle Ages universities developed in Europe and provided a new setting for the study of theology. Dr Gillian Evans has traced the medieval development of theology as it became an academic discipline. In the twelfth century theology as *'speculatio'* was understood as a 'gazing on the divine' which was seen as 'essentially a devotional exercise'. By the late twelfth century, Dr Evans argues, speculative theology had been stripped of all such elements: it became 'an activity of the mind in which religious emotion had little or no place ... the divorce of contemplation from abstract thought of an academic kind was complete'.[2]

Throughout the Middle Ages, theology was generally regarded as the *Queen of the Sciences* in universities which were, almost without exception, ecclesiastical foundations, whose *primary* task was the training of clergy and the critical formulation of church teaching. All academic studies clustered around theology like bees in a swarm around their queen. Non-theological subjects were understood as servants of theology, or preludes to theology, and they sought to find a theological justification, grounding or rationale for their specific studies. University subjects and university personnel were arranged hierarchically, with theology as the crown. Questioning this ordering was often seen as subversive of the whole structure not only of the academy, but of the ecclesiastical and social body as well.

Was theology as such, perched on the peak of the academic mountain, a theoretical science in the Aristotelian sense, or a practical science – again as understood by Aristotle? This question and how it was answered related directly to the assessment of the value of action. Was the *summum bonum* the contemplation of God simpliciter or were action, practice, a settled life-style, a lived-out holiness essential components of a true relationship to God? After all, did not John's

---

[2] Gillian Evans, *Old Arts and New Theology: The Beginnings of Theology as an Academic Discipline.* Oxford: OUP, 1980, p. 93.

gospel declare that 'Those who live by the truth come to the light so that it may be clearly seen that God is in all that they do'? (John 3:21 REB) Thomas Aquinas endeavoured to demonstrate that theology was a theoretical science, a *sophia*, in Aristotle's sense because it is an end in itself, whereas practical knowledge is directed towards other ends and other goods.[3] Other medieval theologians, such as Duns Scotus and the nominalists who were so influential on the protestant reformers, taught that theology was a form of *phronesis*, a practical wisdom, close to Aristotle's understanding of that term. Scotus taught that theology was concerned with God as the supreme good and therefore the ultimate goal of human life. Objective knowledge of this goal was necessary for believers engaged in the way of discipleship, to aid them in moving towards their true goal and destiny.[4] The protestant reformers tended to follow in this Scotist tradition, regarding theology as a practical science with central pastoral and existential elements.

In a medieval Christian university the Christian faith was the ultimate norm, and all other subjects were expected to serve and find their *telos* in theology. Theology and indeed the university as a whole were involved in and tied to the magisterium, or teaching office of the Church. The medieval university was expected to do far more than clarify and transmit the teaching of the Pope and the bishops; it was along with Pope and bishops an integral part of the magisterium, expected to examine, update and articulate the tradition and the deposit of faith. But from the beginning there was an ambiguity at the heart of the medieval university. At its best, it held that education was for the whole person, body and soul, for time and for eternity, that community mattered, that Christian truth must be expressed in loving practice. At its worst, it encouraged an arrogant thought police which stultified the enquiries and the teaching of the whole university.

Post-Reformation and Enlightenment universities continued to have theology at the heart of their enterprise, ruling as Queen. And they saw the task of theology in the university as essentially a practical one, particularly concerned with the education of ministers for the service of the church. The theological faculty now stood alongside medicine and law as one of the three 'higher faculties', with explicit remits for the formation of professionals, a kind of triple crown for the early modern university. The university as such was concerned with struggling with truth and also educating for good practice. The university understood its concern with theory as directed towards the goal of excellence in practice.

---

[3] W. Pannenberg, *Theology and the Philosophy of Science*. London: Darton, Longman and Todd, 1986, p. 232.
[4] W. Pannenberg, op. cit., pp. 232–3.

In Scotland, for instance, there developed an Enlightenment tradition which insisted that at the heart of the academic enterprise there was a queen, now understood not as 'pure' theology, or theology understood as the education and formation of priests and church leaders but as a theologically informed moral philosophy which had as one of its central concerns the education of good practitioners, the promotion of professional excellence. This tradition continued in Edinburgh at least up to John Macmurray's tenure of the chair of moral philosophy in the 1940s and 1950s, and was for many years influential in American colleges and universities which shared the Scots intellectual tradition, where characteristically the President would give lectures on moral philosophy to the whole student body.

Over a number of centuries the idea of theology as the 'Queen of the Sciences' was gradually eroded, except in the more conservative Christian lands, where it survived through blood transfusions as part of the struggle against modernity, liberalism and modernism. The modern university was either a fragmented, pluralist republic without an acknowledged queen, or there was ongoing conflict as to which discipline or disciplines could claim the crown. A recent attempt by John Milbank to reaffirm for today theology's queenly role in the modern university is thoroughly quixotic.[5] In typically swashbuckling style, Milbank declares that the secular atheist or agnostic suspicion of theology must be challenged:

> And the grounds for this challenge would be simply that they have got every thing the wrong way round. They claim that theology, alone among purported academic disciplines is really 'about nothing'. But theological reason, if it is true to itself, replies to this with a counter-claim – all other disciplines, which claim to be about objects regardless of whether these objects are related to God, are, just for this reason about nothing whatsoever.[6]

Milbank advocates 'the most extreme mode of counterattack', arguing that unless other disciplines are ordered to theology they are 'objectively and demonstrably null and void, altogether lacking in truth'.[7] I find it hard to take this sort of thing seriously. It is just not an option today for theology – or indeed for any other discipline in the modern university. And that is surely just as well, since the 'Queen of

---

[5] John Milbank, 'The Conflict of the Faculties: Theology and the Economy of the Sciences', in Mark Thiessen Nation and Samuel Wells, eds., *Faithfulness and Fortitude: In Conversation with the Theological Ethics of Stanley Hauerwas*. Edinburgh: T. & T. Clark, 2000, pp. 39–57.

[6] Milbank, op. cit., p. 41.

[7] Milbank, op. cit., p. 47.

the Sciences' model precludes in various ways theology fulfilling a serious servant role, or intellectual ministry, in the diverse, pluralistic modern university.

Practical theology as the crown of university study

The foundation of the University of Berlin in 1809 was a notable turning point in the development of the modern university. Berlin became a model for other German universities, and increasingly for higher education outside Germany on both sides of the Atlantic as well. In this tradition the university is properly concerned only with *Wissenschaft*, a scientific commitment to relate everything to universal rational principles. Theology now had to justify its place in such a university. And the scholar who did this most effectively was the eminent theologian, Schleiermacher.

Theology, Schleiermacher taught, is both scientific and has a practical task which should be pursued within the university – the preparation of leadership for the Church. In justifying the place of theology within the university, Schleiermacher suggested that there were three levels in theological study. The foundation was philosophical theology, which established and examined the first principles of Christian theology, on the unquestioned assumption that Protestant Christianity was the crown and epitome of all religion, and religion was a universally human phenomenon, in which people encounter the transcendent. Then comes historical theology, which examines the development of the Christian tradition. Finally, as the 'crown of theological study' comes practical theology, which is the 'technique' of church leadership. But Schleiermacher's allocation of the 'crown' to practical theology does not indicate special honour to that discipline, let alone an attempt to reassert that theology and particularly practical theology is the queen of the sciences. It is simply that practical theology is the last stage in the education of clergy in the university, before they go out to their parishes.

Ministers and church leaders should, according to Schleiermacher, combine a 'scientific spirit' and what is called 'ecclesial interest', or a commitment to serve the Church. Those who are most successful in combining ecclesial interest and the scientific spirit are aptly to be called 'princes of the Church'! The scientific and the practical endeavours interpenetrate, for '[e]ven the especially scientific work of the theologian must aim at promoting the Church's welfare and is thereby clerical; and even those technical prescriptions for essentially clerical activities belong within the circle of the theological sciences.'[8] Theology, for Schleiermacher, is a function of church leaders, not of the whole people of God. Accordingly, it is equipment for clergy, just as medicine or jurisprudence are the studies necessary for physicians or lawyers.

Schleiermacher tends to take as a given the existing structures of Church and ministry; it is not, as he sees it, part of the responsibility of theology, or indeed of practical theology, to criticize, change or reform them – a strange position for an heir of a Reformation, which included the reformation of the universities high among its priorities, to take! Schleiermacher's thought thus becomes 'a blueprint for the clerical church, and almost its apologia'.[9] His is not a 'church theology' with a built-in critique of the visible Church, but a clerical theology which assumes that within the Church the non-clerical members will be in a dependent capacity, like patients seeking healing from their physician, or clients asking the help of their lawyers.

Despite problems such as we have outlined above, Schleiermacher's vindication of the right of theology to a place in the modern academy, and his account of the internal organization of theology still have influence today, although many people believe he produced a not wholly satisfactory resolution of the still continuing tensions between what he calls 'ecclesial interest' and the 'scientific spirit'. If ecclesial interest is abandoned, academic theology loses its roots in a particular community of faith in 'the real world', and with that it often abandons a concern with relevance. If the scientific spirit is set aside, theology becomes the in-house private discourse of small and declining Christian communities without sustainable claims to possessing public truth with something to offer in the public square. A balance or tension needs to be maintained for the sake of responsible and relevant theology, to save the church from becoming a ghetto incapable of communicating with the culture and society in which it is embedded, and for a healthy and lively university which does not dodge or marginalize fundamental issues which are admittedly difficult to handle and almost impossible to resolve consensually. Perhaps the task of theology in the university today is to be like the grit in the oyster around which the pearl may gather, by asking in the academy the hard unfashionable questions which are often a productive irritant, by affirming the continuing significance of the tradition of faith, and by reminding the intellectual power structures of their responsibility for the weak and the poor.

---

[8] F. Schleiermacher, *Brief Outline of Theology as a Field of Study*. Trans. T.T. Tice. Lewiston, NJ: E. Mellen Press, 1990, p. 8.

[9] W. Jetter, cited in Pannenberg, op. cit., p. 429.

Maps of learning and their dangers

Maps are important, for without them we risk wandering and getting lost. But maps can distort or misrepresent reality, and confuse the pilgrim on her journey. No projection is a perfect reflection of reality, and all projections have a heartland and a periphery. But it is becoming increasingly difficult, if not impossible, to prepare an acceptable map of the postmodern academy. The postmodern university and even (with appropriate qualifications) most seminaries, reflect and reinforce the increasing specialization and fragmentation of modern life. The tidy ordering of the medieval university, with theology as the 'Queen of the Sciences' at its heart, is unrecoverable, but we are faced today with various and conflicting endeavours to give some kind of coherence to the academic enterprise as a whole. The way the definition and relations of disciplines are arranged, the way a university is structured, express implicitly or explicitly an ideology, a world-view, an overarching interpretation, a map.

In pre-modern days the general effort was to locate specific studies within a biblical grand narrative; in modern times the Bible, religion, the Christian faith, theology and ethics are to be fitted into the project of an 'encyclopaedia', ordering all knowledge in terms of some more or less secular principle. But the postmodern university is a collection of fragments struggling for some kind of coherence and community in the search for wisdom and understanding. Alasdair MacIntyre argues that the Ninth Edition of the *Encyclopaedia Britannica* (1873 ff.) pointed towards a time when '[t]he Encyclopaedia would have displaced the Bible as the canonical book, or set of books of the culture'.[10] Accordingly, the Bible (and all thinking rooted in the Bible), 'is judged by the standards of . . . modernity in a way which effectively prevents it from standing in judgement upon that modernity'.[11] And the post-modern university, having given up the map-making project, teeters on the edge of disintegration.

It is here, I think, that central problems lie: is it possible for theology to be *in* the university, but not domesticated or tamed by the university? How can theology maintain a distinctive critical distance from the increasingly secular and confused values of the university so that it can play a specific sort of constructive role? Is a dual responsibility, to church and to the academy, any longer viable? What service can theology render in a fragmented and confused academy?

---

[10] A. MacIntyre, *Three Rival Versions of Moral Enquiry*. Notre Dame: University of Notre Dame Press, 1990, p. 19.

[11] MacIntyre, op. cit., p. 179.

MacIntyre suggests that in the nineteenth century there was a mounting tendency to ascribe priority to morality and to ethics or moral philosophy, on the assumption that there was a 'social agreement, especially in practice, on the importance and the content of morality', which none the less 'co-existed with large intellectual disagreements concerning the nature of its intellectual justification', although almost everyone concurred in the belief that such justification was in principle possible.[12] General consensus about the nature of right conduct, and a bracing degree of difference about the philosophical foundations of morality were believed to give coherence to the academic enterprise.

The position of theology which takes practice seriously in the academy has been much challenged in recent times. MacIntyre is surely right in suggesting that moral and theological truths became increasingly regarded as belonging in the realm of privatized and arbitrary belief: 'Questions of truth in morality and theology – as distinct from the psychological or social scientific study of morals and religion – have become matter for private allegiances, not to be accorded ... formal badges of academic recognition'.[13] Ethics has accordingly been moved to the periphery of academic life, and has increasingly nervously stressed its autonomy, from theology in particular. This has left an ominous vacuum at the heart of the academy. As a consequence academics and professionals interested in issues of public policy or social responsibility have sometimes begun to look with expectation towards theology and in particular theological ethics for help and a sense of direction. We are therefore at a time of particular opportunity for a theology which is not afraid to attend to, to interpenetrate, and to inform other disciplines. If MacIntyre and others are right in suggesting that the post-encyclopaedic university in a postmodern world is in a crisis in which it is confronted on all sides with questions it lacks the resources to answer, perhaps an ethically informed theology may be able to suggest some possible ways forward towards a greater relevance and a better sense of being a community of shared purpose.[14]

I believe that, at least in relation to his encyclopaedia project, Schleiermacher's position is irretrievable. We do not today have agreed maps of the academy, and I do not believe that theologians should spend their time and energy asserting a claim to a place in the heart of a non-existent atlas. After all, if the university throws us out, we can operate quite happily in the Church – only, as I shall argue, the

---

[12] MacIntyre, op. cit., p. 26.
[13] MacIntyre, op. cit., p. 217.
[14] MacIntyre, op. cit., p. 271.

university would be the poorer for it. And an even more pressing problem today is perhaps the increasing anti-intellectualism of many branches of the Church, and their unwillingness to take theology seriously. In the fragmented postmodern university much energy is wasted on boundary maintenance between disciplines, with sometimes absurd consequences. But theology should have a central concern for community, and for communication across boundaries and through barriers.

Let me give an example of the problems we face today. A leading British social scientist concerned particularly with issues of public policy, Professor David Donnison, despairs of the capacity of the modern university to provide the wisdom that society requires. At the root this is because in a culture where most people believe that God is dead, moral judgements have become regarded as 'little more than approving or disapproving noises – expressions of personal preference or taste, much like the words we use when choosing between vanilla and strawberry ice-cream'.[15] Since there is no academically acceptable way of resolving conflicts about moral judgements, the commonest strategy is to side-step the issue. Academics are concerned with weighing evidence and assessing logical coherence; because morals are now regarded as arbitrary matters of taste and prejudice they are pushed to the margins and deprived of intellectual dignity:

> As for moral dispute – that has been banished from the lecture rooms altogether, for it leads people to say things like, 'You ought to be ashamed of yourself', and this is not the kind of things you say in a seminar. To make the distinction unmistakably clear, politicians and priests are brought into such academies from time to time to conduct moral debate; but on a one-off basis, usually at the invitation of student societies, speaking from a different kind of platform – thereby exposing to everybody the unscientific status of their pronouncements.[16]

This, Donnison concludes, leads to a narrowing and distortion of academic life, which is in many cases condemned to irrelevance or irresponsibility.

In such a situation the place of theology in the university assumes a fresh importance. Getting this relationship right may be significant for the academic enterprise as a whole, and helpful to a range of other disciplines. So I would affirm that *practical* theology exists in the academy to affirm that all theology is practical, just as biblical studies reminds theology of the centrality of scripture, and systematic

---

[15] David Donnison, *A Radical Agenda*. London: Rivers Oram Press, 1991, p. 42.
[16] Donnison, op. cit., p. 44.

theology points to doctrine as an unavoidable element in the theological enterprise.[17] And if theology is a practical science at the service of God and the human community, in the Aristotelian or any other sense, it cannot be detached from ethics. For theology to be a practical science in the classical sense first developed by Aristotle it must be a form of *phronesis*, which is 'a reasoned and true state of capacity – to act with regard to human goods'.[18] The person of practical wisdom is able to deliberate well on what is good for the individual, and on the good life in general. And a decent society desperately needs people of practical wisdom.

If *theology* is wisdom or knowledge orientated towards action and accordingly inevitably pervaded with the ethical, it is important also to affirm that it is *theology*. If theological discourse is primarily about *religion*, it is always in danger of dissolving into study of the context, and becoming a kind of sociology or psychology of religion. But if theology is discourse about God in the presence of God, and discourse with God, we are engaged with something *totaliter aliter*. We cannot talk about God or talk to God while setting aside, even temporarily, the question of practice: What is God calling us to do? How should we respond? We are also involved simultaneously in doxology.

If Alasdair MacIntyre is right – and I think he is – that the modern university is fragmented and lacks the resources to deal with the questions which confront it, partly because it has become incapable of coherent and rigorous moral enquiry, is it possible that a theology effectively related to other disciplines might have a major contribution to offer towards a renewal of academic integrity and responsibility? For this approach the ugly ditch between 'is' and 'ought', fact and value, has been bridged, in however tentative a way, in order to enable reflective and effective practice. Could this be part of our gift to the whole academy, in its postmodern disarray and uncertainty?

Theology and multiple practices

A theology of practice and of practices must first ask questions about God's activity, and consider other agents' practice within the horizon of the divine practice and as actually or potentially participating in God's activity. This proper theological interest in God's activity in history and in nature implies that at the level of human agency practical theology

---

[17] On this see especially W. Pannenberg, *Theology and the Philosophy of Science*. London, Darton: Longman and Todd, 1976, pp. 231–41 and 423–40.

[18] Aristotle, *Nicomathean Ethics*, vi.5, p. 43 of D. Ross edition, Oxford, 1954.

cannot be concerned exclusively with the activity of Christians or of the Church. It applies a theological critique and analysis to the practice of people as such, and people-in-relationship rather than artificially isolated individuals who are assumed to be free from all social ties and forms of conditioning. And because the divine practice of God in Jesus Christ has at its heart passion, with its dual sense of suffering and intense emotion, a Christian understanding of practice must concern itself not only with activity but with feeling and with suffering as well. But with these provisos, practical theology is also concerned with the practice of Christians. At this level it might take as its motto the saying of Kierkegaard that the real problem is not so much what Christianity means as how to be a Christian, adding that in striving to be and act as a Christian one learns what Christianity is.

The specific danger here is that of regarding the Christian as agent in unduly individualistic terms, whether those of pietistic individualism where there is little reference to the Christian fellowship, or of possessive individualism in which the individual is seen as owning herself and defined in terms of what she can gain and what she possesses, in terms of things rather than social relationships. Christian practice, Christian being and Christian relationships must always be understood in the context of the Church and of the Reign of God, and cannot therefore be understood in narrowly individualistic terms.

Practical theology also studies 'practices', or ordered ways of arranging behaviour, like the professional practices of medicine or the law, or indeed of ministry (although there are a number of problems in describing ministry as a profession). Here practice is the behaviour of a class of professionals in accordance with a professional code, and under the discipline of 'the profession'. We are reminded that education is not simply the imparting of knowledge and skills; it is also, and always has been *formation*. The ends or goals of a profession are generally agreed, if in rather general terms: physicians' practice is to maintain or restore health; lawyers are concerned with the proper observance of the law. Each 'practice' has inherent and specific notions of excellence, and all forms of professional practice are to be understood as forms of service, or forms of ministry. Professionals jealously guard their practices against unqualified interlopers. I cannot set up as a lawyer or a surgeon even if I want to, because I have not been trained, accepted and initiated into the professional guild, the craft, or what used sometimes in the past to be called the 'mystery'.

This last term is a useful reminder that there is still a mystique surrounding the practice of professionals. The profession safeguards its practice from others, and rarely allows its proceedings to be scrutinized by outsiders. It prefers to regulate its practices and discipline its members itself. Hence suspicious outsiders constantly echo George Bernard Shaw's epigram: 'All professions are conspiracies against the laity.' And with good cause, for professions can indeed act in a selfish way; practice can be abused for the benefit of the practitioner at the expense of the client or patient.

Patterns of practice with their own in-built standards of excellence are useful for the community as a whole, although sometimes professionals defend their own interests against the common good. Practice is not an isolated matter; it takes place in fellowships, in solidarity with others. And any practice has in-built norms and excellences of various sorts. A dentist, for example, must know the right way to fill a cavity, and how to extract a tooth, and so on. Behind this technical skill there lies knowledge of more than technique – of anatomy, and physiology, and so forth. But the dentist must also obey norms of conduct towards his patients; he must have a precise kind of personal integrity as part of his professional identity. If he is incompetent, or makes sexual advances to patients, he is disciplined, struck off the register and not allowed to practise. A practice has thus built into it standards of excellence, as Alasdair MacIntyre argues in *After Virtue*:

> By a 'practice' I ... mean any coherent and complex form of socially established cooperative human activity through which goods internal to that form of activity are realised in the course of trying to achieve those standards of excellence which are appropriate to, and partially definitive of, that form of activity, with the result that human powers to achieve excellence, and human conceptions of the ends and good involved are systematically extended.[19]

Forming ministers at the frontier

A concern for ministry is surely a necessary and significant part of the agenda of theology, but it is far from being the whole, or the heart, of that agenda. The understanding of ministry should be broad, ecumenical and theologically well-grounded. Nothing is worse than the acceptance of a narrow and outdated understanding of ministry as a pattern of practice to which students are to be taught to conform. But practical theology still has a concern for critical and responsible professional formation. It is right that the ordained ministry should have professional standards of responsibility and skills that are fully professional, but if the ministry regards itself as 'a profession' *simpliciter* it relegates the other members of the church, who share in

---

[19] Alasdair MacIntyre, *After Virtue*. London: Duckworth, 1981, p. 175.

the royal priesthood of the whole people of God, to the status of *clients* or *patients*, recipients of ministry rather than participants in ministry.

Where should the formation and education of ministers take place? The obvious choice is between the *seminary* and the *university*. The seminary characteristically is residential and draws its students from one denomination, church or tradition. Its strengths are that the life of the seminary can effectively be structured around corporate and individual worship; spirituality can be given as much attention as intellectual development; and clergy can be prepared to be faithful servants of the church or denomination. The weaknesses of the seminary include the danger that it may become a spiritual hothouse, encouraging types of spirituality which cannot be sustained in the outside world; that intellectual standards may be low; that the questions and problems of the 'outside world' may be more or less effectively excluded; and that the students and staff may be too similar in theology, personality and understanding of church and ministry. Seminaries are often jewels in the crown of one denomination and effectively obstruct friendship with those of other traditions and the broader ecumenical understanding that friendship makes possible.

In the university, on the other hand, the probing questions, doubts and uncertainties of an increasingly secularized society cannot be avoided. Friendships with other students of varying or no faith are easily cultivated. Vocations are tested more rigorously, and if they survive, the ordinands are more richly equipped for ministry amidst the realities of today's world. The theology that is taught has had to respond to the probing from other faculties, and may as a result become either more resilient and faithful, or more cautious, inoffensive and banal. In the university one learns to communicate the gospel to modern women and men where they are, and to understand the complex situation in which we find ourselves. There are, however, huge problems in sustaining in the modern university a theology which in any sense understands itself as doxology, theology done in the presence of God, and to the glory of God. But that kind of theology *is* possible in the modern secular university, and when it is realized, it is the best intellectual and spiritual formation for ministers and for disciples who will live and work in a radically plural and secular society, fulfilling their varying vocations and ministries. The secular pluralistic university, with all its problems, is surely the best place in which to develop understandings of servant and prophetic ministry relevant to tomorrow's world.

Joint ecumenical formation is of the greatest importance for the future of the Church of Jesus Christ. The friendships and trust which it enables between students of various denominations and traditions are capable of transforming the ecumenical situation 'on the ground'. This can be organized in ecumenical seminaries, or in consortia of denominational seminaries. But it is particularly good if these are deeply immersed in the ongoing intellectual life of a university, and closely involved in local congregations, particularly in areas of multiple deprivation where the challenges and opportunities for the Church are obvious and manifold.

At the theological quarry

What kind of service might theology render amid the confusions and uncertainties of today's world? I suggest in conclusion a kind of parable: serious theological work today is or ought to be rather like working in a quarry, and quite specifically the kind of quarry which one finds in India, where men and women, and quite young children too, in the heat of the day hack away at the rock-face with simple implements, exposing themselves to danger, and committing to the task all their reserves of energy, intelligence, determination and strength.

I am not thinking of the modern fully mechanized quarry, where everything is done at a safe distance, at the flick of a switch, or the pressing of a button, where danger and sweat are minimized, and people do not themselves engage directly with the rock-face. That might be an image of the modern academic assumption that we are most likely to encounter truth in detachment, that objectivity is all, that commitment is a distraction, or leads to distortion of the truth.

No, I am thinking of the kind of quarry that we find in India and elsewhere, where:

- The work is hard, demanding, exhausting.
- The work does not bring high status or tangible rewards, indeed the very opposite. You work because of an inner compulsion, vocation or constraint.
- Most of the work is invisible, rarely noticed or applauded. People in their cars pass by the quarry with hardly a glance as they go about their business.
- The work is sometimes dangerous, full of unexpected hazards.
- Co-operation is essential. No one can work the quarry alone; one must work as a team with others.
- The workers in the quarry seldom see the end-product. The stones they quarry are normally used and fashioned far away.

The cliff-face in our theological quarry is the Bible and the rich resources and insights into truth which are to be found in the Christian tradition, and the other world faiths and ideologies that have interacted with the Christian tradition.

If we are faithful in our quarry work in the heat and sweat of the day, we produce:

- Rough blocks of stone, which others may fashion and shape and use for building strong and lasting edifices – homes and hospitals, schools and churches, places of welcome and of service, places of stability, constancy and love, built of living stones.
- And from our quarry we also produce the small rubble stones called *road metal*, used for making firm, straight paths on which God's people may move forward.
- Occasionally we find a gemstone in our quarry, which delights by its beauty, sparkling in the sun.
- Sometimes we come across a crystal, acting like a lens, helping us to see more clearly into the depth of things, to glimpse another world, to find a vision that others may share.
- And then, as in every quarry, there's loads of grit and dust, apparently useless, untidy, pervasive, irritating the eyes and coating the nose and throat. But if perchance a piece of that grit might ultimately find its way into an oyster, it gathers around the irritant layer upon layer until the grit becomes the nucleus of a pearl. The grit stands for the awkward, probing, irritating questions that a lively theology should address to church, society and culture.

So, back to the quarry, to obtain the fragments that serve as road metal, the living stones that make our homes and churches, the grit that provokes the oyster to produce pearls, the crystals that concentrate light into visions, the fragments that generate utopias, that build up jigsaws of meaning, and that nourish the activity of truthfulness, love and justice which is the practice of God's Reign.

Is that kind of theology the true service of God and humankind today?

References

Carr, W., *The Priest-like Task*. London: SPCK, 1985.

Carr, W., *Brief Encounters: Pastoral Ministry through the Occasional Offices*. London: SPCK, 1985.

Carr, W., *Ministry and the Media*. London: SPCK, 1990.

Carr, W., *The Pastor as Theologian: The Integration of Pastoral Ministry, Theology and Discipleship*. London: SPCK, 1989.

Forrester, D.B., *Truthful Action: Explorations in Practical Theology*. Edinburgh: T. & T. Clark, 2000.

Pannenberg, W., *Theology and the Philosophy of Science*. London: Darton, Longman and Todd, 1986.

Schleiermacher, F. *Brief Outline of Theology as a Field of Study*. Trans. T.T. Tice. Lewiston, NJ: E. Mellen Press, 1990.

MacIntyre, A. *Three Rival Versions of Moral Enquiry*. Notre Dame: University of Notre Dame Press, 1990.

PART FOUR
RESPONSE

To all who have contributed to this book

from
its honoured recipient,
Wesley Carr
2003

An original thought had been that each essay would receive a response to be read not just in technical terms, but to give some illumination to the personal connection between ourselves. The publishers decided against this for good reason, but I still wanted to say something that was both personal and yet also gave something to each author. Old habits die hard!

I hope this may give each contributor a sense of where he or she stands in relation to others. It will also give a sense of the total background to those who operate inevitably in parts.

September 2003

Chapter 14

A Response

Wesley Carr

I imagine that I feel what a dinosaur felt at the end of its era. As I come to the end of my ministry in the Church of England, I look back upon almost 40 years of mostly enjoyment, of making many friends and of learning much. When I come to this collection I feel only humbled. It reminds me of how much time I have spent roaming in the margins between the church and other institutions rather than at the centre of the church's life. Here these worlds are represented by two distinguished psycho-analysts and psychiatrists (Drs Obholzer and Shapiro), one diocesan bishop (Wright), two suffragan bishops (Lowe and Redfern), two pastoral theologians (Professors Forrester and Gill), two parish priests (Emma Percy and Christopher Moody) and two involved in research and training (Drs Ward and Percy), and one teacher from a theological College (Angela Tilby).

This chapter is by way of thanks. I have tried to respond to the overall picture that the authors present as it appears from my current position. The call for theological interpretation of the church's reality is not new. I attempted it several times, most notably in what I consider to be my best book, *The Pastor as Theologian*. There I used the group relations model as a basis for holding the complexity of our psychological aspects, so that neither the perspective of the individual nor the group dimension were surrendered to each other. Instead, they generated a useful model by which to bring together individual and group, society and religion. Just as Freud did not discover the unconscious but made it structurally investigable, so group relations studies do not provide any new information but they do suggest a coherent model for using what is sometimes felt to be disparate. And in terms of such studies as providing a basis for such interpretation, my experience with the Tavistock Institute and associated bodies was always a matter of practical concern, not just an interesting theoretical dilettanteism.

The primary task

One of the principal insights of that tradition in its approach to organizations is the concept of 'primary task'. Yet although essential, it is often misunderstood. This is because it directs immediate attention to the unconscious behaviour of the group or institution and offers itself as a heuristic tool for interpreting dynamic factors within an institution. Every group will have some sort of shared feeling, which makes them members of that particular group and not another team or gang. But there is another level of unconscious sharing, which gives a group a sense of task without which it would cease to exist: that is, its primary task. If an hypothesis about this can be developed, however strange it may sound, we have a tool with which to dismantle the complexity of an organization and restore it for renewed activity (Obholzer, Shapiro. Ward). What is more we can deal with any sort of body of human beings in the same fashion: it is therefore possible around the notion of primary task for an institution to find its unity.

Dependency

In the case of the Church of England, its primary task, even allowing for different contexts of ministry and church life, is in the area of dependence. I have often found, however, that this is a dangerous area, because people naturally associate dependence as a malign state by contrast with autonomy and cannot see the positive aspect to dependence which is essential to any faith, not least the Christian faith. Obholzer, for example, makes it almost an agreed composite statement of intent. Ward thinks of dependence as a malign state and consequently feels it has to be withstood. In conversation it is possible, for example, to draw a useful distinction between 'dependence' (the morally neutral first and last state of human existence) and 'dependency', which is the malign state in which the dependent individual surrenders his or her autonomy and responsibility. Might we be better to drop the word altogether? There are times when I think so. The problem is, however, that there is no other word to describe the dynamic to which this refers. I have tried to distinguish 'dependency' from 'dependence', but this cannot really be done in English. The subtlety is usable, but in American English the two words are so interchangeable with meaning that few would discern the subtlety. And both share the same derivative adjective – 'dependent'.

A model of ministry

Yet there is a reason for the struggle: the need for a coherent model of ministry by which to develop a strategy. Throughout my time of ministry there have been many enthusiasms in the Church of England for discerning and elaborating its distinctive ministry. Indeed, it is a sad reflection that there has been more discussion of ministries (deacons, NSM, MSE, LOM)[1] than outbuilding congregations and ministry to society. But one reason for this avoidance, is the difficulty of determining a model of ministry. The reason is that the models are usually drawn straight from theology for their insights, or from sociology or psychology, while the real question is of a model which works in all these. In my first book *The Priest-like Task*, I tried the consultancy model. It worked (I thought) quite well, but could not be grasped because people did not know what to make of the terminology in this context.[2] Sometimes a strategy is based upon a meaning in the New Testament, sometimes on a different reading of the New Testament and early church history; others on different eras of church history, and others on financial and managerial issues. It is incidentally, at this point of everyday understanding of and work at ministry, interesting to note the number of bishops who give pride of place to a photo of themselves with the Pope: I am unsure what this means!

The parochial system

There is still something fundamental in the Church of England's commitment to the parochial system. It now seems to some outdated, especially at a time of financial stringency and shortage of priests. There seems something of a dinosaur about the continuing argument for the notion of the parish. Stephen Lowe and Alastair Redfern, are two suffragan bishops, both of whom I respect as colleagues and friends, but about whose office I have doubts. I had a confirmatory vision at Rowan Williams' installation as Archbishop in Canterbury Cathedral. Stranded by a slight error on the wrong side of the nave at the beginning of the processions, four deans, including myself, tried to cross the nave of Canterbury Cathedral. It was like the M1 in the rush hour: there was no way of breaking through the processions of the

---

[1] NSM = Non Stipendiary Minister; MSE = Minister in Secular Employment; LOM = Local Ordained Ministry.

[2] In spite of Frances Ward's remark about poetry, I have found people appreciative of the couplet from Keats: The moving waters at their priestlike task 'of pure ablution round earth's human shores.

Archbishop's Council (why them?), diocesan bishops and then the longest of all – suffragan and assistant bishops, all of them fine men but those people in the system with whom the buck never stops. What sort of organization runs so top-heavy a structure at a time of such lean financial parameters? And what is more, considers such a role in many cases preparation to lead a diocese? Is it not the dinosaur with a large and ungainly body and a very small brain? Take some of the salient factors which have influenced the church and my ministry.

Both from inside and outside there has been major experience of change. Everyone is affected by the alterations in the Lord's Prayer, and priests in their celebration and movements have come through a series of changes from the Book of Common Prayer (for many the 1928 version) to Common Worship. Much time has been spent on the liturgy.[3] Like most churches Westminster Abbey is designed for more than one purpose: in this case it is for coronations and between such events we have to manage a liturgy in a rather curious space towards the front of the Quire. However, we are not alone in that and we have something through which we find many people can worship. But the prior question to ask is why has liturgy become so important? There has been the attention to detail in churches, but also a growth in the number of conferences and societies associated with liturgy and its study. Indeed, at times it appears that in the Church of England every so-called new thing has been justified by reference to the fourth century or earlier. But today there are two obvious points. First, the loss of the awesome link between the words of institution and the action, which Cranmer did so well, even if it is liturgically 'wrong'. It was one of the great literary and theological understandings of the Reformation. And in a visual society it again comes into its own. Notice by the way, how many priests now actually put some manual acts at that point. Secondly, the notion that the congregation is the celebrant and the president presides over the celebration by the congregation. I suppose it may possibly be the case, although it seems unlikely, but dynamically I could see no way in which any normal worshipper would ever feel this. Suddenly to start talking about the congregation being celebrant makes the faith a new demand.

I suppose it is this new sense of demand that I find difficult. Yet the experience of clergy and people at the time of the reformation must have been similar. One of my favourites from that period is Robert Parkyn, Vicar of Adwick-le-Street, near Doncaster. He kept a diary

---

[3] I was the new curate in Luton, six of us with Harold Frankham the incumbant. He was later Provost of Southwark. Pointing out that we needed the permission of the Ordinary, I received a simple response: 'I am the ordinary' – good in practice, if wrong in theory.

which emphasizes both change and conservative backlash in the liturgy in the sixteenth century, but after the seventeenth century coalescence into the Book of Common Prayer, apart from the ill-fated 1928 exercise, the prayer book has remained the key form of worship.[4] This is no argument for liturgical conservatism. But it is against liturgical fluttering before the immediate environs of the church. 'Parish' means local area, as defined geographically. But defined dynamically it is different. When training laity in parishes over many years, I used the technique of asking where people would be on Sunday and then where they would be on Monday. From the most mundane places people ran the world, and the notion of the parish as the seat of all ecclesiastical and religious operations is manifestly false. In other words, we need the notion of parish which is where among other things we worship: we also need a notion of parish, which gives our activity meaning.

Lay and ordained

This observation will helpfully draw the distinction between lay and ordained more clearly. To a large extent, the incumbent does spend much of his time in the immediate environs of the church and; in the nature of the case, many of the congregation will not. They are, therefore, free to exercise their lay ministry anywhere they like in the world: they do not need any authority to that, so they can do it. Meanwhile, the priest, however, has been given limited authority for that ministry in a limited part of the world: it is the parish, and he is licensed only to that. The essence of lay behaviour is testimony and the classic scriptural account is the story of the man born blind in John 9: 'Once I was blind, now I can see'.

Clarification of these two roles is continually necessary if the church is to possess a lively theology that 'should address awkward, probing, irritating questions to church, society and culture' (Forrester). He also has interesting things to say about professionalizing. Ward criticizes some of my writings and suggests that there is in them a diminution of the laity. I have always tried to avoid that, but there was that tragic split which emerged. For example, lay people can do administration, while clergy can be spiritual. This is an unfortunate split in the light of St Paul's injunction to hold gifts together. And there are some very good managers among the clergy and some

---

[4] In the light of today's concerns with sex, it is facinating to note that the one change Parkyn could not stomach was a married clergy.

appallingly incompetent lay people. Again, the notion of non-executive being a model for lay behaviour looked fine until the scandals emerged and non-executive director was discovered to be rather impotent role in the face of public scandals. The relationship between lay and ordained people, is not collaborative so much as complementary. Expectations of the church and of its ministers are different: if someone wants a priest they want a priest not a layman. But equally, they want a layman, they do not want a surrogate priest. I have consistently tried to make these points. In *The Priest-like Task*, I was attracted by Keats' words. They seemed to bring together beautifully the idea of healing, which is the priestlike function of the whole church, to be that around the human shores and not just the religious ones.

The occasional offices

Christopher Moody, an experienced parish priest, still sees value in the traditional style of parochial ministry. He, however, goes a little further and begins from our lives outside the church and not inside. The sacraments, too, are natural symbols which belong firstly, to the world of creation. 'Our particular skill as ministers of the occasional offices is in relating the primary realities of birth, marriage and death to the narrative of God's love revealed in Jesus Christ'.

But something odd is happening in the world of the occasional offices, where the church seems to be losing confidence in them and then instils a similar lack of confidence in others. I'm still very struck by this story. An incumbent in a suburban parish became tired of doing baptisms and offered only to do blessings. Nevertheless people kept coming and were blessed. One day, however, overheard in the main street, the following conversation between two young mothers: 'I hear the Rev X. doesn't do babies any more'. 'Oh yes he does', said the other, 'it's just that he doesn't use water now'. It is that sort of reality, which teaching goodness knows what, nevertheless is there that we need to address and be aware of.

Demanding ministry

Another incumbent, Emma Percy, with Martyn, rightly lights on the impact of this sort of ministry on the person. They are looking for more rage about the church and less politeness, which is implicitly raised by the basic part of the minister's question: 'What is happening to me? And why?' These are the core ministerial questions that are asked in role. Psychologically they invite us to check ourselves for feelings, whether permanent or temporary, in order to allow for any bias in the engagement. Sociologically, that is to check out the relationship between ourselves and the people or person with whom we are dealing in the social context. In doing so, we will use what is technically counter-transference, and be more often in touch with the wishes or intentions of the person or persons with whom we are dealing. Theologically they bring to bear the theme of atonement, which allows the expression of anger and aggression to be part of the ministry of Christ and of the Christian. But as a description, the general ground, on which churches in northern Europe work today, the passage from David Martin (published as an appendix in Grace Davie's book) provides an excellent summary.[5] The complexity of scenarios in pastoral ministry is often responded to by the complexity of the pastor. That is why he or she does feel things, often beyond their comprehension. But to restrict that feeling to the rational part of the self, (and make it the basis of protest) will ignore too many other major topics to do with the self, the other, the community and God.

Cathedrals and greater churches

In any talk of the Church of England's ministry today is not possible to omit the cathedrals and greater churches. While we cannot speak easily of 'success' in the religious environment, nevertheless, there does seem that there is something about these great buildings and their larger-than-life scale. They may be carried back and then seek the 'beyond' which is beyond the local and even includes the international church. Cathedrals and greater churches have succeeded more than anybody could envisage in the last quarter-century. Tourism becomes more popular, and tourism is only pilgrimage with a non-religious dimension. In terms of cost and financial management, as well as organization, cathedrals and greater churches have rarely been in better shape. There are obviously a number of anomalies. But what may be going on as the people are coming?

At the Abbey a programme to recover the calm (which meant major reordering of the abbey) and make it more accessible to tourists (and therefore pilgrims) was undertaken. These churches offer a scale of worship that is widely held to be helpful in encountering God. Obviously the greater cathedrals still spend a fortune to maintain the

---

[5] Davie, G. *Believing without Belonging. Religion in Britain since 1945.* Blackwell, Oxford.

choral tradition at the heart of worship, which is widely appreciated. And, while you cannot speak of 'success' in religious terms, nevertheless over the past quarter century or more, these great buildings have come back into a new lease of life. They seemed to be able to represent wholeness for a community, either by expressing what the mind sought, or by addressing broken wholeness and at time of tragedy, apparent helplessness. They are good for sad or joyful occasions, the Abbey, of course, being also suitable for royal events. Most maintain a high level of musical competence in liturgy. From being doomed as mediaeval excrescence on a modern church world, these churches have become places which occupy and preserve sacred space and important routes through the community. They nevertheless still have difficulties in finding their place in the constellation of the church.

An example from the world of cathedrals may help make this clearer. At the Deans and Provosts (now The Deans' Meeting) it was proposed that Chapters might all return to the Commissioners some part, or all, of their grant money. The amount would have to vary according to the proportional value to budgets, but every chapter gave and £400,000 was raised to assist the Commissioners, through the difficult times they were facing. The annoyance can be imagined when the published accounts of the year showed cathedral funds down and bishops' expenses up by precisely £400,000.

Conclusion

This seems an appropriate place to stop. Once again, money is prominent, along with cathedrals, bishops and the Church Commissioners. I hope, however, that all who have read these essays will have recognized that the heart of the ministry is still provided by the parishes and by faithful parish priests. I have been privileged for the past 30 years or so to travel around the country and meet clergy and lay people in different parts. Without being patronizing, I can say that I am impressed by the enthusiasm and competence of our clergy. For every one that appears in a headline, there seems to be a goodly number who are quietly getting on with their ministry to which the Church of England has committed itself and to which I, for one, hope it will remain committed.

This prayer comes from the west wall of the Abbey:

God grant to the living, grace; to the departed, rest; to the Church, the Queen, the Commonwealth and all mankind, peace and concord; and to us sinners, eternal life. Through Jesus Christ, our Lord. Amen.

Dr Wesley Carr
Curriculum Vitae

(ARTHUR) WESLEY CARR
DEAN OF WESTMINSTER

Born: 26 July 1941
Married to Natalie, with one daughter

EDUCATION
Dulwich College
Jesus College, Oxford, MA
Jesus College, Cambridge, MA
Ridley Hall, Cambridge
Ecumenical Institute, Bossey, Geneva
University of Sheffield, PhD
University of the West of England, DLitt (honoris causa)
University of Sheffield, DLitt (honoris causa)

POSTS HELD
1967–71   Curate, Luton Parish Church
1970–71   Tutor, Ridley Hall
1971–72   Chaplain, Ridley Hall
1972–74   Sir Henry Stephenson Research Fellow, University of
           Sheffield
1972–74   Hon Curate, Ranmoor Parish Church, Sheffield
1974–78   Chaplain, Chelmsford Cathedral
1974–82   Deputy Director, Chelmsford Cathedral Centre for
           Research and Training
1976–84   Director of Training, Diocese of Chelmsford
1978–87   Canon Residentiary, Chelmsford Cathedral
1987–97   Dean of Bristol
1997–   Dean of Westminster

OTHER APPOINTMENTS

1980–87	Member of General Synod (Chelmsford Clergy)
1989–97	Member of General Synod (Deans and Provosts)
1984–85	Select Preacher, University of Oxford
1986–93	Chairman, The Media and Theological Education Project, New College, Edinburgh
1987–95	Educational Advisory Group, The Jerusalem Trust
1987–97	Council Member, The Bridge Foundation, Bristol
1987–97	Acting Chairman, Salvation Army Advisory Board, Bristol
1987–91	Governor, Bristol Cathedral School
1988–97	Trustee, Bristol Cathedral Trust
1988–2000	Member of Executive, Association of English Cathedrals
1991–97	Chairman of Governors, Bristol Cathedral School
1991–92	Non-Executive Member and Chairman of External Relations Committee, Bristol and District Health Authority
1991–96	Member of Council, Lincoln Theological College
1992–95	Foundation Governor, Alleyns Foundation of God's Gift, Dulwich
1992–95	Chairman, Chapel Committee
1992–98	Programme Advisor, The Tavistock Institute of Human Relations (Chairman, 1997–98)
1993–94	Director, The Tavistock Leicester Group Relations Conference (many years' association and staffing roles)
1992–97	Member, The President's Group, The Bristol Chamber of Commerce and Initiative
1995–2003	Governor, Dulwich College
1995–	Trustee, the Dulwich Estates
1995–	Chairman, Dulwich Chapel Committee
1997–2000	Chairman of Development Committee, The Lincoln Institute for the Study of Religion and Society, Sheffield
1997–	Trustee, The Lincoln Institute for the Study of Religion and Society, Sheffield
1997–	Member of Advisory Board, The Erikson Institute, Stockbridge, USA
Various dates	Member of ACCM/ABM and Committees
	Member of the Advisory Board of Ministry
	Vice Chairman, Ministry Development and Deployment Committee
	Chairman, Continuing Ministerial Education Sub-Committee
	Senior Bishops' Inspector and Trainer of Inspectors
	Senior Bishops' Selector

Index